Standing Together
in the Community of God

Standing Together in the Community of God

Liturgical Spirituality and the Presence of Christ

Paul A. Janowiak, SJ

A PUEBLO BOOK

Liturgical Press   Collegeville, Minnesota

www.litpress.org

A Pueblo Book published by Liturgical Press

Cover design by David Manahan, OSB. Photo copyright © St. James Cathedral, Seattle, Washington. Cross overlay by Frank Kacmarcik, OblSB.

Library of Congress Cataloging-in-Publication Data

Janowiak, Paul, 1951–
    Standing together in the community of God : liturgical spirituality and the presence of Christ / Paul A. Janowiak.
        p. cm.
    "A Pueblo book."
    Includes bibliographical references (p.   ) and index.
    ISBN 978-0-8146-6024-9 — ISBN 978-0-8146-6257-1 (e-book)
    1. Jesus Christ in the liturgy—Catholic Church.   2. Catholic Church—Liturgy—Theology.   3. Jesus Christ—Presence.   I. Title.
BT575.J36   2011
264'.02—dc23   2011033421

To my family and the Arrupe Jesuit Community
at Seattle University, who have taught me
how to gather faithfully together, regularly and with grace.

The cup of blessing that we bless,
is it not a participation in the blood of Christ?
The bread that we break,
is it not a participation in the body of Christ?
Because the loaf of bread is one, we, though many, are one body,
for we all partake of the one loaf.

—*1 Corinthians 10:16-17*
The Solemnity of Corpus Christi

Contents

Preface

In an earlier work, *The Holy Preaching: The Sacramentality of the Word in the Liturgical Assembly* (2000), I explored a pastoral question that surfaced from my liturgical life as a Roman Catholic at worship and a presider at the eucharistic assembly. Given the richness of our sacramental life and our devotion to the real presence of Christ in the Eucharist, I asked how we might understand the meaning of the Second Vatican Council's Constitution on the Sacred Liturgy that asserts that Christ "is present in his word, since it is [Christ] himself who speaks when the holy Scriptures are read in the Church" (*Sacrosanctum Concilium* 7). I discovered that the sacramental character of the proclamation and preaching of the word of God is embodied in a relational event that takes seriously the locus of revelation within the worshiping Body of Christ. The eventful character of this proclamatory act involves many layers of meaning: the communal and apostolic sacred texts we share as believing Christians, the life situations of the hearers of that Word, the minister as the voice of that dialogue between God and us, and the actual liturgical context in which this revelatory encounter unfolds.

In the intervening years, that interest has widened to include the character of the other modes of sacramental presence the Constitution outlines: "when the Church prays and sings" and "in the person of [the] minister," indeed, in the whole sacramental life of the Church (SC 7). New questions emerged for me. If preaching was such a relational, dialogical, and participative event within the liturgy, is the same character of dynamic presence found in the assembly's praying and singing and in the presider's gathering of the community for this focal act of Christian identity? Do all sacramental celebrations express this real presence of Christ with the same rhythm and harmony that we experience in the eucharistic life of the church? Indeed, if Christ is "always present"—as the document insists—how is this related to the traditional Catholic understanding of "real presence" in the eucharistic elements? My own worship life as a Jesuit and a priest and my teaching in an ecumenical school of theology and ministry all provided me with rich source material for these theological and devotional interests. I discovered how a spirituality and piety surrounding the liturgy would be deeply enriched by seeing these as one presence in four modes. The whole Christ, the *totus Christus*, is not divided up and sacramental presence is not parceled out separately nor are these modes in a "reality" competition with one another. In short, I believe that faithful worshipers have a felt knowledge, enriched by faith and experience, that the sacramental presence we encounter in the eucharistic gifts does not stand apart from all these rich modes of Christ's self-communication *to* us and *for* us and *with* us. The fruit of that study and worship is the subject of this book.

One further point of clarification may also illumine the importance of the liturgical dynamism, and it emerged for me in the particular ecumenical context out of which I live and study. My Protestant and Anglican colleagues and students have impressed upon me the importance of God's sovereignty in all we say and do. God is at the heart of our human desire and our religious hunger. God acts first and we respond. In that light, I saw the importance of situating the relational, dialogical, and participative character of the liturgy within the dynamism of the triune life itself. Our "full, conscious, and active participation in liturgical celebrations called for by the very nature of the liturgy" (SC 14) is in response to the Trinity's own communion of mutual love and self-gift that, in the liturgy, we are invited to share. This simple foundation deepened the awe and gratitude I discovered in the sacred mysteries we celebrate as God's saving acts in Jesus now offered to us in the power of the Spirit's indwelling. Indeed, the Orthodox tradition has been insisting on this dimension in every ecumenical encounter with Christians, yet we have not fully appreciated the gift they bring. I believe a deeper appropriation of the trinitarian foundation of worship provides a way to speak to the hunger and thirst for a eucharistic spirituality in these times, especially acute among many young people today who long for the mystery seemingly so apparent in former ages. It is out of that reflection and ecumenical dialogue that I began to imagine the liturgy as the expressive moment of "standing together in the community of God." I have always prayed "in the name of the Father, and of the Son, and of the Holy Spirit." The depth of that divine embrace seems more real and life-giving to me now.

I suggest that our age requires a fresh eucharistic spirituality and piety for the new reality that is unfolding in this twenty-first millennium. The mystery for which we yearn is alive and in our midst, embraced by our tradition, and articulated with such bold and creative beauty in the vision of the Second Vatican Council. It simply asks for an intentionality and attentiveness in the way we pray together and interiorize our sacramental life. We need not look to another age for this depth out of some sort of pristine nostalgia. God is faithful, Christ is intimate with us, and the Spirit is moving.

I am grateful for the diversity of liturgical voices I have encountered in my life and study that have made the sacramental economy, which is such an integral part of Roman Catholic identity, a source of ecumenical communion in spirituality and piety that hopefully and soon will lead to one table of Word and Sacrament, source and summit of the unity Christ so desired, *ut unum sint*. In addition, I am grateful for those whose life and witness have shaped my faith and informed my thinking, particularly my family, whose fidelity to worship and to gathering at all times and seasons for communion in word and meal on many levels strikes a chord in everything I say in these pages. My Jesuit mentors, John Baldovin, SJ, Patrick Howell, SJ, Jerry Cobb, SJ, and all my Jesuit brothers in the Oregon Province deserve specific thanks for their encouragement and support. The liturgical communities I have served revealed the truth of what I have tried to capture. My colleagues and students in the School of Theology and Ministry at Seattle University have enriched the dialogue and provided a faithful example that our ecumenical convergence can and will bring us into deeper communion. Finally, Hans Christoffersen, Stephanie Lancour, Lauren L. Murphy, and Donna Pierce, as well as Fr. Mike Ryan and Maria Laughlin of St. James Cathedral in Seattle, have all shepherded this project toward its completion through their patient editorial assistance. For all these, I give praise and thanks to the Giver of all good gifts. It is an honor to spend time thinking and writing about something I cherish so much and to have faithful people around me to share in a hunger for God that only deepens with time and mellows with grace.

Acknowledgments

Excerpts from the English translation of the Constitution on the Sacred Liturgy from *Documents on the Liturgy, 1963–1979: Conciliar, Papal, and Curial Texts* © 1982, International Commission on English in the Liturgy Corporation (ICEL); excerpts from the English translation of *The Roman Missal* © 2010, ICEL. All rights reserved.

Excerpt from "The Circus Animal's Desertion" by W. B. Yeats. Reprinted with the permission of Scribner, a Division of Simon & Schuster, Inc., from *The Collected Works of W. B. Yeats, Volume 1: The Poems, Revised* by W. B. Yeats, edited by Richard J. Finneran. Copyright © 1940 by Georgie Yeats, renewed 1968 by Bertha Georgie Yeats, Michael Butler Yeats, and Anne Yeats. All rights reserved.

Poem by Symeon the Theologian from *The Enlightened Heart: An Anthology of Sacred Poetry*, edited by Stephen Mitchell. Copyright © 1989 by Stephen Mitchell. Reprinted by permission of HarperCollins Publishers.

Excerpt from "The Reed Flute's Song," in *The Essential Rumi*, trans. Coleman Barks, et al. (Edison, NJ: Castle Books, 1997). Used by permission.

At the time of publication, the following permissions were in process:

Jean Corbon, *Wellspring of Worship* (Mahwah, NJ: Paulist Press, 1988).

Suzanne Noffke, *Prayers of Catherine of Siena* (Mahwah, NJ: Paulist Press, 1983)

Chapter 1

Standing Together in the Community of God:
Sacramental Worship and the Presence of Christ

Let us begin with what we know together and feel in our bones as a sacramental people. Christ is present to us in the liturgical celebration of the sacraments in a mysterious and nourishing way. Worship provides the privileged arena of grace for the community of faith to proclaim this presence. In the liturgy of Word and Sacrament, we stand together as the Body of Christ, embraced by the triune God at the heart of all that is. In that sacred communion, Christ is in our midst in a real and focal way. Generations of our forebears have chosen to live and die for this belief and the sacramental economy that expresses it.

Such "felt knowledge" is an act of faith that resonates deep within the communal heart of the church. The mysterious depths of this worship in the name of the Father and of the Son and of the Holy Spirit inevitably stammers to reach theological articulation, perhaps more clearly and univocally in some periods and cultural settings than others in our ecclesial history. The fruits of this dialogue eventually return to the level of *theologia prima*, the faith experience of praying together that initiated the reflection. Eucharistic faith in the presence and action of Christ in the sacraments remains so central to our corporate prayer life that even minor differences of theological interpretation or necessary agreements surrounding rubrics and norms easily exacerbate painful divisions and mutual distrust among Christians.

Real communion in the Body of Christ suffers from this, even to the point of smug rejection of eucharistic hospitality among denominations, even to the exclusion of members within a given faith community. In such an environment, liturgical practice becomes a visible litmus test for fidelity and orthodoxy, legislating worthiness to share in the nourishment that flows from the heart of the triune God, in a communion that unites us with Christ's own self-offering, and that is the source and wellspring of Christian identity. Theologians and ecclesial authorities may argue vehemently about such doctrinal differences

1

and philosophical nuances, all of which can be a basis for a lively and spirited interchange. However, for most believers, what we hold most treasured in our faith is expressed in the way we pray and celebrate together week after week. Assaults upon our communion in the Body of Christ, in law or in practice, do not go unnoticed at the level of felt knowledge and scandalize the preciousness of "what we feel in our bones." Standing together in the community of God, it seems, asks more from us.

This much we know: liturgical celebration stands as a visible embodiment of the substantial unity *or* division of the hearts and minds of Christians. Unity or its lack takes flesh not only in the character of shared dialogue among theologians and bishops but also in the practice of the Sunday assembly, indeed, within the worshiping Body itself. Contemporary experience has revealed to us the cost of such fragmentation that reaches down into a local community of faith. Members slowly begin to drift apart from one another over liturgical issues of doctrine and practice, even of style, language, and leadership. Who can cleanse the vessels after the assembly has communed? Is the cup of blessing offered to all? Can anyone preach who feels "called" to do this? What words are faithful to the tradition that is both ancient and ever new? The unity of the Body of Christ dissolves in this intensity of a questioning the very act of our identity as Christians.

If Christian communities become inured or weary from this mutual critique and do not pay reverent attention to the effects of our recurring inability to praise God together in "one heart and mind and voice,"[1] we may reach a time when our division ceases to matter anymore. This "not mattering" is different from schismatic splits or ritual separation or reformation in our history—and perhaps even more scandalous—because of the absence of passion or deep identification with the sacred mysteries we celebrate and the union of hearts and minds they proclaim. In the quest for reunion of and within the Christian churches today, the necessity to argue out passionate differences may be replaced by a simple, sad recognition that it does not matter anymore whether we believe and pray as one Body. The tragedy of such a measure of Christian identity should make us tremble and call us to conversion.

---

[1] "It is truly right that with full hearts and minds and voices we should praise the unseen God, the all powerful Father, and his only Son, our Lord Jesus Christ" is the summons to the people of God in the Easter *Exsultet*.

How, then, can we pray truthfully, in the words of Eucharistic Prayer III, "[Y]ou never cease to gather a people to yourself, so that from the rising of the sun to its setting a pure sacrifice may be offered to your name"? The four decades since the Second Vatican Council have been exhilarating and also very painful. Worship has often been at the center of this great imaginative shift, often replete with battles and scars. A revision of the texts, as divisive and protracted as that has proved in practice, is simply not enough. Perhaps, at this juncture, we need a *refreshed liturgical spirituality*, a piety for the People of God, one that unites us together at the source of Christ's own life in us, and draws the diverse body together as Christians rather than wedges us apart. At the same time, we must remember that doctrines and theological statements must remain necessary partners in this liturgical resuscitation, because praying and believing are constantly interacting with one another.

That is why any exploration of a theology that informs the presence of Christ in the sacraments must be held in necessary and creative tension with the actual liturgical celebrations that embody God's encounter with us in this grace-filled event. In times of transition and cultural shift, that tension rises and can easily become ideologically self-absorbed and lose the focus of its original power and grace. We can forget who we are, what we are doing, and how this is rooted in the One who calls us into this grace. In such times, we need to explore the ambiguous shape of our belief and see what holds it together. This involves *spirituality* and *piety* in the task of *theological meaning*. We have not adequately used liturgical piety in our spiritual imaginations in recent decades, because we fear it will not bear theological scrutiny. Theological meaning, however, needs the human engagement of the sacramental mysteries. *Lex orandi* and *lex credendi* mutually enrich one another.

We emphasize here that liturgical praying is first and foremost a *corporate* action rather than an individual act of devotion. God saves and acts on behalf of a people. We each draw our precious and personal baptismal identity from that primordial and communal grounding. The ecclesial context of this exploration spirituality and piety will continue to reaffirm that theology, ritual practice, and spiritual passion need not be strangers. Rather, the tensive relationship among theory, practice, and meaning keeps the whole liturgical enterprise honest; at a deeper level, it reveals in each a common rhythm and harmony. Shared passion enhances communion and *real communion* is what God is all about.

3

Such a dialogue would affirm that belief in the presence of Christ in the Eucharist, as a foremost example, is not a matter of much disagreement for most of us. Yet, the deeper connections between theology, practice, and passion would nudge us to ask in fresh ways *what quality of presence* the Eucharist bears in our liturgical enactment and how such a *sacred intimacy* shapes the way the assembly, as the primary celebrants of the rite, prays together in thanks and praise to God for Christ's saving deeds among us, the *totus Christus* in whom we are now drawn in mutual communion. Deeper questioning about the dynamics of faith that take shape through liturgical practice moves us beyond the eucharistic mystery of Word and table, into all our shared sacramental life. If the passion stirring within us remains a respected partner in this dialogue, our attention to our worship life begins to strike chords with the pattern of relationships and presence we share with all people and all creation as common inhabitants of this world.

Such exploration between the pattern of the way we pray and the way we live our lives moves into dangerous territory, because much of our faith knowledge comes to us through the rhythm and grace of ritual action, not easily reducible to simple words and explanations. At such a profound and rich symbolic level, we can risk alienating or confusing one another and ourselves in an attempt to be clear and orthodox and faithful to our contemporary experience as believing Christians. Yet the recovery of passion and devotion for the liturgy as source and summit of Christian life[2] impels us. Tending to the fires of Christ's passion for and in us is the risk that sacramental life engenders.

[handwritten margin note: How are we able to have our heads speak our heart]

The Eucharist provides a great metaphor for questioning the relational nature of sacramental life, because the mysterious gift of "abundance in unexpected places" (cf. Matt 15:29-37) seems to be the enduring condition for Christ's presence with the assembly, feeding common hunger for communion in word and meal. How, then, is Christ present to us today in such nourishing abundance? Is the Redeemer's gift of self-offering to the Father and to us in this great sacrament limited in our experience to particles of bread and drops

---

[2] This is the description of the Christian liturgy in The Constitution on the Sacred Liturgy (*Sacrosanctum Concilium*, 1963) of Vatican II (cf. SC 10). This document will be discussed in more detail below.

of wine we consume when we receive holy communion? How, then, can we say, as the tradition affirms and church documents attest, that we also truly know him and encounter him in the assembled faithful who pray and sing, in the presider who gathers the community into a communion with Christ and one another, in the Scriptures proclaimed and preached, indeed, in all sacramental celebrations?[3] Are these real presences or not? Even more important, are these admittedly distinct modes of presence separate from each other, able to be cut off from each other and from their ultimate and unifying context of Christ's promise to be with us always, even to the end of time (Matt 28:20)? The sacramental presence of Christ in the table-sharing at Eucharist, therefore, reveals only the tip of the iceberg. Christ's multivalent presence pervades the other sacraments that express our communion with Christ and one another: in initiation,[4] the anointing of the sick, when we marry or are ordained to priestly service, and when we are reconciled with and for Christ's Body.

This first chapter sets the grounds for a discussion that will encompass this whole study of the rich sacramental dimensions of *standing together in the community of God*. We will begin to explore the ways that these different dynamic actors and elements in the liturgy relate to each other and bear the presence of Christ in a focal and unitive way. We will argue that they do not stand over against one another or compete for the honor of an independent and, therefore, truly *real* presence. Rather, these *modes of presence*, as we will call them, interrelate and mutually clarify one another to proclaim a sacramental encounter with the risen Lord, widening the boundaries of Christ's grace-filled activity in our midst. Furthermore, we will see how the spiraling action of the community that culminates primarily in the table-sharing of Christ's Body and Blood—but also taking place in the baptizing of new members,

---

[3] Cf. SC 7, *General Instruction of the Roman Missal* (GIRM), 27 (International Committee on English in the Liturgy, 2002).

[4] Eucharist as the completion of the threefold sacraments of initiation, which include baptism and confirmation, shows precisely the multivalence and relational quality of sacramental life. Although Eucharist stands at the symbolic center, the other sacramental "life functions" (as theologian Otto Semmelroth, SJ, called them in his studies at the time of Vatican II) flow from the same abiding presence of Christ. Cf. my book, *The Holy Preaching: The Sacramentality of the Word in the Liturgical Assembly* (Collegeville, MN: Liturgical Press, 2000), part I.

the anointing of our sick ones, and other sacramental actions of the church—asks that we refresh all aspects of our celebrations and imagine them as a *significant whole*. The task may seem bewildering, given the ritual stubbornness that has already surfaced a half decade after the reform of the liturgy promulgated by the universal church in the middle of the last century. Such an investigation involves revisiting some of the theological and pastoral groundwork that led to and shaped the theology and spirituality of the liturgy articulated by the Second Vatican Council. Hopefully, this fresh look will uncover a deeper appreciation of a mystery we have already shared on these many levels but whose wellspring is largely untapped and even blocked by stubborn notions and narrowed expectations of its power to consecrate us into the gift we receive, the Body of Christ, a holy communion.

SACROSANCTUM CONCILIUM AND THE RENEWAL OF THE LITURGICAL IMAGINATION

The first document of the Second Vatican Council, interestingly enough, was about the church's life of worship, a culmination of decades of scholarly research by many theologians from many countries. The Constitution on the Sacred Liturgy (*Sacrosanctum Concilium*, December 1963) promulgated a reform of the church's venerable tradition of worship in order to clarify and embrace more faithfully "the nature of the liturgy and its importance in the Church's life" (SC chap. I, pt. I). These proposed and mandated changes to our liturgical life and celebrations were an attempt to recover the dynamism that energized the community of believers since its earliest days and to translate that vibrant faith into contemporary believers' lives. Contrary to the views of those who have mistrusted the fundamental impetus of the council's actions or who have refused to engage the reform on that deeper level of ecclesial and personal transformation, the liturgical renewal was not an attempt to throw out the past or upset comfortable ways of understanding what most Christians still acknowledge as the most intimate revelation of God's presence with us, in Christ, through the power of the Holy Spirit. The reform asked that the church recover a communal act of praise and thanks that corresponded to the revelation of the risen Lord's abiding presence in the baptized community of believers. The council attempted to address what appeared in practice and piety to be a narrowed focus on the changes occurring to the ritual elements, performed autonomously by a figure set apart primarily to mediate these mysteries to a faithful but uninvolved laity, all of which obscured the depth of the holy encounter taking place.

6

Implementing such a profound recovery of the church's worship could never have been adequately understood by those who were shaping this vision. As history has shown us, many faithful and willing worshipers were deprived of the depth of that communal call to grace because those who would be charged with the leadership and catechesis of such liturgical reform simply could not appreciate the cost and commitment of such a charge. Hindsight cannot claim that the council fathers and those who advised them knew entirely the risks of altering centuries of ritual action and language, but the boldness of their action remains a prophetic response to grace. It is as if they were "walking by faith and not by sight" (2 Cor 5:7). The impelling Spirit that was stubbornly nudging them to such a profound step of renewal convinced them that the liturgy (i.e., "making the work of our redemption a present actuality"), and especially the Eucharist, "is the outstanding means whereby the faithful may express in their lives and manifest to others the mystery of Christ and the real nature of the true Church" (SC 2).[5] The valor of such a faith claim speaks volumes, and we may ask whether such a proclamation has borne fruit in our worship experience, and, if not, why that is so. The reflection emerges as a matter of moment for all, because we cannot deny that the desire for such a "rule of praying" (*lex orandi*) still burns in the hearts of the People of God. The task of liturgical and sacramental theology is to fan the flame of that common desire.

Do we truly experience ourselves standing together in the community of God, nourished and impelled for mission and shaped into Christ, because we share this sacramental economy? At the complex and diverse level of our everyday communal practice and of our individual understanding of what we are doing at the liturgy, can we attest to a richer communion with God and one another because we gather to share a sacramental life together? In other words, does our present liturgical practice express with clarity the sacramental mysteries it claims, "a sacred action surpassing all others" (SC 7)? Our mission as the Body of Christ in the world impels us to explore our ritual

[5] For some spirited accounts of the prework of the council and the actual debates that led to the vote on *Sacrosanctum Concilium*, see Annibale Bugnini, *The Reform of the Liturgy (1948–1975)* (Collegeville, MN: Liturgical Press, 1990); and Mathijs Lamberigts, "The Liturgy Debate," chap. III in *The History of Vatican II*, ed. Giuseppe Alberigo and Joseph A Komonchak, Eng. ed., 107–66 (Maryknoll: Orbis, 1997).

and liturgical geography and reflect on its role in shaping a shared baptismal identity and faith. In particular, a sustained dialogue on our central belief in the *sacramental presence of Christ* may help to bring these important questions to the surface of a wider population of faithful believers, who may feel that systematic reflection on the theology of the sacramental life is simply the purview of experts. Yet we all know these truths in our bones. The "grace of the sacrament" stirs deep within the faithful People of God, revealing a passion and piety that can serve and embody theology and practice. We can all start at the often unappreciated well of our felt desire for God, for intimacy with Christ, and for an anointing by the Holy Spirit. The liturgy we celebrate regularly claims to be the privileged arena for all this. We *can* start there at the heart, where the passion resides, "the point where the river of life rises as a wellspring in the midst of human existence," as Dominican Jean Corbon has described the sacramental life we call worship.[6]

THE LIVED AND FELT EXPERIENCE OF THE PROMISE OF WORSHIP

As a church, we know from our own experience as worshipers, teachers, ministers, and pastors that the journey of renewal over the past half century has not been easy. Such uneasiness takes many forms and emerges from very different and complex expectations and claims. A significant number of believers have concluded that the church as a communal body has eclipsed the mystery of the sacred liturgy and trivialized its profound holiness. Younger Christians gaze longingly at worship of another time and long to replicate it, while still eschewing the larger dimensions of Catholic life and discipline that were part and parcel of the liturgical self-identity of a half century ago. Perhaps most challenging of all, others have simply wandered away from faithful, regular liturgical practice because Eucharist, and sacramental life in general, simply does not speak meaningfully to their own lives nor does it adequately engage the world and its questions and needs and struggles. Layers of ambiguous gestures and meaningless claims, such people say, get in the way of their personal desire for God and their hunger for meaning and truth. Some believers, suspicious of an

[6] Jean Corbon, *The Wellspring of Worship*, trans. Matthew J. O'Connell (New York: Paulist Press, 1988), 143. A second English edition was published in 2005 by Ignatius Press, San Francisco.

institution that legislates the rubrics and language of worship from afar, reject even the christological center of the sacramental life and the hierarchical nature of an ordered assembly whose constitution excludes, controls, and hoards power. Doubts about the liturgy's efficacy in our contemporary life and mission, as well as the rush to reassert its unifying hegemony in these matters, has even expressed itself in the church's leadership itself of late, as she reestablishes boundaries of *who* is authorized to do *what* and how the texts and rituals we employ are translated into the language of the common, holy People of God. Added to this unlikely cadre are disaffected Christians, who have wandered away out of an act of personal freedom, only to discover a ritual wasteland in their self-imposed exile that other Sunday morning rituals try to fill but that still leave their longing unsatisfied. All of the experiences of these good and well-meaning Christians attest to *a ritual lack of abundance*, merging together from a variety of starting points.

In short, decades of moving the furniture and changing the rites in language, gesture, and music appear to have led us to the door of a new chamber of grace-filled opportunity, if we would but enter together, with our whole selves. Such widespread tension and ferment about liturgical matters suggest an invitation by the Holy Spirit for *an interior liturgical reform and transformation* that must take place in the heart of the gathered assembly, if the liturgy is truly the "outstanding means whereby [we] may express in [our] lives and manifest to others the mystery of Christ and the real nature of the true Church" (SC 2). Furthermore, this interior consecration of the community as the Body of Christ must inevitably lead to mission in the world, into a search for abundance in unlikely places. The rhythm and harmony of the liturgy of life, it seems, always new and refreshed "from age to age," comes full circle. The crucial issues appropriate to our present time seem to be those of a spirituality of worship in dialogue with theology and ritual practice. The People of God at prayer need more than merely an aggressive argument among theologians and bishops over sacramental terms and meanings, the dynamics of which they observe like an audience at an athletic venue. Our real, shared life of prayer establishes and gives expression to our belief (*Legem credendi stauit lex orandi*). The community's passion and embrace of this prayer and belief holds us together in creative communion.

In the midst of the tension resulting from these diverse responses
to a liturgical life that appears to have given up too much or has not
taken sufficient account of contemporary reality, a call for a liturgical
spirituality that goes beyond moving the furniture and reorchestrat-
ing the prayers and hymns seems in order. How Christ is present in
the liturgy, calling us and feeding us, and walking with us in the
trials and joys of the journey of life, must be engaged with the vigor
of our ancestors throughout the ages, whose faithful practice remains
resonant in our contemporary liturgical words and actions. Faithful
love for our church and for the worship she renders God, so evident
in those who articulated the vision in Vatican II's courageous act of
liturgical reform, needs to be the subject of new and fresh study. This
reflection demands the attention of the whole church, not simply the
professional theologians. A renewed and serious liturgical catechesis
should be prepared for those who preside at the liturgy, for the faithful people who gather as a celebrating community of that mystery of
Christ's grace for us, for those who lead the ministries of Word and prayer
and song and service, and for those who try to pass on that tradition
as teachers and guardians of our sacramental life and worship. Despite
all the tension and differences, we can agree on this one great desire,
which is rooted in God's great desire for us: all believers long for a
renewed commitment and devotion at the level of the heart, so that
we can gather more faithfully to celebrate the paschal mystery—
Christ's life, saving death, and transforming resurrection. We want to
be faithful to the venerable tradition of our ancestors by hearing the
word, celebrating the meal of his covenant promise and sharing the
communion it demands of us, and by joining with Christ in giving
thanks and praise to God by living that Spirit-filled life in service to
the world.

The church stands as the primary sacrament of this revelation of
Christ's saving presence, redeeming the world. Everything else serves
this mission; liturgical divisiveness and individual devotional or political agendas impede the flow of that wellspring of grace emanating
from the heart of God. Our connectedness with God's life flowing
through us is crucial to the efficacy of the church's sacramental life,
as we will discuss more fully at the end of this chapter. Consequently,
charity within the Mystical Body of Christ, as the Jesuit Edward
Kilmartin has insisted, "gives us a common heart. . . . It is impossible

for a Christian to hope uniquely for himself [or herself]."[7] This truth about our individual faith identity as rooted in the church remains largely ambiguous and submerged, only to be teased to the surface by the Spirit in times of symbolic lack or ecclesial betrayal. The Constitution on the Sacred Liturgy emphasized that Christ's abiding presence in the church, expressed most poignantly when she is engaged in common prayer, reveals its power on a variety of levels and is integrated throughout the entire celebration of the liturgy. Often our liturgy battles neglect this crucial sacramental dynamism, preferring to compartmentalize and isolate that rhythmic flow of grace.

Hearing anew the call to communion in our ritual life as an effective instrument of living and preaching the gospel, we would do well at the outset to hear again the council's bold claim on our desire to be faithful to what we know together deep in our bones:

> To accomplish so great a work, Christ is always present in his Church, especially in its liturgical celebrations. He is present in the sacrifice of the Mass, not only in the person of his minister, "the same now offering, through the ministry of priests, who formerly offered himself on the cross," but especially under the eucharistic elements. By his power he is present in the sacraments, so that when a [person] baptizes it is really Christ himself who baptizes. He is present in his word, since it is he himself who speaks when the holy Scriptures are read in the Church. He is present, lastly, when the Church prays and sings, for he promised: "Where two or three are gathered together in my name, there am I in the midst of them" (Mt 18:20).
>
> Christ always truly associates the Church with himself in this great work wherein God is perfectly glorified and the recipients made holy. The Church is the Lord's beloved Bride who calls to him and through him offers worship to the eternal Father. (SC 7)

These four modes of the presence of Christ in the liturgy, in which the church actively labors with Christ's own redemptive work, articulate the framework of meaning for this entire book. Doctrine, liturgical practice, and communal devotion share in the dialogue. These modes of presence are not isolated from or in competition with one another.

---

[7] Edward J. Kilmartin, SJ, "Eschatology and the Evanston Congress," 1958 STD Dissertation, Gregorian University, as quoted in Jerome Hall, *We Have the Mind of Christ: The Holy Spirit and Liturgical Memory in the Thought of Edward J. Kilmartin*, 138–39 (Collegeville, MN: Liturgical Press, 2001).

Furthermore, we will see how a respect for the rhythm and harmony with which these modes of presence interact in the liturgy invites believers into a deeper intimacy and communion with Christ and one another in a way that consecrates a community's self-identity as the Body of Christ, urges that community to a deeper surrender with Christ laboring in the world, and speaks to individual hearts who feel isolated or cut off from the mystery for which they long and hunger with as great intensity as the first followers of the risen Lord.

A liturgical spirituality embedded in this profound call to worship asks that we root ourselves as a community of believers in the very life of God in whose name we say we gather to pray: "In the name of the Father, and of the Son, and of the Holy Spirit." The liturgy begins in this relational, dialogical, and participative way, and so does the interior journey of deeper discovery of the presence of Christ in the liturgy we celebrate. Gathering in the name reveals how we stand together in the community of a loving, healing God, fed by the redemptive presence of Christ, the Word made flesh, and held together and sustained in mission through the power of the Spirit at the heart of all life. The community of the triune God never isolates and so the Body of Christ cannot isolate or separate off into irreconcilable factions if she is to remain a vital sacrament of the God she serves. The Christian community stands in and with Christ Jesus laboring in the world, guided by the power of the Holy Spirit, a rhythmic participation in the triune life itself. This necessary relationship between how God is and how we gather to pray together in our sacramental life deserves a deeper look.

THE TRINITY AS THE MODEL OF CHRISTIAN WORSHIP

> [E]very liturgical celebration, because it is an action of Christ the Priest and of his Body which is the Church, is a sacred action surpassing all others; no other action of the Church can equal its effectiveness by the same title and to the same degree.
>
> —*Sacrosanctum Concilium* 7

Such an expansive claim for liturgical action as the "way of proceeding" for all Christian life risks being an empty claim if the dynamism of the divine life itself does not permeate *why, how,* and *with whom* we gather as the church at worship. This life-giving source roots its power and grace in God's identity as a Trinity of Persons in relationship with each other. Our faith tradition has wrestled from the beginning about what that means and how that happens. Yet, from the earliest centuries, Christianity has insisted that this generative, interpersonal nature of the triune God most authentically expresses the divine mystery "in whom we live and move and have our being" (Acts 17:28). Interdependence and mutual sharing in self-emptying love—characteristics that appear on a surface level of interpretation to be a limitation or a weakness—turn human expectation of power and glory upside down, express God's greatest authenticity, and inform our truest integration as human persons living in the world. We use anthropological names to express this divine community, as limited and gender-biased as they may seem at times, because we are dealing with *persons* and *events*, not merely ideas, concepts, or things. French Dominican Yves Congar, wrestling with what he called the "Principle Monuments of Tradition" that interweave to form our shared legacy as Christians, reminded a Tridentine church on the eve of the Second Vatican Council of this eventful and doxological root of worship and its relationship with doctrine and ecclesial life. The contemporary church needs to hear his insistence again:

> We are here concerned with the liturgy as the expression of a Church actively living, praising God, and bringing about a holy communion in him: the covenant fulfilled in Christ Jesus, its Lord, Head, and Spouse. . . . Not the voice of the magisterium teaching, defining, reproving, condemning, or refuting, but the voice of the loving, praying Church, doing more than merely expressing its faith: hymning it, practicing it, in a living celebration, wherein too, it makes a complete self-giving.[8]

The church immerses herself with heart and mind and voice in loving communion and praise. Our signing ourselves "in the name" says that we believe and choose to be identified, albeit haltingly and with metaphoric humility, by our bonding with Father (as a parental image), Son, and Holy Spirit, as they express this divine relationship in a rhythm of love and mutual laboring whose fruitfulness provides the source of all creative light and life. This is the Trinity we worship and image *through*, *with*, and *in* the incarnate Emmanuel ("God-with-us," Matt 1:23), whom we long to know, love, and serve, and in whose

---

[8] Yves Congar, OP, *Tradition and Traditions* (London: Burns and Oates, 1966), 427–28, reprinted and retranslated in *Theologians Today: Yves M.-J. Congar O.P.* (New York: Sheed and Ward, 1963), 81.

presence we desire to live forever in the power of the Spirit (Rev 22:16-17). This relational quality of God has profound consequences for how we understand ourselves as believers, how that faith expresses itself in our worship, and how we will choose to live the faith we profess as the Spirit-filled, resurrected Body of Christ in the world, in which "we live and move and have our being."

As the image of God created in this triune mystery, the community of human persons is part of this great rhythm and harmony of God's life. Our own presence *to* and participation *with* the Beloved, whose own fruitful, loving reality seeks first to be in relationship with us, would then, it seems, orient authentic living and praying together. This fruitful encounter turns us toward the life of the world, whose stewards and shared inhabitants we are. This pattern announces God's way: "In the beginning was the Word," John proclaims to us, "and the Word was with God, and the Word was God. He was in the beginning with God," without whom nothing has been made (John 1:1-3). The Holy Spirit of that encounter of mutual love and labor between the Father and the Son is poured out upon the whole creation in a harmony of self-giving that expresses an astounding truth about us and all creation. *Intimate relation, mutual sharing,* and *participation* embrace the milieu of authentic human living. We cannot blithely dismiss this grace, neither in our lives, our worship, nor our desire for meaning and fulfillment. Our truest identity as created beings hinges upon and shares in this rhythm and harmony with God and each other. We were made for relationship and loving encounter, and this fact of creative wholeness grounds everything we have and are.

If this communal, participative, and relational ground of our being is true, and our creed and faith tradition insists that it is, then prevailing ritual and rubrical images of lone rangers and isolated monads distort the harmony and shape of Christian identity and worship. Yet, Christian communities often do not experience their foundational act of praise and thanks as intrinsically communal, participative, and relational in its core enactment. The appeal to self-sufficient and individualized metaphors for God and for Christian life and worship still tug at us and draw us like sirens to something that only frustrates the true journey toward God that we so desire. Their seductiveness and appeal stubbornly adhere in some form throughout our shared faith history down to this present new millennium, even as the contemporary church struggles to embrace her identity as the pilgrim People of God and seeks to express that reality in the liturgical reform that has blossomed and sputtered in the years since the Second Vatican Council. Our way of praying together can often appear and be enacted as if everything and everyone were separate entities and actors, isolated elements of a rite, and lone worshipers who happen to be in the same place at the same time. Left to our own isolated desires, we still prefer God to be *up there*, and Jesus now present to us *down here* in *that*, and the Spirit moving primarily in *me* . . . all in order to feel satisfied or comfortable that we have sorted out the way God acts in the world. Such compartmentalization mistakenly assures us that we have corralled the graces that are then portioned out to individuals who gather to celebrate the sacraments, especially the Eucharist.[9] Given the trinitarian life of God, can we honestly conclude that such a privatized, controlled, and compartmentalized expression of the grace of Christ's life in us reveals the mystery of *real presence*? Does Christ become incarnate *for us* as the expression of that divine life in such a static manner, or does the invitation "to become what we receive" involve something much more harmonious with the life of God itself? God's abundance revealed through a sacramental world seems to suggest the latter.

That is why we can begin exploring a refreshed and renewed liturgical spirituality by rooting its dynamism in the triune life of God. Wrestling with such a divine mystery presents more than heady theological concepts that we can comfortably leave to the experts. As worshipers, presiders, preachers, ministers, and educators of the liturgy, we must take seriously and plumb the rich depths of the notion that we share and participate in the life of God as created and baptized beings. Because God reveals God's self as a community of persons, loving and being loved, and surrendering that love in a great redemptive act of self-giving, then our own worship, as an action of Christ and his Body, participates in the same dynamic of loving and being loved, of surrendering and communing, of breaking open and pouring out that Jesus himself incarnates in our world as a revelation of the One who sent him and who is now acting in the world. Look again at the powerful passage from the Constitution on the Sacred Liturgy quoted above and

[9] This attitude certainly holds, as well, for all our sacramental life celebrations, e.g., when we desire to have our children baptized, to be anointed at a time of illness, to come forward at a certain age to be confirmed, married, or reconciled. We will focus primarily on Eucharist, but this holds true for all the sacramental life.

15

see it in the light of what we have been asserting about the relational and communal life of God in the world:

> [E]very liturgical celebration, because it is an action of Christ the Priest and of his Body which is the Church, is a sacred action surpassing all others; no other action of the Church can equal its effectiveness by the same title and to the same degree. (SC 7)

The claim the liturgy makes here is radical. All the actions and participants in the communal act of worship embody *as a whole* the graced relationship that Christ shares with the One who loved him and who spoke his presence into our world. Doing the liturgy's work of remembering the promise enfleshed in the Incarnate Word and offering our praise and thanks together in Christ is the sign and symbol of that pattern of redemptive and revelatory love. Moreover, the Trinity's rhythmic act of dynamic presence shares a generative grace that cannot be for its own sake but a gift of love and mercy poured out upon the church and all creation by the gift of the Holy Spirit. The *community's focal role as celebrants* of God's saving acts in Jesus is neither new theology nor does it denigrate Christ's unrepeatable, unique action of dying and rising to save the world. Paul's Letter to the Colossians proclaims Christ's relationship to the Father as a gift that then, in its fruitfulness, animates all life and worship:

> He is the image of the invisible God, the firstborn of all creation . . . all things have been created through him and for him. . . . and in him all things hold together. He is the head of the body, the church; he is the beginning, the firstborn from the dead, so that he might come to have first place in everything. For in him the fullness of God was pleased to dwell, and through him God was pleased to reconcile to himself all things, whether on earth or in heaven, by making peace through the blood of his cross. (Col 1:15, 16b, 17b-20)

The Trinity as model of Christian worship, therefore, replicates the following dynamic: God the Parent, whom Jesus called Father, is the creative source of life and love, and Christ bodies forth and expresses that relationship to us and for us, by inviting us as friends and sisters and brothers into his own self-offering response of love and adoration to the One who loved him. The Spirit inscripts that way of living and loving into our very nature as a baptized community, bodied forth by us for the healing of the world in the expressive moment of our sacramental life.[10] The more we reverence that rhythmic, harmonic way of praying, offering, surrendering, and giving thanks, the more expressive the proclamation for the life of the world. That is why the liturgy is "a sacred action surpassing all others" and is "the summit toward which the activity of the Church is directed; [and] at the same time it is the fount from which all the Church's power flows" (SC 7, 10).

The liturgy dares to make this claim as source and summit of Christian life because God is source and summit of all redemptive activity. Such power and grace revealed among the believers as pure gift of God does not limit itself to the time and place of the liturgy itself; however, the specific gathering to worship does celebrate in intense ritual density this truth that pervades all aspects of God's mercy and redemption for all time. This means, quite simply, that the church's way of praying together bodies forth the expressive and momentous event in which Christ shares with humankind this life lived in willing and wholehearted surrender to Love, a grace-filled summons, as St. Augustine says, "to become what we receive." The gathered community engaged in the sacramental life proclaims an identity that then becomes the pattern for our communal mission in the world. Worship and mission cannot be separated, and the truth about God they proclaim together is not only redemptive for believers but also revelatory for all reality.[11] We both *receive* the gift and *embody* the grace of the Trinity's life, source, and summit of all that is.

To summarize, then: the Trinity's own eventful way of being—a presence *to*, a relationship *with*, and an encounter *for*—provides the

[10] Christ as bodying forth the life of God is a favorite image of the Dominican Edward Schillebeeckx, especially in *Christ, the Sacrament of the Encounter with God*, 3rd rev. ed., trans. Cornelius Ernst (Kansas City: Sheed, Andrews, and McMeel, 1963), see, for example, 15–16, 59. For the notion of ritual's role of "inscripting" (i.e., writing it upon our hearts), I am indebted to my friend and mentor Edward Foley, Capuchin, especially his essay titled "The Eucharistic Prayer: An Unexplored Creed," in *Assembly* 28.4, Notre Dame Center for Pastoral Liturgy (July 2002). See also Louis-Marie Chauvet, *The Sacraments: The Word of God at the Mercy of the Body* (Collegeville, MN: Liturgical Press, 2001), 166–67.

[11] For more on the relationship between the redemptive and revelatory aspects of Christ's act of self-giving, see Anne Hunt, *The Trinity and the Paschal Mystery: A Development in Recent Catholic Theology* (Collegeville, MN: Liturgical Press, 1997).

dynamism that constitutes this "action surpassing all others" that we call Christian worship. In the church's liturgy, we remember the story of this glorious promise of redemption and mercy and claim its enduring power as our own. We then join Christ in glorious praise and thanks, with all the angels and saints, consecrated into a holy communion of all that has been, is now, and will be forever. Our harmony with God's way of proceeding gives flesh and blood to a desire that mirrors and responds to the divine Desire acting in us, shaping us, luring us into fullness. This proclaims authentic worship in spirit and in truth, to which Jesus invited the woman at the well (John 4:24) and renews in every age, gathering a people to himself, as Eucharistic Prayer III acknowledges, "so that from the rising of the sun to its setting a pure sacrifice may be offered to [God's] name." No lone rangers or isolated monads compose the agents and actors here. A community at worship is in harmony and rhythm with the very life and being of the triune God.

How does this shared passion of the community of God enhance our own communion? Or, in the words of a more formal systematic theology, how does the immanent Trinity (how God is in God's self) share that life as the economic Trinity (God as "for us" in an act of created Love)?[12] The final points of this chapter will look at the particular way that gathering in the name of the Father, Son, and Holy Spirit can draw us as worshipers, presiders, ministers, and educators of the liturgy into a more faithful expression of the divine Desire acting in us.

GOD THE FATHER AS SOURCE AND SUMMIT OF ALL LIFE AND LOVE

> There is a river whose streams make glad the city of God.
>
> —Psalm 46:4

The Eastern churches of our tradition have held fast to liturgy's role as an expression of the trinitarian life of God. In the West, we have

---

[12] The recent theological works of Edward Kilmartin, SJ, such as *Christian Liturgy* (Kansas City: Sheed and Ward, 1988) and *The Eucharist in the West: History and Theology*, ed. Robert J. Daly (Collegeville, MN: Liturgical Press, 1998); of Catherine Mowry LaCugna's *God For Us: The Trinity and Christian Life* (San Francisco: HarperSanFrancisco, 1991); and of Jean Corbon's *The Wellspring of Worship*, trans. Matthew J. O'Connell (New York: Paulist Press, 1988) are but a few examples that provide a wonderful resource for the meaning of this relationship for theology, liturgical practice, and spirituality.

18

gradually become so focused on the doctrinal dimensions of what we do and say in worship that we have diminished the power of our drinking deeply from the source from which all this graced life flows. The cosmic dimension of liturgy, as the Eastern churches have maintained, pours forth from our primal connectedness to this deep desire emanating from the very heart of God, the wellspring of all that is. The Dominican Jean Corbon speaks of this dynamic out of the Eastern Catholic ritual tradition that shapes his theology of worship. His poetic words are themselves a great resource for liturgical piety and imaginative conversion:

> In the river of life there is a current of tenderness, an incomparable element of attraction. The energy of the holy God, his communion of love, is permeated by an impatient desire, a passion: "to be with the children of [humankind]" (Prov 8:31). At the origin of the human person—of each and every human being—there is this outpouring of love within the Trinity, a pierced love that calls us to a life: from the gaze of the Father in his beloved Son there springs up God's thirst, his thirst for human beings. Thus too, in the very beginning the human nostalgia for God is born.[13]

The West is no stranger to this trinitarian dynamism. Spiritual writers speak often of God's passion for humankind as a desire to be with the fruit of God's creation. For example, St. Catherine of Siena, in a mystical reverie recorded in her *Dialogue*, tries to capture this passion of the Trinity of God reaching down into the depths of redemption:

> And you, High Eternal Trinity,
> acted as if you were drunk with love,
> infatuated with your creature.
>
> When you saw that this tree could bear no fruit
> but the fruit of death
> because it was cut off from you who are life,
> you came to its rescue
> with the same love
> with which you created it:
>
> you engrafted your divinity
> into the tree of our humanity.

[13] Corbon, *Wellspring of Worship*, 18.

O sweet tender engrafting!
You, sweetness itself,
stooped to join yourself
with our bitterness.[14]

Religious movements like the Carmelite reform were so attentive to this same dynamic. Iain Matthew, OCD, considering the "dark night" of St. John of the Cross and its radical encounter with the triune mystery, comments on John's mystical canticle "The Fountain":

> *Qué bien sé yo la fonte . . .*
> I know so well the fountain, rushing and flowing
> though it be night.

The stanzas tell of an ocean-sized waterfall, which is the Father surrendering to the Son, Son self-emptying to the Father, Spirit-water spilling out to create a universe; the cosmos comes to sip it, though all—heaven, people, hell—are already drenched in it. John [of the Cross] knows it, believes it; and he sees it welcomed, cupped, and offered to him in the Bread of Life:

> That everlasting fountain comes concealed
> in this living bread, to *give us life*
> though it be night.[15]

Centuries later, St. Ignatius of Loyola, the founder of the Jesuits in the late fifteenth century, begins his first contemplation of the mysteries of our redemption in his *Spiritual Exercises* by asking the retreatant to imagine the Trinity contemplating the world.[16] That love which such engagement engenders remains such that God cannot *not* be with humankind and sends the Beloved One, Jesus, incarnate in the flesh.

We can move too quickly in our liturgical spirituality toward a sustained reflection on the redemptive nature of Christ's life, death, and resurrection without adequately reverencing the passionate source and wellspring that reveals and animates this act of self-giving. God's desire to act out of a Love that defines God's very being is generative,

---

[14] Suzanne Noffke, ed., *The Prayers of Catherine of Siena* (New York: Paulist Press, 1983).

[15] Iain Matthew, OCD, *The Impact of God: Soundings from John of the Cross* (London: Hodder & Stoughton, 1995), 73.

[16] *Sp. Ex.* 102–9.

as a mother tenderly gathers her children to herself. This parental love, by its sacrificial nature, gives kenotic (i.e., self-emptying) shape to the act of worship we do because God's desire is "taken, blessed, broken and shared." It provides the template for our own being-in-the-world. How *is* that and what does that mean for us? A few aspects of this divine way of proceeding may help to clarify the liturgical character of our own lives.

God remains true to Love by simply loving. The divine source of all that is acts on that truth by the desire to share this "God-ness" with creation. So we can say that God "takes" that identity, "blesses" it, giving thanks and praise for the goodness of creation that is its shared fruitfulness, by delighting in what God has made. Divine delight spills over in the creative act of fashioning the earth in Genesis ("God saw everything that he had made, and indeed, it was very good" [Gen 1:31]) and in other biblical books such as Proverbs, the Song of Solomon, Wisdom, Deutero-Isaiah, and Revelation. That utter joy thunders from the Jordan River (Mark 1:11) and the mountain at the transfiguration (Luke 3:22; Mark 9:7), and begs the disciples to "listen to him." The Scriptures read in the liturgical assembly trumpet God's joy so that Christ's paschal "transitus" (his coming passage back to the Father) will be experienced, through the lens of Jesus' triumphant victory over sin and death, as our own call to fullness of life, *per ipsum, et cum ipso, et in ipso*. "Let this place resound with joy," the *Exsultet* proclaims in the darkness of the Easter Vigil, "echoing the mighty song of all God's people!" This joy and delight outweighs all the pains of its coming to birth. We need to recover the spiritual passion at the heart of this desire for us and tap into the refreshment it offers us, even in the most bleak and desolate times of our lives:

> Under the apple tree I awakened you.
> There your mother was in labor with you;
>> there she who bore you was in labor.
> Set me as a seal upon your heart,
>> as a seal upon your arm;
> for love is strong as death,
>> passion fierce as the grave.
> Its flashes are flashes of fire,
>> a raging flame.
> Many waters cannot quench love,
>> neither can floods drown it.
> (Song of Solomon 8:5b-7a)

, to draw again from Corbon, that love is also "broken" and ˌced," because God "'gives away' his Word and Breath, and all ˌgs are called into being." That self-giving is an emptying out, a "love that is pierced," because "[God's] love reveals itself there, but in a shadow of a promise to which no attention is paid."[17] The labor of giving birth is a "kenosis," a self-emptying. The "sharing" awaits reception, but Love cannot hold back until creation responds in kind. The vulnerability of this act should shake us at our foundations at the awesomeness of what God is accomplishing in us, an abundance revealed in unexpected places. Standing together, raising our hands in praise and thanks, gives flesh to that ritual response we utter, often with too light regard: "It is right [i.e., "meet and just" and "right and profitable for our salvation" as the preface goes on to underscore] to give our thanks and praise." Precise words cannot capture its awesomeness. Standing together, singing, gesturing, and moving to the rhythm comes closer. Embodied adoration and delight seem so appropriate here, rather than dour passivity and distance.

From this brief look at the dynamic of the Father as generative, self-emptying, delighted, and involved in the act of loving, we can see the liturgical dynamics of our own lives. A presence *to*, a relationship *with*, and an encounter *for* a deeper communion in God and the community of the Beloved shares in the primal creative act of the One who called us into being. Before any prayer is uttered or song is sung, the gathering has begun in the heart of God. The *assembly's simple presence* gives flesh to that desire at work in us. The congregation is holy because God is holy! "Holy things for the holy people," cries the presider at early Christian liturgies such as Cyril of Jerusalem's fourth-century community.[18] How happy and blessed are we to be called to the Supper of the Lamb! The pattern of our praise and thanks, rooted in God's own self-giving and delight sharpens in focus.

Imagine if *presiders* gathered the Body of Christ with an attentive reverence for this sacred mystery of the Father's unquenchable desire, which is incarnate in the community flowing through the doors and constituting the church on any given Sunday.[19] But the responsibility does not stop there. *Preparing* the liturgy and *ministering* at the ambo

---

[17] Corbon, *Wellspring of Worship*, 17.

[18] *Mystagogical Catecheses*, 5.19.

[19] See Alexander Schmemann, *For the Life of the World* (Crestwood, NY: St. Vladimir's Seminary Press, 1988), 27. Father Schmemann says that the

22

and the altar table with similar attentiveness would be acts of complementary devotion and self-emptying love. Gratitude would shape the whole assembly's gestures and voices and attention. *Teaching the young* these mysteries of our faith might ask more faith-sharing, wonder, and imaginative reflection on what God might be saying to us through simple gifts and faithful people. We might even be more cautious about manipulating the rites for secondary agendas or mere convenience. The words we employ to express God's loving encounter would be more adequately captured in the poetic rather than the explanatory or trivial.

Harmony with the desire of God expresses the dynamic and many-faceted character of holy communion, in which the entire *event* takes spiritual precedence over much of our current concerns regarding power, status, and political correctness. It follows that the sacramentals we use to express this relationship, such as water and light and fire, graceful movement and procession, might matter more to us in terms of quality and abundance. We will speak of this more in the later chapters. Suffice it to say at this point that we are tapping into a deep well of passion, rooted in the source and summit of our lives and worship, taking shape in the great but ordinary fact of our gathering to do the things we do in the liturgy. Recognizing the parental love of God as the wellspring of this healing "current of tenderness" draws people together around important matters of worship rather than wedges them apart.

JESUS CHRIST AS THE ONE WHO BODIES FORTH THIS RELATIONAL, INTERPERSONAL LOVE

> From on high he flowed like a river,
> From Mary he stemmed as from a root,
> From the cross he descended as fruit,
> As the first-fruit he ascended into heaven
> Blessed is his will!
> The Word came forth from the Father's bosom,
> He put on the body in another bosom;
> From one bosom to another did he proceed,
> And chaste bosoms are filled with him.
> Blessed is he who dwells within us!
>
> —Saint Ephrem the Syrian, fourth century

---

mundane act of Christians leaving home and bed and making their way "to *constitute the Church*" reveals that "a sacramental act is already taking place."

On the night before his great passage from life to death, Jesus gathered the Beloved for a meal that recalled the faithful covenant of God's deliverance of the chosen and the abiding invitation to be led by fire and cloud as they journey always as a community of disciples into a new land. Jesus' own eucharistic prayer of thanks and praise to the Father in John 17 includes not only the redemptive nature of his self-offering but also the revelatory moment of humankind's own communion with the One who is source and summit of all that is. John's familiar passage, most familiar to us in the Easter Sunday cycle, may sound simply circuitous and repetitive in content, but its rhythm and harmony reflect the relational, dialogical, and participative quality of the trinitarian life itself, and Jesus' own presence *for us* as the incarnational expression of the dynamic community of God. Jesus prays and intercedes in the context of his own hour of being handed over and poured out for the life of the world:

> I ask not only on behalf of these, but also on behalf of those who will believe in me through their word, that they may all be one. As you, Father, are in me and I am in you, may they also be in us, so that the world may believe that you have sent me. The glory that you have given me I have given them, so that they may be one, as we are one, I in them and you in me, that they may become completely one, so that the world may know that you have sent me and have loved them even as you have loved me. Father, I desire that those also, whom you have given me, may be with me where I am, to see my glory, which you have given me because you loved me before the foundation of the world. (John 17:20-24)

God's desire now melds into Jesus' desire at this most critical juncture, and that passion consecrates us as the Body of Christ for mission. The symbolic density of the *real presence* of Christ in the liturgy stands upon this cosmic interchange of love. The fruitfulness of Jesus' life, death, and resurrection does not exist as a separate divine act that is simply handed to us on a platter and in a cup and simply left on the altars of our churches to be dispensed or venerated for its own sake. At the heart of this great sacramental encounter of presence is the intimate love between the Son and the Father, whose parental generativity bears mature fruit in the loving response of Jesus in offering his own body and blood as testament to that love. In this great act in which he no longer calls us servants "who do not know what the master is doing" but friends, "because I have made known to you everything

Can a formal memorized prayer of the presider ever be as powerful as free prayer?

that I have heard from my Father," Jesus asks us to enter into communion with him, to "take and eat" of the mature fruit of this loving response.

The institutional narrative that we associate ritually with transformation of the bread and wine in the Synoptic Gospels expands even more pointedly in John's context to the community's own summons to be broken and poured out as a sacrifice of praise, in union with her Lord. Yet, even here, the rhythm of this dynamic exchange of obedient love is not complete. The Holy Spirit, the Advocate, will lead us deeper into the mystery of this divine communion and its abundance, so that as the new chosen people, we are then empowered "to go out and bear fruit" in our loving one another (John 15:15-16). The paschal meal expresses the wide dimensions of the gift given, whose very reception consecrates the community itself in its Christian identity.

That is why we insist here that Jesus' redemptive act memorialized in the Eucharist is also *revelatory* of a greater eschatological abundance, a manifestation of the cosmic expanse of divine desire at work in creation. What that means is that the saving deeds of Christ become a moment of our own transfiguration, where we glimpse the passion in the heart of God and experience the Father's invitation to draw from its life-giving stream of grace.[20] What God has given Jesus, Jesus now in turn gives to us. But even more, where Jesus *is* becomes a place where we find our truest home. Redemption is here, *where the Beloved are.* It is "Christ who lives" now in us, through the power of the self-surrender of his life in obedient love (Gal 2:20). Our identity as a people hinges on this connection, rooted in God's primal aspiration: "Father, I desire that those also . . . may be with me where I am, to see my glory, which you have given me because you loved me before the foundation of the world" (John 17:24). A later chapter will explore the presence of Christ in the bread and wine and its significance for the whole liturgy. What concerns us here is that Jesus' identity and presence are inseparable from his presence *to,* his relationship *with,* and his encounter *for* the mission of the Father who sent him. Any consideration of Christ's sacramental presence must take into account

[20] On the transfiguration as a "seeing" by the disciples of the glory of Christ with the Father, see Corbon, *Wellspring of Worship,* 59–62. This is a revered theme in Easter Christian spirituality and worship, one in which Westerners can gain much more clarity regarding the spirituality of participation in the divine mystery that the liturgy celebrates.

the intense relationality and generativity of this paschal context. Jesus knows that he comes from Love and is returning to that Love, and so he longs to share that servant love at the Passover feast with the Beloved (John 13:3-5). The outpouring of that loving relationship of mutual love is the Holy Spirit in which we now participate. Jesus' action redeems and reveals and consecrates, all in the same act.

This web of interrelated realities constitutes what Yves Congar called the "mystery in its fullness," which the church's liturgy actively "celebrates and contains."[21] The eucharistic mystery can never be reduced to the self-enclosed confines of particles of bread and drops of wine in and of themselves. These material elements themselves are dynamic, a visible manifestation of the Word that was uttered by God to us in Christ and revealed to our ancestors in faith. Bread and wine, "which earth has given and human hands have made," are to be taken and blessed, broken and shared in ritual remembrance so that they become the expression of that covenantal promise of God revealed in Jesus. The gathered, praying assembly eats and drinks the holy gifts and she reserves the fragments for the sick and infirm and for the community's post-Eucharist devotion as a testimony to the abiding presence of that desire of God for us. This prolific desire is communicated first to Jesus ("the first-born of those who have died" [1 Cor 15:20]), and now communicated to us as the advent and birth of our own mission for the life of the world. Paul captures this with metaphorical grace in the Letter to the Romans: "If part of the dough offered as first fruits is holy, then the whole batch is holy; and if the root is holy, then the branches are holy" (Rom 11:16).

This dynamic, relational presence also provides the soul of a faithful eucharistic piety and devotional life outside of the liturgy itself. Adoration spills over from a focal presence in the bread to the holiness and efficacy of the gift coursing through the veins of this whole Body and through the creation God loves and Christ redeems. For Congar, the liturgy must always move from the zeal of devotion to its special role as a *locus theologicus* that attempts to announce the mystery in ways beyond doctrinal formulation. Hence, Congar notes the words of W. S. Vorsier, his contemporary, when speaking of the church's act of worship as a "witnessing to or a profession of faith":

ion and Traditions, 82.

The Church did not begin by saying that bread was being changed into Christ's Body and that wine was being changed into Christ's Blood; what it began by saying and still says, is: "This is my Body, this is my Blood"; the additional change may almost be called an afterthought.[22]

This "witnessing" is more than observing a miraculous transformation. Christ's Body and Blood are gifts to nourish the People of God in order that the gathered church may communicate that passion and desire of divine connectedness into every aspect of creation. To imagine the quality of sacramental presence without that eventful quality of "taking, blessing, breaking, and sharing," which reflects the dynamic character of Jesus' own life and mission, masks the depth of its holiness as "Blessed Sacrament." Regarding the Body and Blood of Christ as static objects at which we gaze and marvel stops terribly short of the blessedness present in this sacrament. This static understanding of Eucharist as a *thing* rather than an *event* mutes the Father's eternal word spoken in the pregnant hush of creation, in the flash and furor of deliverance from exile, and in the redemptive suffering that results from a love that is "pierced" and poured out. Christ's "yes" to the Father echoes in Mary's kenotic response in joy to the angel: "Let it be done to me according to your word" (Luke 1:38). The sword of love that will pierce her own heart (Luke 2:35) does not spare her own child, nor should it spare us. "All mine are yours," Jesus says to the Father, "and yours are mine; and I have been glorified in them" (John 17:10). This whole redemptive "mystery of our faith" comes to fruitfulness in the sacramental presence of Christ, when we "receive" him. Such a generative birthright courses also through the veins of martyrs and saints whose own witness to the Word made flesh became the seeds and nourishment of the church down to the present day. This is the *real presence* of Christ born out of the community of God.

Theologians at the time of the Second Vatican Council, followed by much sacramental reflection in decades since the reform, have noted this presence of Christ as "the sacrament of God," the sign and the reality of the communion between Lover and Beloved in which we are invited to share. Roman Catholic theologians, such as Karl Rahner, Edward Schillebeeckx, in particular, and Bernard Cooke, Kenan Osborne, Ghislain Lafont, David Power, and Louis-Marie Chauvet, in recent years, go back to this primal sacramentality that underlies all

[22] Ibid.

sacramental and liturgical theology.[23] Jesus is not simply a model to be "imitated," as Chauvet has noted, but a grace-filled presence in relationship that announces and offers that same intimate communion in the divine life from which he comes "as the gratuitous gift of God and, more precisely, as Savior." Moreover, as Chauvet goes on to explain,

> He is our ferryman to God's shore. We do not have to desperately run after him to join him: he himself comes toward us, as at Emmaus, and takes us in his boat to carry us to the other shore. It is, before all else, this truth that the sacraments are witnessing to us: a pure gift from God deposited in our hands (The body of Christ—Amen).[24]

Once again, the liturgical dynamic and the foundation for a liturgical spirituality in Christ's "bodying forth" the gift of God's way of being provide us with a rich treasure of reflection for our corporate worship, as well as our individual soul-making. In communion with his Father, Christ's mode of presence is always a loving surrender *to* the One who loved him, and *to* the community *with* whom he walks and is received as guest, and whose real presence among us we come to know, as Luke recounts, "in the breaking of the bread" (Luke 24:35). Christ lived and died and rose *for* our holy communion, both with God and one another, and participation in the mystery (our reception of the sacrament) asks no less of us.

[23] For example, see Karl Rahner, *The Church and the Sacraments* (New York: Herder and Herder, 1963); Edward Schillebeeckx, OP, *Christ the Sacrament of the Encounter with God* (Kansas City: Sheed and Ward, 1963); Bernard Cooke, *Sacraments and Sacramentality*, 2nd ed. (Mystic, CT: Twenty-Third Publications, 1994); Kenan Osborne, *Sacramental Theology* (New York: Paulist Press, 1988); Ghislain Lafont, *Eucharist: The Meal and the Word*, trans. Jeremy Driscoll, OSB (New York: Paulist Press, 2008); David M. Power, OMI, *The Eucharistic Mystery: Revitalizing the Tradition* (New York: Crossroad, 1992); and Louis-Marie Chauvet, *The Sacraments: The Word of God at the Mercy of the Body* (Collegeville, MN: Liturgical Press, 2001). See also part I of my book *The Holy Preaching*. This is a recovery of a patristic notion of sacrament that Eastern Catholic and Orthodox theologians have articulated consistently. Cf. Schmemann, *For the Life of the World* (Crestwood, NY: St. Vladimir's Seminary Press, 1988); and John Zizioulas, *Being as Communion* (Crestwood, NY: St. Vladimir's Seminary Press, 1985).

[24] Chauvet, *Sacraments*, 53–54. Quotations from this source are used with permission of Liturgical Press.

in the community of God. The liturgy enacts the sign and reality of the community's conscious, public act of *identity-making in the Spirit*, because God's desire and Jesus' bodying forth of that Love transform those who gather in its power and grace.

The Spirit's guidance into truth that Jesus promises (John 16:13) is not some private revelation that can be hoarded but a willingness to be led with Christ into the dynamics of the heart of God. Christian tradition calls this conversion. Individualism, self-contempt, and any form of oppression that divides the human family express the decayed fruits of our choosing our own individual ways, rather than the way of proceeding grounded in the names of God. The Father's desire for us takes flesh in Jesus' own desire to offer fitting praise to the One who loved him and sent him as the redemptive, revelatory gift of Savior and Lover of the world (John 17:5). The Holy Spirit's presence is the sharing of that dynamic self-offering with us on behalf of all creation, inscripted into us as our truest identity. The church's presence in the world announces the sacrament of that divine love that, in turn, loves, heals, forgives, and transforms the world. That gift of the Spirit, written upon our communal heart, provides the fire that fuels our mission, a fire passed on to us through the Spirit of the risen Christ, and nurtured through the faith of our ancestors who have gone before us in faith. Jesus' priestly prayer begs that the Father send the Spirit and "sanctify" the Beloved (John 17:17-19), and this *epiclesis* enkindles a desire in us that lures the community continually toward the promise. The fruit of our gathering in faith seals the new covenant, and the liturgy provides the time and space where the Spirit tends the flame of that love that shapes our identity as a Christian community.

Jerome Hall, SJ, pondering the thought of the late Edward Kilmartin, SJ, articulated the power of the Spirit's role in *all human longing* that is rooted in God:

> Through the sending of the Spirit the fulfillment of humankind is also realized. Human persons, created with an orientation toward the Transcendent, yearn for the perfect happiness of personal union with God; this yearning is fulfilled in the gift of communion with the Trinity. Jesus' greatest act of love of neighbor, therefore, is his invocation of the Holy Spirit.[26]

---

[26] Jerome Hall, *We Have the Mind of Christ*, 134.

The Christian liturgy, therefore, provides the strings for the harp of the Spirit to sing of the cosmic dimension of this in-gathering that Jesus invokes now that his "hour" has come (John 17:1).

Once again, we see that the Spirit's role reflects the inner dynamism of our worship. The fruitful and mutual love of the Father and the Son revealed at Word and table and font spills over into their relationship with the created world. The Spirit's action takes the humanity that Christ loves and inscripts that way of loving and being into the enfleshed community, which is the basic sacrament of the community of God. Henceforth, our way of being in this mystery is *participative, dialogical*, and *interrelational* if we are to live into the grace and gift of the Spirit that identifies us as the Body of Christ. The thanks and praise that characterize Jesus' attitude toward the Father becomes the eucharistic people's attitude and way of prayer, through the bond we share in the power of the Holy Spirit. The loving presence that each baptized member of the worshiping community bodies forth to the others becomes the truth of Christ's life and the model of the church's life as she embraces the world. Consequently, the pattern of liturgy inscripted by the Spirit becomes clear to us in the doing of the deed (*ex opere operato*), and our presence *to*, and our participation *with*, and our loving service *for* the world God loves must shape the way we offer fitting thanks and praise to God.

Conversion and transformation at these profound depths require "spiritual direction," in the widest sense of that term. We have the Holy Spirit to "guide us in this truth," as Jesus promised (John 16:13). We may resist such a call to conversion, or mask that mode of Christ's presence by the scandal of our corporate and personal witness, yet the longing of Love—Christ's Spirit in us—will not rest until it rests in its truest identity, the Body of Christ, as Augustine reminded us with such clarity. Communion in the power of the Holy Spirit, in this sense, reveals Christ as Lover of God and of those to whom he is sent. The Lover says to the Beloved that we "*do this* in memory of him." The grace of eating and drinking in grateful memory means that we receive the *totus Christus*, an intimate sharing of both head and members of the Body he claims as his own. This activity further announces "the gift of participation in Christ's covenant sacrifice and [our] resulting communion with the Trinity and all the saints," as Hall later notes. [27] *Christ-for-us and we-for-Christ* describes the dynamic, and, as Kilmartin

---

[27] Ibid., 146.

himself insisted, "this reciprocal personal relation is grounded on the work of the Holy Spirit who both brings Christ to the faithful and the faithful to Christ."[28]

Such pneumatological considerations make it clear that a liturgical spirituality that takes seriously the gift of the Holy Spirit as the bond of our holy communion deserves more careful focus than we have given it in the West in recent centuries. The reform of the liturgy after Vatican II seems only now to bring those questions to the fore in a way the church never imagined forty years ago. Any form of sacramental worship whose unspoken motivations and outward expression exclude, fracture, and individualize clashes with the deeper life-giving stream that emanates from the heart of God. Radical engagement and surrender in the power of the Spirit is the only way that our worship will harmonize with the passion of God from which it springs. Longing wistfully for a mystery to be performed at a more comfortable distance from our communal heart and that sees actual participation of the whole *totus Christus* as peripheral increases the ritual dissonance. Perhaps this distancing provides an insight into the wide range of ritual discontent among a variety of believers that currently characterizes our ecclesial life. The fact that the tension exists at all could well provide the greatest evidence of the persistence of that Spirit of Christ's faith and love now taking hold in us.

BROTHERS AND SISTERS, WHAT ARE WE TO DO? (SEE ACTS 2:37): LITURGICAL PRAYING AS AN ACT OF CONVERSION AND TRANSFORMATION

It is important to affirm here that we need not be paralyzed by our struggles as a contemporary church, especially with regard to the role the liturgy plays in our ecclesial identity. The community of God—Father, Son, and Holy Spirit—takes our communion in this mystery so seriously. The presence of Christ we experience in sacramental life "bodies forth" God's desire in our actions of "taking, blessing, breaking, and sharing." Attention and reverence to these holy things in the liturgy exercises our ecclesial identity and renders Christ present as sacramental food and drink that we need to live. They build up hope and cast out fear, because the muted signs and symbols of that divine connection are alive again. This paschal shape of the liturgy, born of Christ's incarnation and the Spirit's gift in our midst, gives a hallowed

---

[28] Kilmartin, *Eucharist in the West*, 371.

role to the *elements* we use, the *assembly* who gathers to pray and sing, the *Word* that is proclaimed and preached, and the *presider* who gathers the community into communion. All these dynamic actions and actors are interconnected, revelatory of a presence whose various modes exhibit a rhythm and a harmony of the Spirit hymning the life of God in us. Standing together in the community of God, singing and moving to the rhythm of the triune life: this is the shape of a worship whose participants are willing to be taken, blessed, broken, and shared for the life of the whole world. Christ is present in a powerful way. In the years before Vatican II, Thomas Merton spoke of this sacramental presence as a "peace" that liberates and leads into even deeper reaches of communion we could never have asked for or imagined. It is a "sign that we have opened the door that leads to the inner sanctuary of our own being, the secret place where we are united to God."[29] Our experience of engaged eucharistic praying in the past fifty years has expanded that landscape of the "inner sanctuary." This is not simply an individualist piety but a spirituality of our communion as a people.

As the great twentieth-century theologian Henri de Lubac, SJ, reflected in the years after the council, our *ecclesial life* then becomes "a prolonged *epiclesis*, or prayer for the coming of the Spirit."[30] The calling down of the Spirit consecrates and transforms what is ordinary into a vessel to bear the Holy. The map of our way, our truth, and our life has been written upon our hearts and in our bodies, minds, and spirits. Its focal expression is enacted at the gathered event of our communal act of worship. The rest of this book explores the rich depths of that summons to hear again the covenant promise offered to our forebears and to join around the altar of Christ's abundance, in which our own surrender becomes a fruitful offering of thanks and praise. It is all about "real presence," as we stand together in the community of God.

[29] Thomas Merton, *The Living Bread* (New York: Farrar, Straus and Giroux, 1956), 69.

[30] Fergus Kerr, OP, "French Theology: Yves Congar and Henri de Lubac," in *The Modern Theologians*, 2nd ed., ed. David F. Ford, 108 (Oxford: Blackwell, 2001). Quoting de Lubac in *Je crois en l'Esprit Saint* (1978–80).

34

"O Sign of Unity! O Bond of Charity!": The Presence of Christ in the Liturgical Assembly

> You yourselves are our letter, written on our hearts, to be known and read by all; and you show that you are a letter of Christ, prepared by us, written not with ink but with the Spirit of the living God, not on tablets of stone but on tablets of human hearts.
>
> —2 Corinthians 3:2-3

Once again, we start with what we know together deep in our bones, particularly so when considering the presence of Christ in the worshiping assembly. The spiritual passion that keeps theology and liturgical practice in creative tension takes on a very human and subjective character here, because we are talking about ourselves. The baptized faithful locate in time and place the Spirit-filled, resurrected Body of Christ that is inseparable from the desire pouring from the heart of the community of God. That grace-filled bond has deepened and expanded through the social energy that has gathered as it has streamed through the lives and deaths of the communion of saints who have brought our living faith to this present day. We will start with a common experience of an ordinary community. That commonness both reveals and hides a great mystery, and it takes a little reverent attention in order to allow it to give up the treasure embedded there.

Imagine this scene. At approximately ten minutes to nine on any Sunday evening at a Jesuit university in the northwest United States, students begin to pour out of the residence halls and make their way to the college chapel to celebrate Eucharist. A similar event of gathering takes place in parishes and chapels throughout the Christian world on the *Dies Domini*, the Day of the Lord. Careful attention to this particular place and context is helpful to illustrate the sacramental character of Christ's presence in the assembly and its relationship to all that will follow in the celebration of these sacred mysteries. *Sacrosanctum Concilium*, the Constitution on the Sacred Liturgy of Vatican II, ascribes a dynamic nature to this particular mode of Christ's active presence in the liturgy: "He is present . . . when the Church prays and sings, for he promised: 'Where two or three are gathered together in my name, there am I in the midst of them' (Mt 18:20)" (SC 7). Given the rhythm and harmony of the relational life of God that founds the nature of the worshiping community, we emphasize that the simple act of gathering is already rooted in the passion of God for us. An attentive reflection on the simplicity of this act has meaning for theology, liturgical practice, and the spirituality that binds it all together. So let us return to this university community gathering on a Sunday evening.

The wellspring of the life of God, poured out upon each person in baptism, begins to make the simple act of rising from the desk, the television, or the spirited conversations of students relating their weekend exploits into an effective sign of the presence of Christ in the liturgy. The spiral toward the great act of holy communion in the Body and Blood of Christ draws a disparate group of young people out into the cold and often rainy night, despite the fact that there are many other alluring and competing invitations to which they could acquiesce. One could simply marvel at the discipline of these students or posit a host of reasons why other factors can explain the great in-gathering of the People of God that makes up this local church. We must be cautious at assigning the "Catholic guilt" response to such marvelous deeds. Young people today do not share that particular obsession of their adult forebears in the faith. But they do feel impelled, often against their more immediate desires to be about other things. Let us simply leave the psychosocial issues there. What happens concretely almost needs to be seen rather than analyzed. Descriptive words with a poetic intent must suffice, so an appeal to the imagination ensues as we continue this narrative.

Imagine these individuals debating with themselves about whether they should go, deciding for some reason to make the effort to get up and begin the journey down the mall toward the chapel, whose lights and colors and open doors provide an inviting beacon that orients their unfocused desire. Some have already negotiated the journey with a group of friends; others walk alone, deep in thought; still others meet up with friends and acquaintances as the common path brings them together. They discuss life and school, parents and love relationships, struggles and joys. This reveals the primary stuff of Eucharist, the encounters and events and elements of our lives that make up the persons who will find a common unity and identity in the ritual Word and Sacrament to follow. Even if individuals are attending for personal reasons, intending to pray for particular needs and people, that common grace of coming together still flows from the heart of God, revealed in Jesus' own longing to eat the Passover with his Beloved *ut unum sint*. This procession toward the sacred mysteries burns with the same zeal of the Spirit that stirred the hearts of the dispirited disciples at Emmaus, which culminated in their unexpected decision to invite the bearer of this burning hope into the midst of their own darkness: "Stay with us," the travelers say, "because it is almost evening and the day is now nearly over" (Luke 24:29).

Gathering to "Constitute the Church"

The Father's desire has a focused end of bringing the disparate into communion and of gathering social energy into graced sustenance. The liturgical celebration provides an expressive moment of that gathering energy of God that redeems and reveals itself in Jesus' paschal mystery, and that communicates its nourishment to us in the power of the Spirit. That is why the document on the liturgy insists on what it calls the *communal nature of the liturgy*:

> Liturgical services are not private functions, but are celebrations belonging to the Church, which is the "sacrament of unity," namely, the holy people united and ordered under their bishops. (SC 26)

The "ordering" here does not mean a compelling, forced march by higher authorities. The structured nature of the assembly into different ministries and gifts under the guidance of the bishops simply intends to state the universality of the church present in this simple, concrete, localized gathering of students late on a Sunday night. The source of that unity and diversity remains firmly in the desire emanating from the heart of God, the Trinity of Persons relating *to*, participating *with*, and mutually offering Love *for*. As Augustine said so ecstatically, "O sign of unity! O bond of charity!" Presiders, ministers, and those who prepare the liturgy need to attend to the immediacy of this bonding taking place as the community gathers. This particular "celebrating assembly," Chauvet reminds us, is "the primary locus of the church," for the *ek-klésia* (*kaleō*, "to call") defines the gathering as "called or convoked by God or Christ." Indeed, as Chauvet asserts, "a church without an *assembly* would be a contradiction in terms."[1] Hospitality certainly enters into the pastoral scenario here, but it is not merely the demands of etiquette. A liturgical spirituality that honors the theology and practice sacramentally expressed in the gathering asks that the atmosphere of the "church" welcome the wanderer and the pilgrim and the guest as Christ himself, sent as the Father's own self-expression (Matt 10:20).[2] Seeing Christ in all is a spiritual attitude that allows us to celebrate the truth of the Eucharist. All are welcome here, the old and young, rich and poor; all are to be received in an attitude of reverence and thanks for what God is doing in our midst. Respect for the time of day, the efforts of these holy ones to arrive, and the sacredness of the unfolding mysteries suggest that last-minute duties and personal attentions of the ministers take second place. Grace is flowing.

This reimagination and shift of focus to the primacy of the ecclesial gathering acknowledges that these students, and any other Sunday assembly of Christians, constitute the *primary celebrants of the liturgy*, ordered as one Body by liturgical ministers entrusted with this responsibility of acknowledging the unity of the assembly. Remembering this keeps the locus of the grace on what God is doing and clarifies the liturgical principle that those who preside, prepare, and minister are but servants of this mystery. "The Eucharist and the Church are both *corpus Christi*," as Henri de Lubac stated so clearly.

> The ambiguity is intentional and significant and has a forceful doctrinal impact. It conveys the idea of real continuity that exists between the head and the members of the unique body, and it simultaneously expresses the symbolic bond between the sacrament and the community.[3]

We must ponder de Lubac's use of the words *intentional* and *significant* concerning this multivalent use of the term *corpus Christi*. God's desire for mutual sharing of life now takes concrete form in the union of

---

[1] Louis-Marie Chauvet, *The Sacraments: The Word of God at the Mercy of the Body* (Collegeville, MN: Liturgical Press, 2001), 34.

[2] Saint Benedict's advice in the Rule, chap. 53, sees the guest as the disciple on the journey: "Let all guests who arrive be received like Christ, for He is going to say, 'I came as a guest, and you received Me' (Mt. 25:35)."

[3] Henri de Lubac, "Christian Community and Sacramental Communion," in *Theological Fragments* (*Théologies d'occasion*, 1984) (San Francisco: Ignatius Press, 1989), 72.

Christ and his church, what he calls a "real continuity." Could we not consider this a *real presence*? Truly, the assembly is not the head of the Body. And yet the Body does not exist without the head. The gathered church is "distinct" but not "separate" from Christ, in much the same way that both the bread and wine (*sacramentum tantum*) as material substances are distinct but not separate from the consecrated Body and Blood of Christ (*res tantum*) in the traditional scholastic theology of the Middle Ages. The biblical passage in *Sacrosanctum Concilium*, paragraph 7, affirming the presence of Christ in the praying and singing assembly, needs to be acknowledged here with greater emphasis: "'Where two or three are gathered together in my name, there am I in the midst of them' (Mt 18:20)." This is *real* and *true*, and such a revelation transforms the relationship between everyone and everything that we do as a sacramental people.

THE ASSEMBLY AS A FOCAL PARTICIPANT IN A MATRIX OF SYMBOLIC RELATIONSHIPS

To explain this with another metaphor, de Lubac emphasized elsewhere the marital imagery in St. Paul's writings as a way to speak about the union of Christ with the church and its symbolic expression in the Eucharist, which is the reality of that union effected in and through our self-offering with Christ and one another.[4] We receive communion as the sacramental sign that expresses the reality of our communion in the *totus Christus*, the fullness of Christ, the head with the members, and we taste the promise when sin and death are wiped away and God will be all in all. The Pauline imagery emphasizes how Christ "nourishes and tenderly cares for" the church "because we are members of his body," just as a husband loves and cares for his wife as for himself. These two become "one flesh" in this mutual care, Paul goes on to say, and concludes with the meaning of this great analogy: "This is a great mystery, and I am applying it to Christ and the church" (Eph 5:29-32). Husband and wife are not the same person, yet their union is profoundly one. Such is the living mystery the Eucharist celebrates: Christ the glorified Lord who, in communion with the lov-

---

[4] Cf. de Lubac, *Corpus Mysticum: L'Eucharistie et l'Eglise au moyen age* (Paris: Aubier, 1948). Susan Wood's *Spiritual Exegesis and the Church in the Theology of Henri de Lubac* (Grand Rapids: Eerdmans, 1998) discusses de Lubac's understanding of this, especially in chap. 3, "The Eucharist/Church Correlation and Spiritual Exegesis," 53–70.

ing intent of the Father, chooses radical intimacy with us, active now in the Spirit's bonding love, animating us now and luring us into the fullness to come. The sacramentality of married life is not captured in its depths by the static outline of a ceremony or the isolated words of a vow. The marriage event bodies forth the longing for union that began this courtship, the present love that is willing to surrender to a life radically transformed, and the future deepening of that gift that can only happen by "being married." The church's union with Christ also shares these rich depths of dimension and time, and the liturgy embraces them all and holds them in creative tension as the source and summit of Christian life (see SC 10). We are baptized into Christ; we share communion with him in Word and Sacrament; and the relationship deepens by "being church."

When Paul speaks in a similar vein in First Corinthians about the unity of head and members, of husband and wife, and the divisions that can arise when the mutual love of members is forgotten, his authority is the reality of Christ's own loving obedience to the Father (1 Cor 11:3), whose way, truth, and life is alive in the community through the power of the Spirit. Chiding the community for its significant disunity "when you come together," Paul then feels compelled to narrate their foundational identity in the Eucharist for which they assemble:

> For I received from the Lord what I also handed on to you, that the Lord Jesus on the night when he was betrayed took a loaf of bread, and when he had given thanks, he broke it and said, "This is my body that is for you. Do this in remembrance of me." In the same way he took the cup also, after supper, saying, "This cup is the new covenant in my blood. Do this, as often as you drink it, in remembrance of me." For as often as you eat this bread and drink the cup, you proclaim the Lord's death until he comes. (11:23-26)

Christ's life in them makes the way they live and the Eucharist they celebrate inseparably joined. Their struggle to live the communion they are necessitates that they gather and remember not only what Christ did in his paschal offering but also how that has been handed on through the communion of saints down to the present day. Both the communion of the church and the sacramental gifts are a real and active presence of Christ, each a sign that effects the reality of the other, a mutually relational, ever-deepening dialogue of absorption into the *totus Christus*, the fullness of Christ, our hope of glory.

Therefore, the "intentional and significant ambiguity" about the reality of *corpus Christi* that de Lubac noted cannot be passed over lightly but needs to be intensified in our spiritual reflection as a worshiping church. The melding of grace-filled presence—relational, dialogical, and participative—remembers, rests upon, and looks forward to Christ's saving deeds, which sanctify past, present, and future emanating from the desire flowing from the heart of God ("intentional"). At the same time, this cohesion of the Body of Christ, head and members, *totus Christus*, emphasizes that God has acted, is acting, and will act to effect the "symbolic bond" of the communion we celebrate ("significant"). The gathering announces that God "takes" the receptive community to be broken, blessed, and shared in these mysteries. And that saving truth can be trusted because God, amazingly enough, has been "taken" with us. The worshiping community matters because God matters (exhibits desire) for us and in us through Christ. The Spirit's drawing of disparate people on an ordinary night in a regular way becomes, as a result, consecrated and transformed into a sacramental action.

The Orthodox and Eastern Catholic traditions have always respected this dynamic. The Roman tradition lost a sense of the graced nature of this "matrix of relationships" that make up the dynamism of *corpus Christi*, focusing instead on metaphysical explanations for the real presence in the bread and wine.[5] Alexander Schmemann's description of the sacredness of the simple act of gathering stands as a wonderful corrective and a renewed foundation for a contemporary liturgical spirituality that holds theology and liturgical practice in creative tension. He speaks of this "journey or procession" on any given Lord's Day as "our sacramental entrance into the risen life of Christ" and "into a fourth dimension which allows us to see the ultimate reality of life" rather than providing an escape from it. Such claims should shake the foundations of our communal identity and open up a place in the community for the heart to respond to the blessing, breaking, and sharing to come. Listen to the almost musical strains of Schmemann's passionate description here:

> The journey begins when Christians leave their homes and beds. They leave, indeed, their life in this present and concrete world, and whether they have to drive fifteen miles or walk a few blocks, a sacramental act is already taking place, *an act that is the very condition of*

[5] Wood, *Spiritual Exegesis*, 62.

everything else that is to happen. For they are now on their way to *constitute the Church*, or to be more exact, to be transformed into the Church of God. They have been individuals . . . the "natural" world and a natural community. And now they have been called to "come together in one place," to bring their lives, their very "world" with them and to be more than what they were: a *new* community with a new life.[6]

The rites in the liturgy should express this giftedness of the assembly rather than distance the primary celebrants from the actual core actions that express the sacramental presence of Christ. We will explore this in greater detail later in the chapter. The ambiguity that may result from *intentionally* honoring such a real presence in the assembly as *significant* should be mined and tended and allowed to open up a place where the Spirit's activity can flourish. We need to listen to the Eastern churches when they invite us to recover the dynamism of the Body of Christ in the liturgical enactment of the sacred mysteries, as Schmemann and others have described. Roman Catholic liturgical theologian Bruce Morrill, SJ, in a similar vein, calls the Vatican II reform a return to the patristic sources that sacramental traditions of both East and West shared for six centuries:

> When Christians assemble for the divine worship they, the Church, participate in the *paschal mystery*, that is, Christ's life, passion, death, resurrection, and conferral of the Holy Spirit. To do the liturgy is to share in the very life of God revealed in the saving deeds of Jesus Christ.[7]

Morrill goes on to highlight the different but not conflicting foci of the two liturgical traditions as Eastern Orthodoxy's emphasis on the "mystical heart of the liturgy" as an ascending movement into "the perichoretic (mutually shared or inter-penetrating) love of the Trinity" and the West's focus on the "sacramental presence of Christ."[8] What we have been asserting here uses this matrix of relationships as an invitation to uncover and relish the multidimensional arena of encounter in the liturgy that unites us with Christ's paschal mystery at

---

[6] Schmemann, *For the Life of the World* (Crestwood, NY: St. Vladimir's Seminary Press, 1988), 26–27 (emphasis mine).

[7] Bruce T. Morrill, "Hidden Presence: The Mystery of the Assembly as Body of Christ," *Liturgical Ministry* 11 (Winter 2002): 31.

[8] Ibid.

the vertical, horizontal, and depth levels of our communal experience as worshiping believers.[9] Employing a relational, dialogical, and participative perspective in the theology, practice, and spirituality of worship helps us to see that such mutually enriching foci need not force a choice between the two emphases of East and West. They each keep the other grounded in the grace of the sacramental presence "hidden"[10] within the assembly, that is, that the grace flows from the heart of God and also streams into the incarnate world that Christ came to redeem and save in the paschal deeds that *now* are present to this Body, in this time and place of celebration. The grace-filled event fulfilled in our midst is mystical and transcendent, neither too-worldly nor beyond the reach of personal encounter. Again, the "way through" the seeming contradictions of the reality of the *corpus Christi* here remains a reverent attention to the rhythm, harmony, and balance of all actors and elements that make up the liturgy as a sacramental action.

Schmemann goes on to speak of the power of eucharistic memorial and presence, and the fullness to which they call the gathered assembly:

> The Eucharist has so often been explained with reference to the gifts alone: what "happens" to bread and wine, and why, and when it happens! But we must understand that what "happens" to bread and wine happens because something has, first of all, happened to us, to the Church. It is because we have "constituted" the Church, and this means we have followed Christ in His ascension; because he has accepted us at His table in His Kingdom; because, in terms of theology, we have entered the Eschaton, and are now standing beyond time and space; it is because all this has happened to us that something will happen to the bread and wine.[11]

---

[9] These three dimensions were outlined by Otto Semmelroth, SJ, in his book *Church and Sacrament*, trans. Emily Schossberger (Notre Dame: Fides Press, 1965), 19–28.

[10] Morrill's work cited above (32) highlights the important categories of Peter Fink, SJ, on the liturgical experience of Christ's presence: "In Word, Christ comes; in presider, Christ leads; in food, Christ abides; in assembly, Christ lives hidden" (*Praying the Sacraments*, Worship Series [Washington, DC: Pastoral Press, 1991], 84).

[11] Schmemann, *For the Life of the World*, 37.

In Christ, we have been "taken" as part of the great self-offering that emanates from the heart of God. The Spirit impels the movement toward communion and writes the script of this great interchange of mutual love and self-offering into the very fabric of our being as church. The Word proclaimed and preached situates us in the midst of the story of this great unfolding of the Father's redemptive, revelatory plan in Christ, whose narration confirms again the fidelity of the promise and the role our lives and witness play in this paschal mystery we are about to share for the life of the world. The presider and the ministers reveal Christ as Gatherer and Shepherd of this treasured flock, and everything we have received as pure gift. All of these modes of presence begin to coalesce and shape the liturgy into a significant whole, a proclamation of Christ's promise to his Beloved to be in their midst as reconciling communion in the world, binding up, letting loose, and pleading for the life of the world (Matt 18:18-20).

Paying attention to this matrix of symbolic relationships that happens because the community is faithfully gathering to do the work of liturgy transforms a one-dimensional act of gathering into a multilayered event of grace. Praying together out of that matrix allows the familiar words of the preface to come alive for the primary celebrants of these events, the common holy People of God: "You have no need of our praise, but our desire to thank you is itself your gift." Grateful hearts in communion with a generative God, source of all desire, body forth Christ in the power of the Spirit and utter words of thanks and praise in us. This constitutes the essence of eucharistic praying. The consequences of such praying together are immense. Unless the community is gathering to hear the Word by which they are convicted and to eat and drink in grateful memory, there is no Blessed Sacrament! And yet there really *is* a Blessed Sacrament; we can attest mightily to that, knowing it together deep in our bones. The simple, historical fact of the faithfulness of that gathering for the past two thousand years renders moot any misunderstanding of the intentional and significant ambiguity between the presence of Christ in the Eucharist and in the assembly. As Dom Gregory Dix reminds us at the end of his great masterpiece, *The Shape of the Liturgy* (1945), the faithful coming together of Christians through struggle and joy, persecution and victory, the mundane and momentous calls forth an attitude of awe and wonder of the magnificence of the God who is source and summit of all these faithful deeds: "The sheer stupendous *quantity* of the love of God which this ever repeated action has drawn from the obscure Christian multitudes through the centuries is itself an overwhelming thought."[12] It is God's communication of that love to the world through the community who, as "the letter of Christ, written not with ink but with the Spirit of the living God" (2 Cor 2:3), communicate the Lord they serve.

THE ASSEMBLY "DIVINIZED" IN THE LITURGY

The Eastern churches, for which the term *divinization* describes the process of all creation being taken up into the victory of Christ, provide an important balance for us if we doubt the worshiping assembly as primary locus of the theological act. The union of love between Christ and the church remains pure gift; it yields a humble awe and reverence and joy within the Body's gathering, not a self-focused attention on worthiness, communal or individual. "O Lord, we *are* not worthy," and a sacramental community with hands outstretched insists that all this grace and power finds its fontal energy in God. The Western habit of establishing a starting point solely from the "liturgical signs" and working back to the God who is the source tends to establish a ritualism that can easily be seen as efficacious in its own right. This in turn can focus theological and pastoral concern on proper performance and on metaphysical analysis of correct matter and form of the celebration. The churches of the East certainly maintain high regard for correct practice and ritualization, but the starting point is entirely different: "We must move rather from the mystery as revealed to us in the economy of salvation to its concretization in the liturgy," the Dominican Jean Corbon has noted. The sacramental life becomes the time and place "when the signs split open (and) they become transparent" and this fontal river of life can "stream out." This gradual unfolding of the life of the Trinity becomes transparent in the church, the believing community, as "the meeting place of two freedoms—that of faith and that of the Spirit"—which is concretely experienced in the liturgy, a moment of embodiment of "the life of God living in our flesh and the life of our humanity living in the Word."[13]

[12] Dix, *The Shape of the Liturgy* (Westminster: Dacre Press, 1945), 745. The whole passage that culminates in this section is one of the most moving passages in contemporary liturgical theology. "Was ever another command so obeyed?" permeates Dix's reflection. See pp. 743–45.

[13] Corbon, *The Wellspring of Worship*, trans. Matthew J. O'Connell (New York: Paulist Press, 1988), 92–93.

This is *real presence*—relational, dialogical, and participative. The ambiguity here is, as de Lubac argues, "intentional and significant."

Corbon's point about beginning with the salvific mystery is important for our discussion here because, for him, the "synergy" of that communion of God-with-us and we-with-God provides the energy of the Spirit for Christ's eventful presence, "real and active," which feeds our hunger and slakes our thirst. "The whole mystery of the sacraments resides in this synergy," he says. The church is the "firstfruits" of this grace poured out upon the whole creation by the Spirit, and the liturgy announces the harvest with and in Christ. As a result,

> this is not a creation *stuck on to* the first creation, nor first creation itself *after* the rough-draft stage; rather it is the body of Christ *in* and *with* our first creation. "With" and "in" are stammering efforts to express the synergy of the new covenant: his dwelling with us; he is in us and we in him. When his life-giving energy meets ours, when these two gratuitous freedoms become one, when the signs of his covenant are recognized by our faith and welcomed into our flesh, then creation becomes that which it was called to be.[14]

THE SACRAMENTALITY OF THE CHURCH AS BOTH "HOST" AND "WAITER" AT THE EUCHARISTIC GATHERING

Before we move to a consideration of how the rites themselves can clarify this presence of Christ in the assembly and its relation to the proclaimed Word, the gifts of bread and wine, and the presider who gathers this Body into communion, a final, cautionary note on the immensity of this claim we place upon the constituted church as primary celebrants, fully active and participating, appears in order. The dangers of self-focus have been acknowledged, noting that we must start with God and not ourselves. Yet, the sacramental life nudges us to take the risk of claiming our identity as the Body of Christ, which the consecrated bread and wine causes and effects by its sheer giftedness. Louis-Marie Chauvet calls this mystery a "scandal" that has profound pastoral consequences for liturgical practice and spirituality. Once again, we would do well to note the passion in his words:

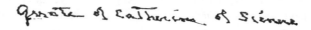

quote of Catherine of Siena

---

[14] Ibid., 93.

"It is great, the mystery of faith!" Before it applies to the Eucharist, the expression applies to the concrete assembly as church. Here there is both mystery and scandal. This is what is not self-explanatory, and for the believing intelligence the scandal of the presence of Christ in the Eucharist risks serving as a mock scandal (that is, merely intellectual) if one ignores this primary scandal, an existential one: the encounter of the living Christ which is possible only through the mediation of a church, indeed holy but composed of sinners, indeed body of Christ but made up of divided members, indeed temple of the Holy Spirit but so parsimoniously missionary. The concrete assembly of every single Sunday confronts Christians with the harsh reality of this mediation that everyone seeks to forget.[15]

The powerful sign of Christ as food and drink for the journey into the fullness of the kingdom will remain simply an interesting religious phenomenon if we sever that mode of presence from the community who receives him, for which Christ lived, died, and rose to announce the beginning of the new age for all creation. Rather than demean the mystery of the eucharistic presence, the insistence on the presence of Christ in the gathered assembly gives heightened intensity to the power of the Word that continues to be "fulfilled in our hearing" and moves us along gracefully toward the table, to be fed by Christ's Body and Blood, all of it a holy communion. Rites that express the depth of this great gift can then be seen truly as "the summit toward which the activity of the Church is directed" and "the fount from which all the Church's power flows" (SC 10).

The ritual actions in the liturgy that body forth the church as basic sacrament, as well as reveal the communal worship act as the expressive moment of her true nature as sign and reality of the total Christ, underline how the ecclesial starting point for the sacramental life reflects what Karl Rahner called "the unambiguous, abiding promise irrevocably made by God" to the world. That grace-filled promise *is* the church, and the church gathered to pray is the quintessential moment of that profound union with God, in Christ, through the power of the Spirit. As Rahner said so forcefully in *The Church and the Sacraments,*

For we have already seen that the Church is the visible outward expression of grace, not in the sense that she subsequently announces as it were the presence of something already there without the announcement, but

[15] Chauvet, *Sacraments*, 38–39.

in the sense that in the Church God's grace is given expression and embodiment and symbolized, and by being so embodied, is present.[16]

This sacramental character of the church stands, then, as the foundational presence of Christ's saving mysteries from which, as we mentioned in the first chapter, her sacramental life functions flow.[17] The gathering of the assembly "embodies" and "symbolizes" (to use Rahner's terms) that presence of grace in the world whose ultimate completion will be fulfilled at the end of time. Yet, because sacraments express the interrelationship of past, present, and future—what de Lubac called "memorial, presence, and anticipation"—the graced encounter in the gathering provides a focal moment of that grace-filled encounter flowing from the heart of God's desire. Susan Wood sums up de Lubac's rich synthesis on this when she comments on the eucharistic origins of the *corpus mysticum*, the Mystical Body of Christ:

> In terms of the Church/Eucharist correlation, the Church in union with Christ is the truth signified by the Eucharist when considered not merely in terms of the sacramental species, but the entire liturgical rite within the historical matrix of memory, presence, and anticipation.[18]

It is only when we forget the fundamental sacramentality of the church as a starting point that we begin to compartmentalize the church as a *mystical body* whose identity flows from its union with Christ, as opposed to the *visible society* of the faithful, a hierarchically ordered community of believers, who make up the visible church.[19] A final nod to de Lubac in his own words will usher us into the rites themselves as expressive of this mystery of union and communion between the eucharistic presence of Christ and the assembly as Christ's faithful Body, the locus of revelation. He is reminding a church in the mid-1950s that the focus on an isolated *real* presence in the bread and wine apart from the deeper interrelationships between the Trinity in communion with us must be avoided in our theology and spirituality. Vatican II would later take up this theological shift and move it to our

[16] Karl Rahner, *The Church and the Sacraments* (New York: Herder and Herder, 1963), 34.

[17] See Janowiak, *The Holy Preaching: The Sacramentality of the Word in the Liturgical Assembly* (Collegeville, MN: Liturgical Press, 2000), part I.

[18] Wood, *Spiritual Exegesis*, 68.

[19] Ibid., 64.

liturgical practice as well. De Lubac says, in *The Splendour of the Church* (1956),

> The Church, like the Eucharist, is a mystery of unity—the same mystery, and one with inexhaustible riches. Both are the body of Christ—the same body. If we are to be faithful to the teaching of Scripture, as Tradition interprets it, and wish not to lose anything of its essential riches, we must be careful not to make the smallest break between the Mystical Body and the Eucharist.[20]

His historical approach and his respect for tradition lead him to a spiritual vision that broadens and deepens our understanding of how we worship and the spirituality that shapes that practice. Commenting upon the patristic passages relating to Paul's commentaries on the one Body in First Corinthians, de Lubac gathers together everything we have been saying about the gathered assembly and presence of Christ in the liturgy:

> St. Leo, with his usual forcefulness and profundity, says the same, and in his words we can hear the voice of all the great Catholic Doctors: "The participation of the body and blood of Christ effects nothing short of this, that we pass over unto that which we receive." The head and the members make one single body; the Bridegroom and the Bride are "one flesh." There are not two Christs, one personal and the other "mystical." And there is certainly no confusion of Head with members; Christians are not the "physical" (or eucharistic) body of Christ, and the Bride is not the Bridegroom. All the distinctions are there, but they do not add up to discontinuity; the Church is not just *a* body, but *the* body of Christ; man must not separate what God has united—therefore "let him not separate the Church from the Lord."[21]

A liturgical spirituality and practice that reverences the sacramentality of the church eagerly stands in the middle of this relational presence, whose ambiguity is intentional and full of significance. Worship that

[20] Henri de Lubac, *The Splendour of the Church*, trans. Michael Mason (New York: Sheed and Ward, 1956), 110.

[21] Ibid., 112. The Scripture passage from which he draws these commentaries is 1 Corinthians 12:27, whose context is the rich multitude of ministries that come together to form the community, where Paul states: "Now you are the body of Christ and individually members of it." The patristic references are to Leo's Sixteenth Catechetical Homily, no. 24, and Origen's *In Matt.*, xiv, 17.

flows from the synergy of this relational encounter and communion discerns the activity of the Spirit animating and breathing in a harmonic polyphony: in the drawing together of the dynamic assembly, in the proclamation and preaching of the word, in "taking, blessing, breaking, and sharing" food, and in the presider's prayerful gathering of the communities into communion into a significant whole. This continues to gather grace and energy in the rhythm and harmony of liturgy and life, where ordinary time becomes holy and sacredness permeates the mundane to create, in this symbolic matrix, something new. Oblate theologian David Power suggests that "Gathering to Worship" announces the advent of God's grace and mercy, breaking into the "passage of life" that entails both struggles and joys, beginnings and endings, and proclaims the redemptive memorial of Christ as an ongoing event. Citing the events in the lives of the community that mark our gathering, he concludes:

> None of this happens without a call to come together and to ask that lives be taken into God's care. So people are called by the rhythm of life and of time itself to mark the sense of these transitions, to seek direction, to ask what God's beneficence gives to them in giving life, what there is to lead them on, stopping for a while from their own efforts to drive themselves and others forward. Yet, though a rhythm of time has been established, the act of coming together for worship, to hear God's Word, ask God's blessing, remember the divine saving action, breaks the rhythm. It is God who calls, and time is interrupted/disrupted by an extraordinary intervention of grace and promise.[22]

THE RESONANCE OF SIGNS AND SYMBOLS AS THE ASSEMBLY GATHERS

In light of the theology we have discussed concerning the Body of Christ and the symbolic exchange of God-with-us and we-with-God,

---

[22] David N. Power, *Sacrament: The Language of God's Giving* (New York: Crossroad, 1999), 314. See also chap. 4, "Ritual Action: The Sacramental Body," 120–48, for a rich discussion of the ritual dynamics of "Social Body, Physical Body, Body of Christ." Power shows the need to reimagine the communal notion of offering as a proclamation of communion, reconciliation, and solidarity in Christ and one another, instead of an overemphasis on a priestly offering that appears to substitute Christ's offering "in place of" our own. The latter misses the complete gratuity and self-emptying of this offer of grace and mercy in which we are invited to share. See esp. 134–39.

a liturgical commentary on this action of gathering must give special note to the importance of *procession and reverent movement through the assembly* as the liturgy begins. *Entry psalms* praising God's fidelity as the people enter the temple or return from the fields rejoicing, as well as *songs of God's gracious invitation* in our midst, provide musical resonance with the theological act taking place. "Who shall ascend the hill of the LORD? And who shall stand in his holy place? . . . Lift up your heads, O gates! and be lifted up, O ancient doors!" (Ps 24:3, 7a). *Rites that recall our baptism,* such as stopping at the font on the way into the body of the worship space and using that water to bathe the assembly, enhance this action of God's passionate calling and the acknowledgment of that desire in the gathering of believers who share this baptismal identity together. Rather than a peripheral "option," blessing and sprinkling and recalling the mighty deeds of God in the womb/ tomb of our baptism catechize prayerfully and gesturally the power of this act of coming together to pray and sing as the Body of Christ. The communal *call to penance in light of this great mercy* acknowledges solidarity both in our need and in the confident grace that binds us together. This attitude stands in stark contrast to a ritual reversal we often experience today, which asks the worshipers to abandon the community and go back into the privacy of one's heart to search for sins and failings. And yet most communities celebrate in that individualistic modality, clear evidence that this spirituality of the presence of Christ in the assembly needs to permeate the deeper depths of our praying and our acknowledgment of the gracious and merciful God in whose name we gather in the first place. The *introductory rites* of the liturgy, therefore, need much more attention and reverence to address the current practice of unfocused prehomilies leading to perfunctory acts of personal penance. The church has gathered, invited to stand together in the mercy of the triune God, and we now beg God to share the gifts of the divine bounty. God's glory is summoned. Now, "let us pray." Theology, practice, and spiritual passion need to come together in harmony on this issue.

We will close this chapter on the assembly by looking with a ritual eye at the community's prayerful engagement at certain key points of our worship, and noting how this presence of Christ in the assembly expresses itself significantly in the invitation to "that full, conscious, and active participation in liturgical celebrations called for by the very nature of the liturgy" (SC 14). First, we will explore the "Liturgy of the Word."

THE BODY OF CHRIST AND THE HEARING AND PREACHING OF THE WORD

> May the praise of You vibrate within us.
>
> —Saint Ephrem, fourth century

The Church as the Context for Hearing the Word in the Story of Their Lives

The gathered assembly, collected in prayer and voicing their common identity both by recognizing their need and offering glory to God in one voice, now settles in to hear the Scriptures from the Hebrew and Christian testaments. The present discussion opens up this area of ritual of proclamation precisely in its relationship to the gathered assembly, one of the three agents of the Word's efficacy in the liturgy, along with the dynamic sacred texts of the Scriptures themselves and with the preacher who gives voice to this Word uttered in their hearing.[23] A more focused discussion of the sacramental presence of Christ in the Liturgy of the Word will follow in chapter 3. This interweaving of themes reflects the rhythm and harmony of these modes of presence, which are always interrelating and playing off of one another throughout the whole celebration.

The revealed word of God, uttered in love to the world, finds the context of its liberating message within the lives of those who long for redemption and liberation—a community constituted in past faithfulness, leading to this "present," and oriented toward a future fullness, all the recipients of the Father's wellspring of desire. The act of gathering *to do something* involves the liturgical community in an active engagement with the community of God in its dialogue of love and mutual sharing of life. Just as Jesus took flesh as the Word spoken to him by the One who loved him, the gathered church assumes the same posture of Christ's own attentive listening and expectation for the Word incarnate in their lives. "This text is being fulfilled today even as you listen," Jesus notes in Luke's description of this ritual, public reading of the sacred texts. "And all eyes in the synagogue were fixed

---

[23] For a complete discussion of these points and the dynamism of the Liturgy of the Word and its relationship to font and table, see Janowiak, *Holy Preaching* (2000), part II. For the notion of the three "agents," I am indebted to my colleague Sr. Mary McGann, RSCJ, whose work on the cultural components of liturgical enactment have been very helpful when considering the liturgy as an "event" rather than a "thing."

on him" (Luke 4:20-22). Something is happening in this dramatic encounter; it involves more than the simple reading of a static passage from the past. The community of listeners is part of the revelation in this moment of Jesus' proclamation of the divine plan of redemption and his embodiment of its saving power, now inscripted by the Spirit into their communal identity as worshiping Christians. The ongoing action of fulfillment circulates through this time and space and gathers depth, penetrating into the lives of believers and strengthening the bonds of intimacy with their Lord.

The sacramental union of Christ and the church, therefore, draws the assembly's contemporary story into communion with the saving mystery unfolding in Christ's life, death, and resurrection. Their receiving of the story and allowing its transforming call to conversion to enter into the fabric of their own lives participates in that fulfilling action that Jesus described in the synagogue. "Indeed, the word of God is living and active," as Paul describes this encounter, "sharper than any two-edged sword . . . it is able to judge the thoughts and intentions of the heart" (Heb 4:12). By entering into the spaces between soul and spirit, joint and marrow, the dynamic Word labors with the Father to yield a harvest of fruitfulness, the gifts of the Spirit and the renewed life that our communion with Christ engenders.

Ritual Actions That Accompany This Theology

How can the ritual action at this point in the celebration faithfully express this dynamic rhythm of God's desire circulating with grace through our lives, revealed for us in the story of our ancestors in faith and the paschal events of our salvation? Taking seriously that profound union with Christ signified by the gathering, the proclamation of the Scriptures must be experienced, first and foremost, as *a communal, unified action in many voices.* The lector and the preacher tell the community's story of the living faith that binds the assembly as God's own. Their particularity as individual persons in these roles is secondary to the priority of God's address first to a *people.* That relationship between individual and communal continues within the assembly as well: each person hears that saving message out of the context of her/his "distinct not separate" relationship to Christ and one another. This communal hearing and proclaiming of the Word patterns the dynamism of the triune life itself. "The words that I say to you I do not speak on my own; but the Father who dwells in me does his works," Jesus says to the Beloved in his farewell discourse in John. But there is more, because that action is always dialogical, relational, and participative: "Very truly, I tell you, the one who believes in me will also do the works that I do and, in fact, *will do greater works than these*, because I am going to the Father" (John 14:10, 12-13). That saving message will continue to circulate through the lives of the believers to reveal "greater works than these" in the manner of life and witness that flows from these mysteries. This fruitful, continually revealing Word results from that promised gift of the community of God, "the Advocate, the Holy Spirit, whom the Father will send in my name, [who] will teach you everything, and remind you of all that I have said to you" (John 14:26).

The assembly's active role as hearer and receiver of the Word, therefore, asks something of the Body. Together they are invited *to expect a word of grace*, precisely because of their living faith that called them to gather "in the name of the Father and of the Son and of the Holy Spirit" in the first place. Such an attitude of surrender and trust does not happen in a community immediately but *over time with faithful practice*. Preaching the Word of God is not about one homily. It is a repeated, liturgical pattern that becomes engraved in the bones and marrow of the assembly. Week after week, the introductory rites of gathering a dispersed community into a sacramental expression of one Body hopefully have enhanced their willingness to hear something that is critical to the community's self-identity. Care for the seemingly mundane elements of *clear proclamation, adequate amplification, and graced presence* in the ambo by the readers of the Scriptures honors the importance of the assembly's ability to hear the Word of God and cooperates with the longing and desire that brought them to seek nourishment in the community's celebration of Word and Sacrament. Expecting to hear a word of grace develops in an assembly who is schooled in the careful enactment of the Liturgy of the Word and the role of the *totus Christus* in the proclamation. The result cannot be quantified, but an active worshiping Body knows when that grace is circulating, and presiders, lectors, and cantors must reverence that liturgical knowing and enter into its expectant rhythm.

Preaching that builds upon that dynamic, breaks open the Word and inserts it into the midst of the community's "soul and spirit, joints and marrow," seems constitutive of this communal event of the Liturgy of the Word, rather than an option among rhetorical techniques or topics to be "covered" by some talk divorced from the graced event now taking place. The relational, dialogical, participative nature of sacramental presence in the assembly gives importance to all this: the collecting of the Body into one, the settling in and expectation, the artful proclamation, and the poetic struggle to bring that Word into dialogue with the story of Christ's paschal mystery, even now being inscripted into their lives through the creative fashioning of the Spirit's breath. Respecting all these necessary "voices," the sacred story of salvation finds its harmony within the concrete life of the assembly who hears it, and so we can say that the presence of Christ in the worshiping community participates in the *kerygma* (Jesus' own preaching) and its power to reconcile the world, transform her, and make her whole again.

Simple gestures and actions speak volumes in this regard and liberate the communal energy at work here. The way the ritual *procession of the gospel book* takes place or how it is carried among the assembly afterwards, as in the Eastern traditions, to touch and kiss in a reverent act of reception and honor, shapes an assembly over time, especially when the proclamation and preaching share this communal perspective. The *general intercessions that follow should flow* from all that has taken place. The cries of the People of God would then be in harmonic balance by addressing a relationship with God and the world that is an intimate and truthful exchange, in dialogue with the real needs and concerns that are part of the ambiguity of real life. The Scriptures of the day should provide the prevailing images to voice them. The opportunity for the assembly to call out names of the sick or deceased in a spontaneous murmur of intercession actualizes a communal nature to this praying that is often lost in dry, generic prayers prepared without a specific people and context in mind. The presider, of course, gathers these prayers and insures a timely ordering of this part of the rite, but the focus should remain on the people's need to voice the concerns that ultimately stream forth from the heart of the God of desire who has gathered them and "fulfilled the Word in their hearing."

We will return to the dynamic nature of Christ's presence in the ritual proclamation and preaching of the Word in the next chapter, focusing on the shared grace of the sacred texts themselves as an eventful enactment within the liturgical celebration. We have established so far the gathered assembly's rhythmic role in this mode of presence from the perspective of its relational, dialogical, and participative action of coming together to "constitute the Church." The ambiguity between the mode of presence of Christ in the praying assembly and the proclaimed Word here is "intentional" and "specific," and the rite can enhance that mutually affirming sacramental presence, as we have seen, with care and attention and faithful practice over time. Once again, this is God's way and it ushers from the desire in the heart of God. Our common praise of God revealed in the story of our salvation and redemption does vibrate within us and is fulfilled in our hearing.

THE BODY OF CHRIST EXPRESSED IN THE EUCHARISTIC PRAYER AND COMMUNION RITE

> Therefore with fullest assurance let us partake as of the Body and Blood of Christ . . . that thou by partaking of the Body and Blood of Christ, mightest be made of the same body and the same Blood with Him. For thus we come to bear Christ in us, because His Body and Blood are diffused through our members; thus it is that, according to blessed Peter, "we become partakers of the divine nature."
>
> —Saint Cyril of Jerusalem, fourth century, speaking to the neophytes baptized at Easter[24]

We now consider the praying and singing assembly and its active participation in the eucharistic prayer, as well as the focal action of eating and drinking in grateful memory, since both the prayer of praise and remembrance and the meal together form a significant whole. We begin with some theological considerations about the symbolic rift that occurred over the course of history that distanced the assembly from its proper role as primary celebrants of the rite and necessary communicants of the eucharistic gifts, which *signifies* and *effects* the union between Christ and the church. Without that experienced, ritual communion of all the actors in this rite, the elements and the prayer surrounding them become something extrinsic to the community's shared identity and lead to passive observance rather than active participation. As we have been arguing throughout this book, such an isolating effect mutes the inherent relational character of God's communication with those God loves. We will then look at specific ritual solutions to this distancing that currently exists in many liturgical celebrations. But first, we return to the shift in the assembly's self-understanding that resulted in the type of passive participation that

---

[24] St. Cyril of Jerusalem, Mystagogical Catechesis IV, "On the Eucharistic Food," 3, in *St. Cyril of Jerusalem's Lectures on the Christian Sacraments*, ed. F. L. Cross (London: SPCK, 1951), 68. The Scripture reference is 2 Peter 1:4.

still seems so hard to shake, even years after Vatican II promulgated these reforms for "full, conscious, and active participation in liturgical celebrations called for by the very nature of the liturgy" (SC 14).

The Roots of the Assembly's Distance: The Gradual Separation between the Body of Christ as Sacramental Elements and as Ecclesial Communion

Henri de Lubac's historical approach to theology uncovered for the twentieth century the riches of the early church tradition, especially the patristic teaching and practice of the first four centuries. The importance of this approach for a theology of the liturgy that takes practice and spirituality as necessary components stands out clearly here, because it asks us to rethink and reimagine common misunderstandings and assumptions about what our early ancestors said, how they prayed, and what significance their ritual acts carried. Later periods of liturgical history and its controversies inevitably place their own interpretations on an earlier age, and de Lubac's recovery challenges us to use a fresh lens on current liturgical practices and meanings. True respect for the sacred tradition demands this (SC 4).

The patristic appreciation for the *totus Christus*,[25] for example, suggests new understandings for our contemporary church identity, practice, and devotion, especially in regard to the intimate and necessary identity between the church and the Eucharist as "the Body of Christ." The underlying insistence in the Constitution on the Sacred Liturgy on this intrinsic relationship between the gathered assembly and the sacramental life she celebrates owes its debt to such a patristic recovery. However, contemporary practice and the "liturgy wars" in recent decades also honestly remind us that the reception of such a key liturgical dynamic simply has not penetrated into our corporate or individual imaginations regarding the sacramental presence of Christ. Lacking that intimate connection, the focus on the priest/presider's

[25] The fathers of the church and Augustine in particular, commenting on the letters of Paul and other epistles, refer to the *totus Christus* as the whole Christ, or, Peter Fink describes the different perspectives, "Christ in the midst of the Church, together with the church that is gathered to himself." This stands in contrast to *Christus solus*, "Christ alone, present in the ministry of the priest, acting on behalf of the people." For Fink's discussion of the importance of the terms in Vatican II sacramental theology, see his article in *The New Dictionary of Sacramental Worship*, ed. Peter E. Fink, SJ (Collegeville, MN: Liturgical Press, 1990), 1107–14.

..rate" (as opposed to "distinct") role in the ordered assembly, as well as the gestures and words he uses to "confect" the Eucharist, naturally become the essential actors and actions in the eucharistic mystery we share at the table. Whether the assembly communes fully under both species or participates fully in ministries at the Word and table do not warrant the same efficacy and attention. They are "extraordinary" rather than essential elements of the rite. The dialogic nature of the eucharistic prayer as the whole church's prayer of praise and thanks loses its dynamism when the assembly is reduced to passive observance. The roots of all this lie historically and theologically in the distancing between the Body of Christ in the sacramental elements and the self-offering of the ecclesial community formed in the act of eating and drinking in grateful memory. The restoration of the sacramental presence of Christ in the "praying and singing" assembly needs deeper appropriation in our liturgical piety and practice.

Here is where liturgical scholarship can be of service to the whole church and its rich spiritual legacy. Germane to this discussion of the assembly's reception of its proper role as primary celebrant are de Lubac's writings about the interesting evolution of the sacramental terms *corpus verum* (the real or true body) and *corpus mysticum* (the Mystical Body, incorporating its relational, spiritual significance and not just its "consecrated" presence alone). *Corpus verum* and *corpus mysticum*, he notes, were mutually enriching terms, ambiguous and interdependent, in whose polarizing shift "the Church loses its eucharistic foundation."[26] Contrary to what we would imagine today, *corpus verum* in the early centuries usually referred to the church in union with Christ, while *corpus mysticum* was used in reference to the eucharistic Body as an effective sign of this communion with Christ and one another. Both of these terms, as they are described here, inform one another; they are "distinct" but not "separate," to use the

[26] Wood, *Spiritual Exegesis*, 63, 65–66. Wood cites de Lubac's extensive analysis of this in *Corpus Mysticum*, op. cit. Edward Kilmartin, SJ, in *The Eucharist in the West: History and Theology* (ed. Robert J. Daly [Collegeville, MN: Liturgical Press, 1998]), uses examples such as Fulgentius of Ruspe (462–527) to show the accepted inherent connection between the worshipers and the eucharistic species. Kilmartin notes in this disciple of Augustine's teaching "that the baptized are not only participants in Christ's sacrifice but are also the holy sacrifice itself (*ipsum sanctum sacrificium*), the 'true bread and true body' (*verum panem verumque corpus*)." See p. 59.

familiar sacramental terms. Because the church gathers to be faithful to the sacramental life, the eucharistic presence abides as the sign and reality of that union of head and members. This mutually enriching interrelationship of terms for the church and the Eucharist lived in a fluctuating rhythm and balance with each other for almost twelve centuries, as de Lubac learned from his historical study of early texts. But the upheaval, controversy, and misunderstandings that began in the early Middle Ages concerning how Christ was present in the Eucharist slowly broke down the multivalent relationship between the historical body of Christ born of Mary, the sacramental Body in the Eucharist, and the ecclesial Body as a communion between head and members.

Fergus Kerr, OP, notes de Lubac's regret that what he called "symbolic inclusions" often evolved, especially during times of crisis and cultural shift, into "dialectical antitheses." What this means is that words we use in theology that are used in an illuminating relationship with each other—that precisely together can reveal rich layers of meaning—begin to atrophy when they are considered as not only "distinct" but *also* "separate," a danger signal, as we have seen, where sacramental mysteries are concerned. Such a disconnection focuses primarily on the differences, on realities and truths set over against each other, rather than as terms mutually enriching and necessarily in relationship. One such migration de Lubac regrets particularly effected the terms noted above, *corpus verum* and *corpus mysticum*. Kerr describes de Lubac's historical findings that reflect a changed relationship between the Eucharist and the church (the Body of Christ), and says,

> Whereas the eucharist had been regarded as the mystical body of Christ (*corpus mysticum*), the expression was gradually transferred to the Church—and the original term for the Church, namely the true body of Christ (*corpus verum*), migrated to the eucharist. The Church as people of God and community of believers had been regarded as the "real" body of Christ while his "mystical" body was his body in the eucharist. . . . For some time both the eucharist and the Church were referred to as *corpus Christi*, with the adjective *mysticum* floating between the two. In the second half of the twelfth century, in order to distinguish the ecclesial from the eucharistic body of Christ, the Church came to be qualified as *corpus mysticum*.[27]

[27] Fergus Kerr, OP, *The Modern Theologians*, 2nd ed., ed. David F. Ford, 110 (Oxford: Blackwell, 2001).

Part of this evolution and separation were the natural result of controversies such as that involving Berengar of Tours, whose position in the eleventh century appeared to deny the inherent relationship between the sacramental Body in the sacrament and the body of Christ that was born and died upon the cross. Such speculation led to a reliance upon metaphysical explanations about the "substance" of bread and wine changing into the sacramental body while the "appearances" remained the same.[28]

Our contemporary context may have forgotten the figures and the exact details of the heated debates, but practice and piety still bear their marks. Practice and piety had begun to lean toward an isolation of the sacramental bread and wine as entities of focal importance in and of themselves, irrespective of the ecclesial blessing prayer at the table, the dynamic act of eating and drinking in grateful memory, and the gathered Body of Christ signified by the sacramental presence in the species. It is interesting to note that the popular rise of eucharistic devotions, such as Corpus Christi, highlighting the physical presence of the sacrament as an object of devotion to be seen and carried in procession, rather than broken, poured out, and shared, demonstrates rituals that stem from these somewhat heady controversies.[29] Even more, the growing lack of the assembly's participation in the action of communion seemed theologically and ritually unimportant compared to the priest's act of confecting the eucharistic wafer, which would then be placed in a monstrance for adoration, fostering seeing rather than eating. We can note here that such devotional piety is understandable and genuinely fueled the passion and love of people for the Eucharist, but the inevitable shift from the assembly's foundational role as the *corpus verum* (the *real* body) to a somewhat isolated and separate *mystical* body (understood now as a figurative term somehow not "the very

[28] For an understanding of the many sacramental controversies and subsequent metaphysical distinctions made as a result of these eleventh-century controversies such as Berengar's, see David Power, *The Eucharistic Mystery: Revitalizing the Tradition* (New York: Crossroad, 1992), esp. chap. 11, "Developments of Eucharistic Doctrines from the Condemnation of Berengar to the Council of Trent," 241–65.

[29] For a fascinating historical account of popular devotion to the Eucharist, see Miri Rubin, *Corpus Christi: The Eucharist in Medieval Culture* (New York: Cambridge University Press, 1991).

reality" of the Eucharist[30]) shows the effect of what de Lubac regretfully discovered as the movement from "symbolic inclusions" (actors in dynamic sacramental relationship and mutual identity) to "dialectical antitheses" (the *real* presence as opposed to some less revered one).

This separation remains with us now in the third millennium, after more than fifty years of a liturgical renewal that tried to incorporate such historical and theological insights of faithful scholars like de Lubac, Congar, and others writing in the years before Vatican II about the nature of the church as a sacramental reality.[31] What their studies show should humble us and correct our assumptions about orthodoxy and fidelity to the tradition. Our early ancestors would never have imagined such exclusivity for terms that, for us, have become conflicting notions of the revelatory grace of Christ that function in isolation from one another.

Perhaps this is why most faithful worshipers do not see themselves as primary celebrants and focal actors in the eucharistic mystery, nor does our eucharistic piety in the West reverently embrace that. The reformed liturgy has been largely unsuccessful in articulating in practice the theological fact that the eucharistic prayer around the altar table clearly remains, first and foremost, the focal prayer of the assembly, voiced by the presider in their corporate name, and not a privileged prayer of a mediating figure who then dispenses the fruit of that sacred deed to the observing recipients. The 2010 revision of the *General Instruction of the Roman Missal* does insist that the eucharistic prayer be prayed alone by the priest "in virtue of his Ordination," but the assembly is also called to "associate themselves with the priest in faith and in silence, as well as by means of their interventions as prescribed in the course of the Eucharistic Prayer" (147). If one subscribes to an isolating notion of roles, where some actors appear to be not only "distinct" but *also* "separate" from others, this injunction in the Instruction might give the impression that this is the presider's prayer. But the Constitution on the Sacred Liturgy clearly emphasized the mutual relationship of all members of the hierarchically ordered body, each

---

[30] Wood, *Spiritual Exegesis*, 66, notes de Lubac's discussion of this in *Corpus Mysticum*, 187–88.

[31] For a fuller treatment of this sacramentality, cf. Janowiak, *Holy Preaching*, chap. 2, "The Church as *Totus Christus*: A Renewal of Sacramentality and Proclamation," 19–64.

with her/his own iconic place in this harmonic, significant whole. The General Instruction itself reinforces this:

> In the celebration of Mass the faithful form a holy people, a people of God's own possession and a royal Priesthood, so that they may give thanks to God and offer the unblemished sacrificial Victim *not only by means of the hands of the Priest but also together with him and so that they may learn to offer their very selves.* . . . . Moreover, they are to form one body, whether in hearing the Word of God, or in taking part in the prayers and the singing, or above all by a common offering . . . at the Lord's table.[32]

This is not a bow to contemporary sociological notions of inclusivity. Because the church is "the sacrament of unity," the Vatican Constitution reminds us, "liturgical services involve the whole Body of the Church; they manifest it and have effects upon it" (SC 26). The Instruction continues, regarding the eucharistic prayer and its role in the rite as a whole:

> Now the center and high point of the entire celebration begins, namely, the Eucharistic Prayer, that is, the prayer of thanksgiving and sanctification. The Priest calls upon the people to lift up their hearts towards the Lord in prayer and thanksgiving; he associates the people with himself in the Prayer that he addresses in the name of the entire community to God the Father through Jesus Christ in the Holy Spirit. Furthermore, the meaning of this Prayer is that the whole congregation of the faithful joins with Christ in confessing the great deeds of God and in the offering of Sacrifice.[33]

The directives are clear, but the practice and interiorization that flows from it still hold back. Such a self-offering in union with Christ costs something, asks for conversion, and shakes the foundations of sacramental presence that have shaped us through practice for so many centuries.

The tone of recent Vatican curial documents and new translations of texts and rubrics seems to be shifting back to a symbolic focus on the *separateness* of the priest in this communal action. Perhaps there are issues of power and the loss of presbyteral status in some circles. Such fears have been exacerbated by instances of poor liturgical leadership,

[32] GIRM 95–96; emphasis mine.
[33] GIRM 78.

which in some instances have led the ordered assembly to appear rudderless and left to act on its own, diminishing Christ's presence as the leader of the church's offering, effectively signified in the person of the priest. Rather than greater interiorization of the multivalent mystery into which we are embraced, we take the safer route of demarcation of roles in order to clarify what is happening and maintain some control or order. Legitimate as these concerns may be, de Lubac's caution about the migration of "symbolic inclusions" into "dialectical antitheses" seems to be a contemporary warning that needs more reflection and attention. The issue of the mutuality of liturgical roles as generative and expressive of the presence of Christ is at stake here and calls us to honest and prayerful assessment and reception.

We will look more closely at the issues of the presider's role of acting "in the person of Christ" in chapter 4. Suffice it to say at this point that such fears and indecision from a variety of sectors of the church concerning the unique role of the presider—over against the gathered, praying, and singing assembly—reflect a deeper mistrust and dissonance in the Body. We still resist the reimagination required of the relational, dialogical, and participative modes of sacramental presence that, together, enhance the powerful proclamation of Christ's invitation for *all* to join in his obedient self-offering to the Father in loving surrender. We must affirm in the midst of this ecclesial doubt that from the earliest days of the church down to the present faithful gathering, the entire eucharistic prayer voices the grateful praise of the *totus Christus*, the fullness of Christ, in every time and season, acknowledging the Father's gift of redemption and liberation in the Word made flesh. God's saving acts in Jesus recounted in this prayer not only fulfilled the new covenant promised to our ancestors but also continue to unite the whole worshiping assembly through, with, and in Christ in this memorial of "making present" this saving reality. As *we* pray to the source and summit of all desire in the preface,

> Through him the Angels praise your majesty,
> Dominions adore and Powers tremble before you.
> Heaven and the Virtues of heaven and the blessed Seraphim
> worship together with exultation.
> May our voices, we pray, join with theirs
> in humble praise, as we acclaim.[34]

[34] Common Preface II, "Salvation through Christ."

Theological and curial documents alone will not address this problem of ritual dissonance and lack of interiorization. Our bodies, minds, and spirits have to wrap themselves around this fundamental truth: the eucharistic prayer is the church's prayer, "our voices joined with all the communion of angels and saints," and the ritual celebration must be *experienced as a communal action,* or else ritual dissonance ensues, theological dishonesty prevails, and the hunger remains undernourished. The sacramentality of the church as the Body of Christ emerged in the mid-twentieth century as a primary insight of the theological method called *ressourcement,* the return to the originating sources and energy of the early church and her texts. The liturgical reform of Vatican II rests upon this recovery work and anchors its vision. The decades of historical and textual research that preceded the council affirmed this *ecclesial context of liturgical prayer* and figured prominently when the time came, in light of *Sacrosanctum Concilium,* to revise the rites that bind us as a church. Cardinal Benno Gut, prefect of the new Sacred Congregation for Divine Worship, called the new texts of eucharistic prayers commissioned by the Vatican council "a new canticle placed on the lips of the praying Church by the Holy Spirit."[35]

This return to the sources and energy of early Christian praying and singing addressed an isolating shift that the Jesuit liturgical historian Josef Jungmann traced back to the eighth-century "Roman Mass in France," whose "silent praying was alien to the tenor of the old Roman scheme." The individualistic focus of both priest and members of the assembly reflected the increasing control of eucharistic praying by the clergy, who were among a select few who knew the Latin used in the rite, and a gradual muting of the voice of "the communion of the redeemed bound together with a glorious Christ in one Mystical Body," as Jungmann so forcefully stated. The whole understanding of the eucharistic action slowly shifted to a tacit acceptance of the table prayer as the utterance of an "I" instead of the communal "We." As a result, he goes on to say,

> In the earlier periods of liturgical life we saw the emphasis placed
> on the Mass as a *eucharistia,* as a prayer of thanks from the congrega-
> tion who were invited to participate by a *Gratia agamus* [We give you

[35] Cardinal Gut's letter is quoted in Annibale Bugnini's *The Reform of the Liturgy: 1948–1975,* trans. Matthew J. O'Connell (Collegeville, MN: Liturgical Press, 1990), 464.

thanks] and whose gifts, in the course of the Mass, were elevated by the words of the priest into a heavenly sacrificial offering. But now an opposite view was taking precedence in [people's] minds. . . . The Eucharist is the *bona gratia* [gracious gift], which God grants to us, and which at the climactic moment of the Mass, the consecration, descends to us.[36]

These attitudes of separation and distancing between the sacrament *we receive* and the real union with Christ in his Body that *we are* have stayed with us through the centuries. They were reinforced by ritual practices that highlighted the presider's activity at the expense of the assembly's reverent and silent passivity, all of which deepened that fractured understanding regarding the proper "celebrants" of the rite.

Renewed catechesis on the liturgy occurs most effectively in *actual practice* and in *a renewed attitude* on the part of all the celebrants that *we* are praying in relationship, participation, and mutual dialogue. The unity of the eucharistic assembly as "filled with the Holy Spirit . . . one Body, one Spirit in Christ"[37] must be experienced as a practiced reality, inscribed into our ritual bodies, rather than proposed as a comfortably held idea that remains static in documents and texts. Practical suggestions that enhance the assembly's role as the primary celebrants lure theological ideas into the sphere of experienced fact, which then shapes our prayer and further catechesis on what is taking place when the church gathers to worship.

ATTENTION TO RITUAL ATTITUDES AND GESTURES THAT ENHANCE THE COMMUNAL NATURE OF SACRAMENTAL SHARING AT THE TABLE

The primary attitude of renewal and a refreshed sense of Christ's presence in the celebrating assembly begin with the dynamic description that the *Sacrosanctum Concilium* (7) uses to describe this eventful mode of presence: "He is present . . . when the Church prays and sings." The simplicity and power of such a communal dynamism in prayer cannot be overestimated, nor can the attention that must be given to achieve it be ignored. The presider, liturgical directors,

---

[36] Josef Jungmann, *The Mass of the Roman Rite: Its Origins and Development*, trans. Rev. Francis A. Brunner, CSSR (Dublin: Four Courts Press, 1951; 1986 ed.), 78, 82.
[37] See Eucharistic Prayer III.

and those entrusted with the ritual music play key roles in this. The leader's calling of the assembly to pray implies that all are invited into a reverent stance before the living God who has invited this gathering into a loving embrace. That truth remains muted when a presider appears to pray alone while the rest of the assembly watches in passive admiration, as if the community cannot or will not do this themselves. Communal praying in one voice evolves out of an interior clarity in both leader and assembly that God's desire for communion with us remains the source of our thanks and praise, and that the people of faith are the present sacramental expression of that great mystery, bodied forth for us in the saving acts of Jesus. John Paul's exhortation to American bishops On Active Participation in the Liturgy (November 1998) emphasizes the Vatican Council's intention that prayer and song and silence form one liturgical whole for all celebrants:

> Only by being radically faithful to this doctrinal foundation can we avoid one-dimensional and unilateral interpretations of the Council's teaching. The sharing of all the baptized in the one priesthood of Jesus Christ is the key to understanding the Council's call for full, conscious and active participation in the liturgy (*Sacrosanctum Concilium*, 14). Full participation certainly means that every member of the community has a part to play in the liturgy; and in this respect a great deal has been achieved in parishes and communities across your land. But full participation does not mean that everyone does everything, since this would lead to a clericalizing of the laity and a laicizing of the priesthood; and this was not what the Council had in mind. The liturgy, like the Church, is intended to be hierarchical and polyphonic, respecting the different roles assigned by Christ and allowing all the different voices to blend in one great hymn of praise.
>
> Active participation certainly means that, in gesture, word, song and service, all the members of the community take part in an act of worship, which is anything but inert or passive. Yet active participation does not preclude the active passivity of silence, stillness and listening: indeed, it demands it.[38]

---

[38] *Ad Limina*, Address of Pope John Paul II to Bishops of the United States, On Active Participation in the Liturgy, Discourse of the Holy Father to the Bishops of the Episcopal Conference of the United States of America (Washington, Oregon, Idaho, Montana, and Alaska) at their *Ad Limina* Visit, October 9, 1998, no. 3.

John Paul's nuances are important, but they must be applied first to the *whole* Body. Out of that relational fullness, an ordered assembly that moves in "polyphonic" rhythm and harmony must remain in tension. Our current exploration would ask that such nuances be applied to both presider and assembly; presiders must sing and not be "sung to" and members of the assembly need not compete for more "active" roles as a measure of full participation. All are called to respect the dynamic of praying and singing and resting in silent awe, or else the blending of different voices of praise are reduced to one note and one singer.

Other ritual attitudes and gestures flow from this principle. The dialogue between presider and assembly that takes place at the preparation of the altar and the gifts, and continuing in the eucharistic prayer itself, must be *prayed as if it is a proclamation and response* whose growing synergy fuels the common words and action. This necessitates a different dynamic than the leader simply reading words and waiting for the next part to recite. The assembly has a participative responsibility as well. Although elderly persons and those with sight and hearing disabilities may need a text to engage in this action, proper attention to the mutual energy that spirals forth from liturgical proclamation and response lessens the need for all assembled (presider, musicians, and assembly) to have their primary focus on a book rather than on the deepening encounter taking place through the power of the Holy Spirit.

> *P:* Lift up your hearts.
> *R:* We lift them up to the Lord.
> *P:* Let us give thanks to the Lord our God.
> *R:* It is right and just.

As the church's eucharistic prayer continues, gathering energy from "every time and season, always and everywhere," the liturgy reaches back into the past and makes the promise of divine hallowing and presence ever new, culminating in the doxology of our union and communion in the trinitarian life, whose fullness we await and whose promise we are. Words of love spoken and obedient love in response: there are many levels and rich depths of communion taking place in every dimension of mind, body, and spirit.

In the acknowledgment of all the grace abounding here, as John Paul II affirmed, *shared silences* seem to be a crucial expression of this sacramental mystery of bonding through, with, and in Christ. Such a respect for spaciousness ~~within the rite allows~~ the whole community to be ~~caught up in~~ an attitude of expectancy and hope. Moreover, it flows from the leadership of a presider who embodies that humble expectation of God's visitation and takes the role of "gatherer of the praying community" seriously. *Reverent gestures ~~of inclusion~~,* such as bowing ~~graciously to acknowledge~~ those who set the altar table and all celebrants using outstretched hands (the ancient *orans* position) as a medium of God's embrace, enhance the commonality of the eucharistic table as an experienced reality of a liturgical Body standing together in the community of God. Representatives of all ages in the assembly, especially the young, doing important ritual actions of liturgical service for the assembly proclaim unequivocally that what we are about flows from a participative effort and action. In the course of this common prayer around the table of the Lord, the presider cannot seem more intent on reciting the words in a sacramentary than on holding the assembly's heart and voice together in an act of praise and thanks. Without this reverent attitude, the connection of assembly and table action becomes ritually severed. More will be said about all this in the following chapters, but in terms of the presence of Christ in the praying and singing Body, *the leader of the liturgical community must carry the body of the assembly in his/her body* when that attitude of common praying and singing remains as an active and essential mode of Christ's presence.

Music shapes this attitude of praying and singing as well. *Festive psalms and hymns* for the preparation of the altar and the gifts, which pertain specifically to the community's gathering of the harvest, to their common hunger for the food in the wilderness, and to their common procession to give praise and thanks harmonize with the liturgical action most effectively when they employ simple tones and refrains that invite a congregation's active participation.

> How precious is your steadfast love, O God!
>> All people may take refuge in the shadow of your wings.
> They feast on the abundance of your house,
>> and you give them drink from the river of your delights.
> For with you is the fountain of life;
>> in your light we see light. (Ps 36:7-9)

The principle holds as well for any point in the liturgy when the communal attention of the assembly on the action intensifies their communion with Christ in their midst. "O taste and see that the LORD is good" (Ps 34:8) and "My soul thirsts for God, for the living God" (Ps 42:2) proclaim so much in so simple a manner. The repetitive character of ritual music serves to gather the heart of the assembly, rather than send them back into themselves to negotiate a wordy, complex text or simply to escape from something that seems best left to professionals. *Simple and rhythmic sung texts of eucharistic prayers* that invite proclamation and the assembly's chanted response can be a consistent, patterned practice, and they need not be the preserve of Easter Vigils only. The Eastern churches can provide a model for the West in this regard. The same holds true for songs that accompany the communion procession.

Primary symbols that are clearly experienced as shared signs of unity speak to the sacramental truth of communion in Christ and one another more than a presider's endless didactic digressions about them can ever achieve. Such explanatory descriptions only serve to peek around the rite and call the assembly out of the liminal time and space to which they have been invited. The same holds true for elaborate themes and distracting side rituals, which exhaust the community's attention and hide the centrality of the table action and communion. The *gifts of bread and wine*, presented in common vessels that express that unity whenever this is possible, locate the primacy of the community's single offering of praise and thanks during the eucharistic prayer. Ciboria, small bowls and patens scattered over an altar already cluttered by papers, eyeglasses, and other distracting elements, simply hide the primacy of the gift of bread broken and wine poured out as the effective sign of the *corpus mysticum* in all its symbolic richness. Needless to say, separate gifts for presiders and a select few speak volumes about distancing and ritual separation from the focal action. Recent liturgical directives (the pouring out of the cups before the fraction rite is an example) have placed such visual union of the sacramental offering at risk. Respect for the elements is important; however, attentive care by all should take precedent over exaggerated solutions for a few, all of which suggest a separation of the unity of gifts and the Body of Christ who receives them. One could argue even further that true respect for this principle also demands a diverse complex of ministers who prepare and share these gifts. Any injunctions that the presider and other concelebrating priests embody "all ministries in one" debilitate the ritual sign of the unity and diversity of the assembled Body of Christ. As the Constitution on the Sacred Liturgy states so clearly, such a respect for the sacramental unity of the *totus Christus* is warranted because worship bodies forth the truth of the action and of the foundation of communion in Christ expressed in this holy gathering:

> In liturgical celebrations each one, minister or layperson, who has an office to perform, should do all of, but only, those parts which pertain to that office *by the nature of the rite and the principles of liturgy.* (SC 28; emphasis mine)

The doxological nature and the shared "bodying forth" of the community's self-offering in the eucharistic prayer suggests that *standing as the posture for the liturgical assembly* is the most appropriate and significant sign of the church's eucharistic act. Obviously, architecture and the size and context of the gathering may alter that. However, as a principle of eucharistic praying, standing is not an act of defiance but of proclamation and honor toward the One in their midst.[39] Rather than suggesting irreverence or a lack of humble surrender, standing harmonizes with the euchological nature of the prayer, a proclamation of God's saving acts now inscripted into the heart of the church when she prays, "We thank you for counting us worthy to stand in your presence and serve you." Recent scholars such as Nathan Mitchell, John Leonard, John Baldovin, and others have argued so persuasively for the historical and ritual foundations of this communal gesture.[40] Their concerns have not been appreciated in recent directives. Debates and conflicting interpretations over reverence and cultural taste regarding posture will continue, but whatever the decision in different

---

[39] The 2010 GIRM, 20, seems to suggest such a nuance: Since, however, the celebration of the Eucharist, like the entire Liturgy, is carried out by means of perceptible signs by which the faith is nourished, strengthened, and expressed, the greatest care is to be taken that those forms and elements proposed by the Church are chosen and arranged, which, *given the circumstances of persons and places,* more effectively foster active and full participation and more aptly respond to the spiritual needs of the faithful (emphasis mine). The principle is not uniformity but the effective union of the Body. For a detailed work regarding the issues in the revision of the Missal by the Catholic Academy of Liturgy, see Edward Foley, Nathan D. Mitchell, Joanne M. Pierce, eds., *A Commentary on the* General Instruction of the Roman Missal (Collegeville, MN: Liturgical Press, 2007).

[40] Nathan Mitchell and John Leonard, *The Postures of the Assembly during the Eucharistic Prayer* (Chicago: LTP, 1994) and Richard McCarron, *The Eucharistic Prayer at Sunday Mass* (Chicago: LTP, 1997), 86–92.

parts of the world, the 2002 General Instruction notes that liturgical gestures are *communal actions of a unified body* and not an expression of private devotion. It is interesting to note the change in emphasis from the 1975 version and the later adaptation in the section titled "Movements and Posture." The 1975 text read:

> The uniformity in standing, kneeling, or sitting to be observed by all taking part is a sign of the community and the unity of the assembly; it both expresses and fosters the spiritual attitude of those taking part. For the sake of uniformity in movement and posture, the people should follow the directions given during the celebration by the deacon, the priest, or another minister. (1975 GIRM 20–21)

The 2010 version states:

> The gestures and bodily posture of both the Priest, the Deacon, and the ministers, and also of the people, must be conductive to making the entire celebration resplendent with beauty and noble simplicity, to making clear the true and full meaning of its different parts, and to fostering the participation of all. Attention must therefore be paid to what is determined by this *General Instruction* and by the traditional practice of the Roman Rite and to what serves the common spiritual good of the People of God, rather than private inclination or arbitrary choice.
>
> A common bodily posture, to be observed by all those taking part, is a sign of the unity of the members of the Christian community gathered together for the Sacred Liturgy, for it expresses the intentions and spiritual attitude of the participants and also fosters them. (2010 GIRM 42)

A faithful critique of the changes in this document over the past few decades may note that "symbolic inclusions" have migrated a bit to the "dialectical antitheses" that de Lubac's concerns highlight. The 1975 version simply highlights the liturgical principle of unity; the latter one immediately begins by delineating roles in which they are enacted. Yet, in both texts, the commonality of gestures still remains the generative principle. A contemporary gloss on this development may note that the "unity of the members of the Christian community gathered for the Sacred Liturgy" is not just the assembly alone but includes all the celebrants of the rite. This can only enhance the effectiveness of signs and symbols in this "sacred action surpassing all others" (SC 7).

One of the practical reasons for this ongoing conflict of posture lies in the *arrangement of the assembly and its relationship to the altar* for this prayer and, indeed, during the whole liturgy. Uncritical use of architectural dimensions that are long and cruciform can hinder the participative nature of the assembly throughout the rite and often lull them into passive observance. Yet, creative solutions always remain, and many cathedrals and large churches shape the enactment to reflect this challenge. But they will never be broached if the gathered assembly as a *primary symbol of the presence of Christ* remains an idea and not a foundational principle. Discussions of this nature, from the perspective of inherent harmony of liturgical theology, practice, and spirituality, need to begin there—with the primary symbols—rather than adding the assembly to the liturgical mix after everything else has been decided in stone. Issues regarding the reservation of the Eucharist and the need for devotional space within church architecture are important and necessary, and we will address them further in chapter 5. The argument here remains the need for harmony and rhythm of the presence of Christ in the "praying and singing assembly," of the ritual enactment of that theological fact, and of a reverent spirituality that focuses on what God is doing in us as one Body of the church, rather than on the self-focused attention or concerns of either the presider or the participating assembly. Any building and any situation holds a creative solution when the primordial symbols are accorded the place and focus they deserve.

Communion rites that speak of *an organic procession in a common journey* and the affirmation of each member of the community as "the Body of Christ" differ according to community culture and custom. However, the same principle of inclusion in a rite of community nourishment for pilgrims who are living together into the redeeming, liberating life of Christ still stands as a common attitude we can all share. Diversity in local communities in the midst of this shared principle respects the creative Spirit that binds us and demonstrates that de Lubac's "symbolic inclusions" need not migrate to "dialectical antitheses." With communion rites, as well as with all liturgical gestures, the importance lies in their enactment as *expressions of the one Body of Christ* and not primarily signs of personal devotion, whose action within the rite often isolates the participants. Gestures of individual piety certainly can stir the heart and feed one's passion, but their ritual place lies in other important spiritual practices, not in the community's focal act of identity making and expression. We process to receive and embrace the gift together; communing to become what we receive provides the foundational impetus for this gesture. At the same time, *suitable time for a reverent, shared silence after the assembly's communion* in the Body and Blood of Christ, a time in which the presider and all the ministers take part, should be experienced regularly as "the way we pray." This quiet space of being together as the Body of Christ, as we have noted before, plays a particularly important role at this time of sacramental communion and actually nourishes personal devotion. Before our entrance into the ordinary time of a busy and frenetic world, grateful acknowledgment of the gift received needs to go beyond words, because it announces the kingdom of peace that Jesus embodied and focuses the consecrated Body on the transforming call to change the structures of our lives that blind us to its possibility.

Finally, at the end of the liturgy, *announcements of the community's living out of the mission* they have renewed in the gathering can be folded into the dynamic of the liturgical enactment itself. The assembly's weekly agenda of prayer and social outreach easily flows from an intentional use of the images and grace-filled moments of feast and season in which the sacramental action is embedded. The believing people continue to act in faith and justice after they depart only because God has first acted out of righteous love, shared that love with the Beloved in Word and table, and poured out the Spirit of that paschal mystery into the lives of the church as primary sacrament of the risen Lord Jesus. Self-congratulatory lists of a community's accomplishments need not provide the primary impetus for this sharing of the common life throughout the week. However, praise and thanks that the life of God, flowing from a heart of passion and connection, roots their identity and fuels their mission always makes any further desire to pray and act in justice a humble response to a prior grace and gift.

THE BODY OF CHRIST SEALED AND SENT IN MISSION

The images and context of the "Solemn Blessing for the Dedication of a Church" provides but one example of all the dynamics of an assembly's life lived in relationship with the community of God. Imagine a presider with hands outstretched in blessing and commission, an assembly standing in reverent expectation and hope, and the church's words in the following prayer, which together provide a perfect example of the rhythm and harmony of theology, liturgical practice, and a passionate spirituality of engagement with the world in, through, and with the Lord she serves:

May God, the Lord of heaven and earth,
who has gathered you today for the dedication of this church
make you abound in heavenly blessings.
R⁊. Amen.

May God, who has willed that all his scattered children
be gathered in his Son,
grant that you become his temple
and the dwelling place of the Holy Spirit.
R⁊. Amen.

May you be made thoroughly clean,
so that God may dwell within you
and you may possess with all the Saints
the inheritance of eternal happiness.
R⁊. Amen.

And may the blessing of almighty God,
the Father, ✠ and the Son, ✠
and the Holy ✠ Spirit,
come down upon you and remain with you for ever.
R⁊. Amen.

As the procession winds its way through the Body of Christ, it bodies forth a flow of grace, renewed and refreshed with the celebration of these mysteries, and begins its necessary and organic movement back into the world Christ loved and redeemed. This transition into ordinary time deepens the truth of the sacramental celebration and the redemptive act the church proclaims. Dominican Edward Schillebeeckx once called this ecclesial summons, "Nulla salus extra mundum, 'There is no salvation outside the world.'"[41] Christ is really present in ways we could never have asked for or imagined.

A sacramental assembly that worships with such attention expands the boundaries of memory and mission. David Power, OMI, calls this regular, faithful enactment of the liturgical memorial "the relation of the remembered event to the present and its continued influence on history." As such, the members of the assembly are immersed in a transforming event "that gives them power to change the horizon of existence and offer future generations new possibilities of

[41] Edward Schillebeeckx, unpublished address at the Dominican School of Theology, Berkeley, CA, 1981.

being."[42] The liturgy's eventfulness engenders a "presence *to*" more than a "presence *of*" in the heart of Christ and in those who are faithful to these mysteries, a situating of mission that unapologetically privileges the "weak, the suffering, the underprivileged, [and] the children."[43] The multivalent language of the liturgy—in story, symbol, and gesture—expresses the celebrating assembly's solidarity with her broken and poured out Lord, "the presence of Christ given through the medium of narrative, blessing, bread and wine, eating and drinking, within a community of service." At the same time, Power insists, "there is a continued absence that qualifies the presence," because the focus does not rest on the localized elements in and of themselves but moves through them to the relational presence they signify and that flows into the life of the community, enlivening that matrix of relationships in service to the world God created as good.[44] This is the true and dynamic life that liturgy makes present, he notes elsewhere, "a witness to the sending into the world of the love of God, embodied in Christ and in his disciples, and active through the power and gift of the indwelling Spirit."[45] The community of God has signed and sealed that "letter of Christ written on the tablets of human hearts" (2 Cor 3:3) and takes seriously their deepening mission to "become what they have received." Catechesis on the liturgy, Power concludes, must connect the circle of this relational, dialogical, and participative encounter we have described as the church's liturgy:

> At the end of each sacramental liturgy, the congregation is sent forth in Christ's peace, with a mission to witness to him, to the power of the Spirit, and to the gift of God's love. . . . As they go forth, in the fullness of the gift received, the congregation expects their faith to be tested and their words challenged. They also expect to be met by the other who awaits them, finding in them the Christ who awaits.[46]

Christ's presence in the assembly, therefore, reveals itself as fruitful and generative, "hidden" within the lives of those who have been gathered, blessed, broken, and shared by the God of love. Jesuit Peter

---

[42] Power, *Eucharistic Mystery*, 305.
[43] Ibid., 313.
[44] Ibid., 318–19.
[45] Power, *Sacrament*, 324.
[46] Ibid.

Fink's categories, mentioned above, of the "Christ who comes in Word, leads in the presider, abides in food, and lives hidden in assembly" maintain the creative tension that dynamic encounters require. The fact of Christ's presence cannot be controlled or manipulated, but, at the same time, the sacramental reality of that ineffable gift draws close and accessible precisely within the matrix of these symbolic relationships in which the assembly celebrates.[47] Immanence and transcendence are the crux of the mystery being enacted here. The "hidden" Christ now takes flesh in the concrete way we choose to live our lives, focus our energies, and interpret the meaning of all reality. We "recognize him" alive and risen in the burning Word in our hearts and in the breaking of the bread together.

The liturgical actions of gathering, of proclaiming and breaking open, and of praising and giving thanks prepare the assembly for communion at the altar but also at the "altar of the world," as Teilhard de Chardin called it,[48] a reception that is part of a densely rich web of mutual self-offering. Mission and sending in this context organically flow from the events and testify to their truth. In this sense, "the Mass is ended" begs the reality here a bit. "Missio"—sent—continues the rhythmic dance with fresh grace and renewed zeal, only to impel the Body of Christ to gather back time and again, because impassioned identity with the world and her suffering, the stirred grace of the

---

[47] Fink, *Praying the Sacraments*, 84.

[48] Pierre Teilhard de Chardin, SJ, *Hymn of the Universe* (New York: Harper & Row, 1965), chap. 1, "The Mass on the World." The integral connection between sacramental presence and mission are clear in this opening passage:

> I have neither bread, nor wine, nor altar, I will raise myself beyond these symbols, up to the pure majesty of the real itself; I, your priest, will make the whole earth my altar and on it will offer you all the labours and sufferings of the world.
>
> Over there, on the horizon, the sun has just touched with light the outermost fringe of the eastern sky. Once again, beneath this moving sheet of fire, the living surface of the earth wakes and trembles, and once again begins its fearful travail. I will place on my paten, O God, the harvest to be won by this renewal of labour. Into my chalice I shall pour all the sap which is to be pressed out this day from the earth's fruits.
>
> My paten and my chalice are the depths of a soul laid widely open to all the forces which in a moment will rise up from every corner of the earth and converge upon the Spirit. Grant me the remembrance and the mystic presence of all those whom the light is now awakening to the new day.

Spirit's urging, the encountered Christ in the other, and the face of the Creator in the created persistently are making all things new.

IMPLICATIONS FOR A LITURGICAL SPIRITUALITY ROOTED IN THE ASSEMBLY

> In the Christian liturgy, it is the assembly itself, encountering Christ in word and sacrament, that becomes a hole in the fabric of things, through which life-giving power flows into the world. But this hole is in this world and for this world. Indeed, the structures of the world urgently need such a hole.
>
> —Gordon Lathrop, twentieth-century liturgical theologian[49]

"O sign of unity! O bond of charity!"[50] This relational, dynamic metaphor is Augustine's description of the church's gathering as the Body of Christ at Eucharist. The student eucharistic community at the university who rise from their desks to "constitute the Church," and all the diverse communities of faith who struggle with the "hidden" grace at work within them as they gather, "effect the reality they signify." This humbling truth can be communicated reverently and beautifully when the rites we celebrate honor the assembly as the primary celebrants of the liturgy. Presiders and those who prepare and serve the liturgical life stand first in responsibility for assuring the clarity of that grace and mercy. There involves a certain powerlessness and ambiguity on the part of all in acknowledging that mystery. We cannot ultimately control this pure gift of Christ's presence "through us, with us, and in us." To that, we can only say, "Praise God!" Christ's example models for us the vulnerability of love, which differs from

---

[49] Gordon W. Lathrop, *Holy Things: A Liturgical Theology* (Minneapolis: Fortress Press, 1993), 212.

[50] Augustine exclaims, "Believers show they know the Body of Christ if they do not neglect to be the Body of Christ. Let them become the Body of Christ. . . . It is for this that the Apostle Paul, expounding on this bread, says: 'Because the loaf of bread is one, we, many though we are, are one body' (1 Cor 10:17). O sacrament of devotion! O sign of unity! O bond of charity! He that would live has where to live, has whence to live. Let him draw near, let him believe; let him become part of the Body, that he may be made to live. . . . Thus, the Lord would have this food and drink to be understood as meaning the fellowship of his own Body and members, which is the holy Church." See *Io. Ev.* 26.13, 15.

a passive and voiceless surrender to oppression. The freedom of the Spirit that mutual self-offering embodies—through, with, and in—Christ—sets a people free to love, to testify to the truth of God's dynamic presence in the world as a Word that liberates, redeems, and proclaims favor. This is the dynamism of the sacred assembly at worship. Is this not what the world seems to desire with such unfocused abandon, relentlessly seeking it in so many guises of riches, honors, and power that, in the end, cannot save? The utter simplicity of a "consecrated" life, which is truly what the assembly at liturgy becomes, speaks volumes to this unmet human desire and need.

Faithful practice, attentive preparation and enactment, and the continual pause to stand in reverent acknowledgment of the grace and mercy being offered here give deeper meaning to the term for the praying and singing assembly that the liturgy documents often employ: "the faithful." Past experience has tended to make us view such a name as disempowering, a label for passive creatures who blindly follow the leaders who herd them. But how refreshing and renewing it would be if we could take back the oppression of our communal descriptor, *the faithful*, and revel in its deep connection to the God who is faithful to us, to Jesus who is faithful to his Father and the mission to which he is sent, and to the Spirit's faithful breath that enters into the very marrow and fiber of creation to offer life, sustenance, creativity, and hope for a reign of justice and peace that only Love can author! The sheer grace of the name and the sure presence of Christ in the symbolic inclusions of *Corpus Christi, Corpus Mysticum* redeem *the faithful* as our truest identity. And we realize it, are consecrated in it, and enact it fundamentally as one body, head and members, together.

In the late second century (150–215 CE), the patristic theologian Clement of Alexandria preached about the nature of the church at prayer, and he captures the intimate and integral relationship between the Word and the eucharistic sacrifice of praise. In his homily to the Christians at Alexandria, he expounds upon the organic nature of the ecclesial activity of Word and Sacrament and its relationship to the praying assembly:

> Breathing together is properly said of the Church. For the sacrifice of the church is the word breathing as incense from holy souls, the sacrifice and the whole mind being at the same time unveiled in God. (*Stromata*, VII.6)

The faithful breathing . . . a spirituality of devotion rooted in the liturgy can truly find depth and spaciousness in this dynamism from which she can contemplate and draw life from the power of God, the abiding intimacy of the Lord Jesus, and the Spirit's refreshment. A contemporary Orthodox theologian, attempting to describe for Roman Catholics the Orthodox focus on the "Interpenetration of the Liturgy" into every aspect of the life of the triune God *and* the community of faith, gives us a reflection on that depth and spaciousness that the living and breathing faithful can bring into the confines of the communal heart at worship:

> "That which everything partakes yet without its being diminished
> by the participation of those who partake in it: this is indeed that
> which truly is." The love of the Trinity expands space into paradise;
> a paradise into freedom, released from care, fear and hatred. There
> is no opacity: everything shines like crystal. There is no lack of space
> caused by impenetrability; everyone has ample room: "What you have
> commanded is done, and there is still room" (Lk 14:22). Each new ar-
> rival does not make for discomfort, which provokes mistrust, but for
> increased breadth, the provision of new space and joy: "Joy that a (per-
> son) is born into the world" (John 16:21).[51]

We have such richness in our midst, members of the one Body rising from their sleep and work, coming through the "Porta Coeli," and willing to be sent out again from the banquet hall, transformed in vision and consecrated in mission. A faithful spirituality that revels in the spaciousness of that banquet place, the clarity of its embodiment in simple lives and common longing, and the mystery that "nothing is diminished" in recognizing that the incarnate One chooses this way of being-with-us "is itself," as Dom Gregory Dix said so well, "an overwhelming thought."

---

[51] Archimandrite Vasileios, *Hymn of Entry: Liturgy and Life in the Orthodox Church*, trans. Elizabeth Briere (Crestwood, NY: St. Vladimir's Seminary Press, 1984), 74. He is commenting on a passage by St. Gregory of Nyssa, *Life of Moses*, 2.25, S.C. 1 bis.

Chapter 3

"The Book of Life in Whom We Read God": The Presence of Christ in the Proclamation of the Word

> God's utterance of himself in himself is God the Word, outside himself is this world. This world then is word, expression, news of God. Therefore its end, its purpose, its purport, its meaning, is God and its life or work to name and praise him.
>
> —Gerard Manley Hopkins, SJ, twentieth century[1]

We move now to a different strain in this rhythmic harmony of the liturgy, the presence of Christ in the reading of the Scriptures and the preaching of the Word. The attempt to integrate theology, liturgical practice, and a spirituality that flows from worship remains the same task. The character of this sacramentality of the proclaimed Word shares the assembly's own dynamism, for the liturgical reading of sacred texts is alive and active (Heb 4:12), the present proclamation reaching back from the moment this eventful Word was first uttered by God in the beginning of all time. This divine, revelatory communication streams from the generative heart of the community of God, because this spoken Word of grace was "with God" and "is God" (John 1:1). That web of interrelationship, richly ambiguous and intentional, winds its way into the creative story of humankind's salvation, redemption, and liberation. The Word enters now into our presence, breathing and expectant, waiting to share that dynamism with us: "What has come into being in him was life, and the life was the light of all people. The light shines in the darkness, and the darkness did not overcome it" (John 1:4-5).

---

[1] Gerard Manley Hopkins, "Further Notes on the Foundation," in *The Sermons and Devotional Writings of Gerard Manley Hopkins*, ed. Christopher Devlin, SJ (London: Oxford University Press, 1959), 129.

This chapter focuses, therefore, on the presence of Christ in the liturgical proclamation of the community's sacred texts, the liturgical embodiment of "the Book of Life in Whom we read God," to echo Thomas Merton's words.[2] From the perspective of shared faith and worship we have been exploring, the Scriptures themselves cannot be merely static texts, words consigned to a page that simply record a past event or divine proclamation. Because they emerge as a spoken Word from the passionate heart of God as a symbolic revelation of God's acts of redemption in history, they reveal the power and grace of Christ, "the sacrament of *our* encounter with God." The proclaimed Word in the Scriptures shares the Trinity's own dynamic of relationship, dialogue, and participation that we found in the worshiping community itself. When the Scriptures are understood precisely as a *kerygmatic* Word, "that which is preached," then we begin to uncover the rich depths of connection and social interchange that characterize the words that flow from the mouth of the lector and preacher as he or she stands at the ambo in the midst of the worshiping community who gathers to hear them.

The lively context of a passage proclaimed on any given Sunday, then, streams forth from past saving events and flows now into a present informed and shaped by that grace, which, in turn, impels the hearers into a future and a mission that bear the very life of Christ. The Jesuit theologian Josef Jungmann articulated this *kerygmatic* quality of the proclaimed word as nothing less than "what Christ himself proclaimed and what his apostles proclaimed abroad as his heralds: that the kingdom of God has entered the world, thus disclosing salvation to [humankind]." In the light of the revelatory and communal nature of Christ's self-communication, we insist at the outset of this discussion that Christ is present in the proclamation of the Word as an *event* in which believers are invited to share and so, as Jungmann says, it "is more than just a doctrine."[3] The characteristics of *kerygma* necessitate *engagement*, *interchange*, and *embodiment*. The liturgical implications for this in preaching, in the role of the believing community in the

[2] Thomas Merton, *Thoughts in Solitude* (New York: Farrar, Straus and Giroux, 1958, 1999 ed.), 57. Merton says, "Christ, the Incarnate Word, is the Book of Life in Whom we read God."

[3] Josef Jungmann, *Announcing the Word of God*, trans. Ronald Walls (New York: Herder and Herder, 1967), 59.

proclamatory act, and in the relationship of this word-event to its fillment at the table and font form the key issues of this chapter.

So we begin with the same dynamic of grace that framed the discussion of the liturgical assembly. The living and breathing faithful have gathered to constitute the church, and the stories of their lives have already begun to meld and merge with those of others who have risen from their beds and desks, left their homes in various stages of chaos or tranquility, and assembled in one place to sing of their salvation in Christ. "The Word is in the world," as John's gospel and Hopkins speak it so eloquently, and that Word goes to work in communion with the "work of the people" (*leitourgia*) in a common task of *kerygma*, because, as Hopkins says, "its end, its purpose, its purport, its meaning, is God and its life or work to name and praise him." The proclamation of the Word constitutes a mode of sacramental presence in this eucharistic act, not an adjunct to it or a preparation for it. Word and Sacrament together express the nature of the church, as Karl Rahner said, and express one word and work of God.[4] Rahner's consideration of the relationship between the Word and the Eucharist elaborated upon his colleague Jesuit Otto Semmelroth's declaration that the twofold structure of the Liturgy of the Word and Eucharist embody a "single work" bestowing grace.[5]

Such integration of these focal liturgical actions proved crucial for the Vatican II reform that soon followed and remains a challenging task today. When liturgical communities—through their practice, catechesis, and lived spirituality—begin to see the unity of this revelatory Word at both the ambo and the table, they can start breathing again in unison with the God who uttered them, with the Body of Christ that gives them flesh, and with the Spirit who consecrates and transforms lives and futures in the way, the truth, and the life they offer. We will first look at the nature of this communication event in terms of the divine dynamic they reveal. Then we will look at liturgical practice that is in rhythm and harmony with that desire. Finally, we will explore

[4] See Karl Rahner, "The Word and the Eucharist," in *Theological Investigations*, vol. iv, trans. Kevin Smyth (New York: Crossroad, 1982), 267.

[5] Otto Semmelroth, *Church and Sacrament*, trans. Emily Schossberger (Notre Dame, IN: Fides Publishers, 1965), 38. I have written extensively on Semmelroth and Rahner on the relationship between Word and table in *The Holy Preaching: The Sacramentality of the Word in the Liturgical Assembly* (Collegeville, MN: Liturgical Press, 2000), part I.

the implications of Christ's real presence in the Word as a source for a renewed spirituality that draws from the passionate desire of God to speak a word of grace *to us* and *for us* in the saving deeds we celebrate.

THE LIVING, BREATHING WORD OF LITURGICAL PROCLAMATION

"Your words, Lord, are Spirit and life." (John 6:63b)

—Responsorial Psalm, Monday of the First Week of Lent

The Liturgy of the Word as Part of the Divine Dynamic

The presence of Christ in the reading and hearing of sacred texts, as we said, is an eventful activity, participating in the dialogue of love that flows from the heart of the community of God. This foundational dynamic cannot be underestimated when we consider the proclamation of the Word as a liturgical action that bodies forth the rhythm and grace of the divine movement of encounter with us. "Breathing together," as Clement of Alexandria reminded us, "is properly said of the Church." The Word of God contains that same life, uttered first by God as a word of love for the Beloved and expelled into the world as an offer of grace. Breathing in and breathing out Life describes the sacramental efficacy of the revelatory Word of God that took flesh among us as Jesus' own loving response in faith to his Father and to us. Our forebears' hearing of that Word, followed by their response in faith that God's creative Word communicated power and meaning in their world, finds its natural liturgical fulfillment "age after age" in a communal act of praise and thanks. The rhythm and harmony of this sacramental word-event that leads to *eucharistos* (giving thanks) continues its liturgical pattern "through, with, and in" us, albeit with new lives and situations in dialogue with the faithful promise from of old. The Word, rooted in the triune life of God, continually encountered in the realities of this present world and sent to forge again a wider and wider circle of living and breathing life, consecrates into communion all who encounter this divine life. Notice, for example, the kerygmatic and evangelical quality of John's community proclaiming the Good News:

> We declare to you what was from the beginning, what we have heard, what we have seen with our eyes, what we have looked at and touched with our hands, concerning the word of life—this life was revealed and

we have seen it and testify to it, and declare to you the eternal life that was with the Father and was revealed to us . . . so that you also may have fellowship with us; and truly our fellowship is with the Father and with his Son Jesus Christ. We are writing these things so that our joy may be complete. (1 John 1:1-4)

As we can see, the church's proclamation of the Word embraces the Christ-life, which flows from the heart of God and communicates its power through the community's sensible experience and shared faith life, revealed as a present action now through the grace of the Holy Spirit. Jesus himself, affirming this pattern, stood up to read among his friends and family in Nazareth, "as was his custom" (Luke 4:16), thereby announcing God's fulfillment in the midst of the worshiping assembly. Our reverencing the Word in its ritual vessel of the lectionary, reading from it together, and allowing ourselves to be transformed by its summons fulfill this rich interchange of gracious communication. The reading event as engagement, interchange, and embodiment, therefore, provides a way for us to understand the *real presence* of Christ that labors in the community's proclamation of the Word in the liturgy. The fertility of this divine communication remains sure and faithful, like the rain upon the earth in Isaiah's prophecy, and "will not return to God empty" (Isa 55:11). Furthermore, the communal reading from sacred texts as an invitation to self-offering and solidarity with Christ shapes the mode of this encounter. The Spirit inscripts and expresses this interchange of life between God and humanity within the church's Body in the form of Word and Sacrament. From the gathering of the assembly to the missioning into the world, everything in the liturgy participates in a proclamation and response to the revelatory Word, in whom we read God and God continues the narrative in us.

The proclaimed Word carries a rich ritual density, as contemporary hermeneutics has noted. Benedictine Ghislain Lafont, among others, has written about the role of narrativity in Christian founding stories passed on to a community of faith.[6] He sees sacramental memorial in that context of a *récit*, what Joy Blaylock calls "the oral tradition of narrativity" that is essential to this sacramental consideration of Christ's presence in the Word. Reading and hearing and preaching the Word generate the sacramental bond and consecrate a sacred text into a

[6] See Ghislain Lafont, *God, Time, and Being*, trans. Leonard Maluf (Petersham, MA: Saint Bede's, 1992).

kerygmatic event. Blaylock concludes, concerning Lafont's narrative approach and its relationship to the liturgical ritual as a whole:

> According to Lafont, those listening to the proclamation of the word in *récit* are intimately bound to each other and to the event proclaimed. When this bond is recorded as a written text, it is then handed on in the proclamation of the sacramental memorial and interpreted for the assembled congregation. For Lafont, the importance of the sacramental memorial does not come from the narrative alone. It is inserted into the ritual action, related to other types of scriptural text, and perfected in doxology. This appropriation of the narrative through forms of discourse, biblical and Eucharistic, shapes our relationships within belief.[7]

The eventfulness of liturgy, therefore, provides a context for Christ to be revealed as present within the proclamation that is "distinct but not separate," from the table action with which it is in relational, dialogical, and participative relationship.

"We Read to Meet Each Other": The Ritual Pattern of Presence in Communion

Literary critics in the past decades have been fascinated with this eventful character of reading as a communal act. Denis Donoghue, in his 1981 book *Ferocious Alphabets*, emphasizes how engagement with literary texts leads to what he calls a meeting of persons in "communion"—a complex interchange that describes precisely what we are about in the communal act of proclaiming and preaching the Word. Donoghue says,

> Breath, the rhythm of taking and expelling breath, represents the only understanding of presence, which persists not by staying in one unchanging form but by committing itself to a moving form as vulnerable as the heartbeat. Our bodily presence in the world is equally vulnerable. The aura which suffuses the idea of dialogue, conversation, communication, and communion arises from the sense of vulnerability in common. Communion is an attempt not to transcend the conditions in which we live upon our breathing, moment by moment, but to assent to them completely.[8]

---

[7] Joy Harrell Blaylock, "Ghislain Lafont and Contemporary Sacramental Theology," *Theological Studies* 66 (2005): 843.

[8] Denis Donoghue, *Ferocious Alphabets* (New York: Columbia University Press, 1984), 98.

Three points in these words about the role of voice and speech in reading should resonate with the work of the liturgy and the relationship of the modes of Christ's presence, particularly in regard to the proclaimed and preached Word. (1) There is *rhythm to this breath,* a harmonic of taking in and letting go. God's divine activity in creation provides the source of that life-giving dynamic. God loves (takes in), speaks that Word (lets go), which is the expression of that generative Love, and then listens to the Son's obedient answer of self-emptying surrender to it (takes in), whose life Christ shares with the world in the same rhythm and power of the Spirit (lets go). (2) *Bodiliness* provides the necessary arena of encounter for this hearing and responding in Love. (3) The *vulnerability of such a connection,* which God shares with us in the *kenotic* (self-emptying) offer of the Word-made-flesh, opens up the way for our active participation in this redemptive event to real communion and complete surrender in union with the Trinity. Let us look at these points from the lens of the proclaimed Word in the liturgy.

(1) The Rhythmic Breath of Proclamation and Response

Donoghue's insistence that presence in communion demands a commitment to "a moving form as vulnerable as a heartbeat" shapes the liturgical dynamism of reading the Scriptures together as the inspired word of God. The living metaphor of breathing accurately describes a communication event in which the speaker acts out of desire and the listener expectantly hears, is convicted by, and acts on the message shared between the two. God first speaks because God loves. That love strikes a chord in our human longing that reaches out in its own desire to love and be loved. The viability of this communication between God and humankind rests on the engagement, interchange, and embodiment of those to whom that vulnerable summons is proclaimed. Consequently, the communal reading of the Scriptures by a community gathered in praise and service of God provides the liturgical matrix of symbolic relationship between God's promise and humankind's response—at times an assent and at other times a refusal—as the liturgical cycle unfolds throughout the ages. Although God initiates the communication event, the assembly, as partner in this address, responds by its willingness to hear and act upon what it has heard. The *ruah,* the breath of God, the Spirit, is at work.

The openness to respond in faith ebbs and flows in our ecclesial life, but the struggle itself—the fact that we continue to do liturgical praying at all—is evidence of the allure of God's offer of "a word of grace, reconciliation, and eternal life, Jesus Christ," as Rahner describes the underlying mystery of the church.[9] How else can we explain the enduring power of the Scriptures in religious life? The Dominican William Hill, in his essay "What Is Preaching? One Heuristic Model from Theology," notes the apparent failure of Marx's axiom that his followers should simply leave religion alone because it will soon "vanish of its own failed momentum." Despite the apparent crisis of belief that affects our current age, people *still* wrestle with the truth of Christ or the claims of religious tradition throughout the world. Although the promise of meaning, truth, and life that the Christian Scriptures offer often seems unfulfilled, the desire beneath the struggle remains as a persistent hope. As Hill says,

> Concern for the God of Jesus refuses to go away. This may point to the fact that the crisis of credibility is not really a crisis of faith but one of culture, that is, one of communicating the Good News in a radically changing cultural context.
>
> I suspect that people *want* to believe but find the form in which the message is preached alien to their own experiences. Thus, the task of preaching becomes one of forging a new language that is appropriate to those experiences in their revelatory power, without neglecting the role of scripture and tradition.[10]

The longing is so important here and it begins, not in us, but in God. In terms of a liturgical dynamic that is relational, dialogical, and participative, Hill's claims of finding some meeting point between the enduring message of the scriptural tradition and the cultural context in which people are able to really "see with their own eyes and hear with their own ears this Word of life" uncover the crucial task of reviving of the kerygmatic power of the Word in our day. The necessary "new language" is not a "new word" of our own fashioning—God's word is consistent and life-giving at its source. However, as the assembly faithfully gathers to "constitute the Church," the partners in the

---

[9] Karl Rahner, *The Church and the Sacraments*, trans. W. J. O'Hara (New York: Herder and Herder, 1963), 15.

[10] William Hill, "What Is Preaching? One Heuristic Model from Theology," in *Search for the Absent God*, ed. Mary Catherine Hilkert (New York: Crossroad, 1992), 193.

conversation change, deepen in relationship, and live out the reality and the demands of the Gospel in circumstances *that are themselves part of the revelation*. This means that the Scriptures we hear on the night of the solemn Easter Vigil, for example, or at the funeral of a dear loved one, carry the enduring power and promise as God's uttered word of grace. However, that grace circulates with new energy within the minds and hearts and spirits of believers that hear the proclamation and who allow their own desire and longing to receive the nourishment the Scriptures offer, which gives them flesh and blood they can recognize as Christ's presence in their midst, a burning of the Spirit in their hearts (Luke 24:32-35). This matrix of symbolic relationships provides the context for the "new language," the nourishing Word. In addition, the wrestling of believers with these texts down through the ages, "as vulnerable as a heartbeat," gives life to the present-day communication of the kerygmatic Word, living and active now, in this time and place. We breathe in the same rhythm.

Yet, we cannot doubt the malaise of preaching and the Word in our liturgical gatherings today. People today often experience the proclaimed Word as a past fact, speaking to another age, safely aloof from the doubts and fears and struggles of their own lives. Theology, practice, and the passion that binds them must ask the hard questions this deadening of the Word raises for us. Has God's Word lost its dynamism or have we stopped responding to and breathing in its life, holding our own collective breath out of fear or lack of faithful practice? Has the church lost her voice due to scandal, a desire to accommodate to other idols, or a gradual disconnection from the very chords of the Spirit whose praise of God no longer "vibrates within us," as St. Ephrem prayed? Truly, the lack of power in the proclaimed Word does not hide the insatiable hunger and desire we have as believers, but it may suggest that we have forgotten our own role as focal actors in its incarnation in this time and place. Perhaps a recovery of "breathing in and breathing out" as a participation in the passion of God, revealed to us in Jesus, sustaining the community of faith age after age, and offering life and hope might engender a renewal of expectation that this Good News truly is *to us* and *for us*, for the life of the world. We might appreciate the Spirit's breath if we see our response as part of the divine revelation taking place.

An intentional commitment to dialogical, participative, and relational patterns of liturgical action resuscitates that rhythm of taking in and sharing the life of God and one another. Engaging its rhythm heals soul-weary pilgrims. The responsibility for this faithful practice rests on the whole church (*totus Christus*) as primary celebrant of the liturgy, but those who proclaim and preach the Word "in the person of Christ and of the church" bear a focal role in this rhythmic exchange of life. Both preachers and hearers cannot speak what they do not believe to be our very life and hope. The Word is gracious and must be received in grace, or else it is stifled in its utterance. Surrendering to the harmony of liturgical proclamation and response revives the life God's offer contains. Gathering to hear the revelatory Word and to sing of our salvation in season and out of season embodies the summons to "keep memory" of God's saving acts in Jesus, so that Christ's offer of grace and mercy is really present in our hearing and can consecrate us in its truth (John 17:17). Presence, as we said, persists through engagement, interchange, and embodiment. The communication event in which God breathes life and love into a creation in God's image and likeness cannot remain idly static upon a page of a text preserved in a museum of another time and people.

David Power's work on eucharistic memorial helps us to see the specifically liturgical dynamics of this active presence of Christ when the Scriptures are read in the gathered assembly:

Beauti- ful

> To keep memorial is to relate the present, which is characteristically in flux, to the past and to the future. The past does not repeat itself, but it has left its traces and testimony, and thus transmits its power to change history and lives by a pattern of action that emerges from it.[11]

The "traces and testimony" that the Scriptures transmit take the form of the new covenant that is written upon the hearts of the people that, in turn, establishes their participation in this relationship of love and mutual self-offering in faith. The content of the law takes flesh and becomes a dynamic encounter when communication between Lover and Beloved creates a relationship of mutual self-revelation:

> I will put my law within them, and I will write it on their hearts; and I will be their God, and they shall be my people. No longer shall they teach one another, or say to each other, "Know the Lord," for they shall

---

[11] David Power, *Sacrament: The Language of God's Giving* (New York: Crossroad, 1999), 176.

90

all know me, from the least of them to the greatest, says the LORD; for I will forgive their iniquity, and remember their sin no more. (Jer 31:33-34)

The Christian tradition maintains that this revelatory Word makes present in human history this offer of redemption when the Spirit of the risen Christ pours out the power and grace of Easter and Pentecost upon the community of believers. The resurrection community "sees the Lord" and this communication of the event is part of the Trinity's redemptive mission in the world. That dynamic is alive and celebrated in the liturgy down to the present day. What "we have seen and heard and touched" now lives in us, the Spirit-filled, resurrected Body of Christ in the world (Acts 2:33). This Good News in the world has a sacramental character that is *kerygmatic*—bearing the promise of God and the presence of Christ as salvation for all humankind. Its historical and personal dynamism consecrates believers in the life of God. In our receptivity to this sacramental proclamation (*ex opere operantis*), we now know who we are, we experience forgiveness and mercy, and what had once been an announcement "written in stone" becomes enfleshed in our very hearts. These are the "traces and testimony" that Power says "transmits its power to change history and lives by a pattern of action that emerges from it." A resonance of the original life that inheres in the sacred texts converses with the stuff of our own lives and provides the grace-filled energy that animates the Word as the presence of Christ "fulfilled in our hearing" (Luke 4:21).[12] The lives and witness of the disciples and communities of Christians before us, of martyrs and mystics and prophets through the ages, now spiral through the energy of our gathering, infusing our struggles and hopes and dreams, and invite connection, reception, and self-offering. "Our bodily presence in the world is equally vulnerable," as Donoghue says, and we can now maintain, is as vulnerable as the heartbeat of the divine Love that first uttered it. This brings us to the second point in Donoghue's analysis of presence: *bodiliness as the arena of encounter for our hearing and responding in Love.* Our discussion may open up the hard questions about the community's own responsibility to keep breathing in and breathing out for the life of the world, for the sake of Christ, and for the true praise that proclaims our deepest identity as God's beloved.

[12] Cf. part II of *Holy Preaching*, in which I discuss the relationship between the enduring "life" of literary artifacts and its relationship to the sacramentality of the proclamatory event in the liturgy.

(2) Bodiliness as the Way We See, Hear, and Touch the Word Written upon Our Hearts

Jesus Christ took flesh and lived among us and we beheld his glory (John 1:14). This is the message passed down to us from generations of believers, and so bodiliness provides a way of hearing the Word and encountering Christ as Word-made-flesh. Jesus, the vulnerable instrument of God, invites us to share that intimate relationship born of love so that the Word can continue to be proclaimed and preached in his Body. Edward Schillebeeckx took the historicity and corporeality of the Christ-event as the basis for understanding the sacramental Body of the church. To honor the incarnation of Christ necessarily means that we reverence the church's Body as an instrument of this presence. He says,

> The man Jesus is the presence of the redeeming God among us, though in the mode of a human presence bodying that presence forth to us. Precisely for this reason the plan of incarnation requires, from the moment of Christ's ascension, a prolongation of his bodily mediation in time. We already know that this sacramental body of the Lord is the Church.[13]

Once we admit the body as instrument of revelation, then relationship, dialogue, and participation shape the parameters of this mode of encounter between God and humankind, Christ and the church, and believing Christians with the world. This dynamic, to use Donoghue's images, represents "vulnerability in common." The perennial biblical themes of exodus and liberation, wandering and seeking a home, breaking faith and reconciling with kin, and hungering and thirsting for the real food and drink God offers find resonance in hearers' minds and hearts when they are proclaimed as "here and now" offers of grace and new life. The fact that actual, faithful lives before us had to engage these stories of redemption and to allow their own meaning and future to shape the community of faith rescues the Scriptures from the shelves of past accounts and invites the transformation they offer to happen now, in us and in our world. Our bodiliness in this world characterizes the arena of encounter for this Good News, because the material world and our place in it provide the stage for the revelatory

---

[13] Schillebeeckx, *Christ the Sacrament of the Encounter with God* (Kansas City: Sheed and Ward, 1963), 59.

Word to be proclaimed as living and active, a sacramental symbol that reveals the truth it signifies. The community gathered to hear the Word and to share in the self-offering of the gifts at the table of God's abundance truly testifies to a proclamation that renders present the embodied Word, in the same spirit as John's community:

> We declare to you what was from the beginning, what we have heard, what we have seen with our eyes, what we have looked at and touched with our hands, concerning the word of life—this life was revealed, and we have seen it and testify to it. (1 John 1:1-2a)

Our willingness to stake our search for liberation and a true home in God on the very testimony we give by lives of love, mercy, reverence, and praise speaks volumes to the world. It also is our humble acknowledgment that Christ truly offered himself "for the life of the world" and this life is visible, tactile, audible, and, because of that, very vulnerable. Such is God's way revealed in Jesus, and it asks of the hearers of the Word nothing less. This summons carries particular urgency for those who proclaim and preach this embodied Word in the midst of the faithful assembly. The discernment of their charism and authority must start from there and announce the kingdom from that place of relational, bodily encounter. "*Caro salutis est cardo*"[14] ("It is on the flesh that salvation hinges"), as Tertullian catechized in the third century. Indeed, the intimate locus for the revelatory Word calls forth in all of us a self-emptying and surrender in the manner of Christ, the Word-made-flesh. Liturgical proclamation must never distance itself from this mode of encounter or it becomes disembodied, static, and lifeless. This leads to our final point about the rhythm of the living and breathing Word: the vulnerability that engagement, interchange, and embodiment requires of a community gathered in faith to hear the word of God as a liturgical action.

(3) Communal Vulnerability and the Proclamatory Event

Once we acknowledge the dynamism of God's word as a spoken communication between Lover and Beloved and the Spirit of Love poured out, we begin to see the shape of a worshipful encounter with the Word that shares in the Trinity's own life. God risks a communal dialogue in which revelation occurs precisely in the rhythm of

[14] Tertullian, *De Carnis Resurrectione*, 8: Migne, Patrologia Latina (MPL) 2, 806.

proclamation and response. Mutual self-communication asks something of both the one who speaks and those who hear. This model of divine vulnerability in God's own self-emptying in expressing that Word in the flesh can transform our own hardened hearts and narrow visions, because God's own *kenosis* here is itself a proclamation of the Good News! Our consecration in this truth (John 17:17) as hearers of the Word takes place through the power of liturgical proclamation and preaching as a sacramental action. Christ himself provides for us the pattern of our worshipful response to this gracious act of God, because Jesus' own "obedient love and adoration of the Father [is] the human translation of his divine relationship of origin,"[15] as Schillebeeckx noted about the trinitarian dimension of this mutual self-offering of praise and thanks. As a result, Jesus' own vulnerability in surrendering his life and mission as an act of praise to the One who loved him and sent him results in God's responding exaltation of Jesus as *Kyrios*, the Lord who opens up our way and our truth and our life. In sharing this Spirit upon the world, that cycle of *kenosis* as transformative vision takes flesh and is really present in us. "And I, when I am lifted up, will draw all things to myself" (John 12:32).[16] The whole purpose and direction of human life is consecrated and transformed when the vulnerability of such connection begins to pattern the way we live and worship.

From the perspective of this kenotic pattern, the enfleshed Word is no longer simply a series of laws and strictures, accompanied by stories to tell us how to live. Sacramental proclamation summons a community to engagement with Christ laboring in the world."[17] Unfortunately, our encounter with the Scriptures within the liturgy often assumes a distanced, moralizing perspective, especially when we use the sacred texts to make a point or admonish behavior. This lack of participative engagement mutes the proclamation. The word of God in its relational fullness opens up a richer, albeit costly, fare for those who feast upon it. As Jeremiah reminds us about this Word written upon the hearts of God's very own,

---

[15] Edward Schillebeeckx, "The Sacraments: An Encounter with God," in *Christianity Divided: Protestant and Roman Catholic Issues*, ed. Daniel J. Callahan, Heiko A. Obermann, and Daniel J. O'Hanlon (New York: Sheed and Ward, 1961), 264.

[16] Schillebeeckx, *Christ the Sacrament*, 20–21.

[17] Cf. Janowiak, "*Lex Orandi, Lex Predicandi:* Preaching a Laboring Word," *Journal of Ignatian Spirituality* (Winter 2005).

No longer shall they teach one another, or say to each other, "Know the LORD," for they shall all know me, from the least of them to the greatest, says the LORD. (Jer 31:34)

The proclamatory event is more about revealing what is embedded within the Body rather than assembling information and telling the assembly what they do not "know." We see here that when law is allowed to move from stone to heart, it becomes wrapped in relationship and self-offering. There exists now both a promise of encounter and a vulnerability that comes from knowing the other and allowing oneself to be known. Christ's gift of making known the Father's redemptive grace and mercy still risks being rejected, forgotten, and ignored. Yet, this freedom represents the cost of a vulnerable Word, a fragile treasure shared in the act of giving it away. God's freedom to "let go" of the Beloved at his side, to communicate to us the offer of life, invites us to receive this same liberating speech and to become bearers of a Word of grace. We are not left alone as we participate in this self-emptying vocation. God knows and participates in this cost of love; Jesus lives its truth for us; the Spirit vibrates its rhythm in our very being. Every moment of encounter in the liturgy preaches this Good News and consecrates the hearers in its truth.

Authentic living testifies to the truth of this proclaimed Word. Love as relationship means dying to self and letting go into a deeper life. Parents, for example, know this in their bones. Their fierce love does not lessen their vulnerability; in fact, the vulnerability is itself the grace that allows the love they share with their children to blossom and grow, "to be fruitful and multiply" in acts of love as an expression of God's creative act. This creative fragility in love represents the attitude of communities that allow the vulnerable Word to refashion them into the image of the Lord they serve. Every proclamation they hear, every word they preach, every movement to the table they make comes first from the vulnerable mouth of God (Matt 4:4), spoken to them and for them in Christ (Col 1:19-20), and heard and received in the power of the Spirit (Ezek 2:1-2; John 16:13).[18] Paul's Second Letter to the Corinthians speaks eloquently to us today of the grace that comes with allowing ourselves to know and be known as the Beloved,

[18] Cf. Yves Congar, *The Word and the Spirit*, trans. David Smith (London: Geoffrey Chapman, 1986), 15–16.

and thereby to hear a word written not on the hardened surface of stone tablets but in the fragile encounter between loved ones:

> Such is the confidence that we have through Christ toward God. Not that we are competent of ourselves to claim anything as coming from us; our competence is from God, who has made us competent to be ministers of a new covenant, not of letter but of spirit; for the letter kills, but the Spirit gives life. (2 Cor 3:4-6)

It is in Paul's paradoxical context of "competent vulnerability" that Donoghue's images of breath, communion, and surrender illuminate divine communication in the liturgy. We read the sacred texts to meet each other[19] in a vulnerable sharing of life, whose dynamism flows from the heart of God. "For where two or three are gathered in my name," Jesus says, "I am there among them" (Matt 18:20).

"Communion," as Donoghue said, "is an attempt not to transcend the conditions in which we live upon our breathing, moment by moment, but *to assent to them completely*." God's Word of grace and life, Jesus Christ, is breathed into us in the power of the Spirit when the assembly opens its ears and minds and hearts to this transforming power and "assents completely" to the Word-made-flesh that names our own baptismal identity. Such active engagement characterizes what is meant when we speak of Christ's presence in the living, breathing word of liturgical proclamation. We will explore the shape of this sacramental presence more in this next section and relate it to the "visible Word" of the table. This will help us see how the whole liturgical celebration can more faithfully express this *kerygmatic* presence.

THE CHRIST WHO SPEAKS IN LITURGICAL PROCLAMATION—SACRAMENTAL PRESENCE AT WORD AND TABLE

> We shall understand the meaning of the Law if it is Jesus who reads it to us and makes its spiritual significance clear. Do you not believe that in this way the meaning was grasped by those who said: "did not our

---

[19] In *Ferocious Alphabets*, Donoghue says, "We read a poem not to enlighten ourselves but to verify the axiom of presence we read to meet each other. The encounter is personal, the experience is satisfying in the degree of presence rather than of knowledge. *We read to meet the speaker*" (99; emphasis mine). The sacramental implications of this are immense.

hearts burn within us while he talked with us along the way and while
he opened to us the Scriptures" (Lk 24:32).

—Origen, third century[20]

How, then, does the liturgy body forth the presence of Christ "when
the holy Scriptures are read in the Church" (SC 7)? How does Jesus
"read" to us? What characterizes this mode of presence that participates in the living, breathing Word that comes forth from the mouth of
God as the lector reads from the sacred texts and the preacher breaks
open that Word in the midst of the gathered assembly? The task is not
easy because, on an experiential level, we often isolate Christ's presence to the bread and wine alone. Because of this narrow sacramental
focus, many of us would admit that imaginatively and sensibly we
feel a ritual division between the Liturgy of the Word and the Liturgy
of the Eucharist. At the same time, despite the confusion regarding the
relationship between Word and table, attentive and engaged worshipers would readily acknowledge that the reading of the Scriptures in
the Sunday assembly does tell us something *about* God and Christ's
saving deeds for us. We see this redemptive offer promised to us in
the stories of our Hebrew ancestors in faith. Because of the Spirit of
the resurrected Christ poured out upon the disciples, those covenantal
stories took on new life and meaning in the community that gathered
together in Jesus' name in the early church. Their lived witness to the
faith, recorded in the postresurrection narratives and letters, gives concrete example of Christ's Passover injunction on the night before he
died: "Do this in memory of me." Worshipers today feel connection in
faith and spirit with the biblical stories they hear. The Scriptures, then,
are definitely an inspired word for us. Yet, affirming Christ's sacramental presence in the liturgical action of proclaiming and preaching
the Scriptures would probably be less evident to most worshipers, and
certainly not in the sense in which we speak of Christ's real presence
in the Eucharist. To clarify our theology and practice of proclamation,
this liturgical action as an eventful presence of Christ to the church
gathered in prayer deserves closer scrutiny.

[20] Thomas K. Carroll, *Preaching the Word*, Message of the Fathers of the
Church Series (Wilmington, DE: Michael Glazier, 1984), 44.

Bringing Together the Table of the Word and the Table of the Eucharist

Even after half a century of liturgical reform, we cannot shake the static and isolating notion that the Liturgy of the Word involves a preparatory action that readies us for Christ's gift of self on the altar in the breaking of the bread and the sharing of the cup. Following a theology of worship that is *relational*, *dialogical*, and *participative* of all aspects of the church's gathering to pray and give thanks, this explanation of Christ's preparatory presence in the dynamic Word, though true in many ways as movement toward communion, still is not enough. We need to bridge the disconnect between Word and table, because the contention of this book is that the entire liturgical act and actors proclaim, to use Rahner's words, "one whole word of God." As Edward Schillebeeckx has said, the Liturgy of the Word and the Liturgy of the Eucharist *together* proclaim the sacramental presence of Christ in the church. "Instructed and enlightened by this sacrament of the word, our vision is extended, and we can see the whole wide, continuous sphere of the Church's sacramental life."[21] Both preaching and the sacramental actions that follow, Schillebeeckx explained further, "can be regarded simply as the burning focal points within the entire concentration of this visible presence of grace" that the church bodies forth as the incarnational expression of this intimacy with us.[22] Insisting on the wholeness of the kerygmatic Word of God at ambo and table, along with the image of mutual points of radiant grace, provide important ways to reimagine the proclamation event within the liturgy. They give us a theological model to connect the sacramental grace of the proclaimed Word, which then organically leads to praise and thanks for Christ's obedient self-offering in which all are invited to share, whose efficacy takes flesh in our sacramental communion in the Body of Christ. Notice the interconnection and rhythmic harmony of this liturgical dynamic of Word and Sacrament as a unified whole. How much clearer and effective our symbolic words and actions would be if that wholeness of the proclaimed Word were clearly expressed throughout the whole celebration! Communion would unambiguously express God's passion for union with us at all levels of body, mind, and spirit.

This symbolic matrix of relationships that sacramentally express Christ's presence, therefore, acknowledges not only that Word and

---

[21] Schillebeeckx, *Christ the Sacrament*, 215.
[22] Ibid., 216.

Sacrament are indeed related but that they are also inseparably integral and in harmony with each other. From this perspective, we would have to insist that, like the assembly's focal presence in the eucharistic action, *without the proclaimed and preached Word there is no Blessed Sacrament.* Furthermore, the sacramental presence of Christ in the Word contains rich levels of meaning that come together precisely as the proclamation interacts with the entire liturgical enactment and within the contemporary cultural context in which it occurs. What emerges sounds *a rhythmic pattern of proclamation and response* within the assembly, which harmonizes with Christ's self-offering that we are invited to share as the Body of Christ.

The action of "taking, blessing, breaking, and sharing" at the table—which characterizes the shape of the entire liturgical action—has already been breathed into the worshiping assembly in their communal action of speaking, hearing, receiving, and accepting with gracious assent the *kerygmatic* offer to which the proclaimed Word gives voice. Such attentiveness among the gathered assembly needs to be cultivated, and ignorance of this dynamic mutes its grace-filled power. The assembly, its ministers and preachers, and those who catechize about the liturgy need to understand how the proclamation of the Word originates and participates in the fertile life and love of the community of God, who desires to communicate this divine relationship to all who hear. To aid that deeper appreciation, our present exploration must provide a theological explanation for the dynamics of Word and Sacrament that are in rhythm with this dynamism that flows from the source and fount of the church's life. Liturgical principles follow from that theology and give expression to a spirituality that uncovers and articulates God's passion to speak a Word of grace into the context of our gathering to pray together, in this time and place, as we are and how we hope to be. Christ is present when the Scriptures are proclaimed; there is a hunger stirring in God's heart that matches our own deepest desires. Let us look a little closer at that revelatory dynamic at work in our gathering.

How the Word Proclaimed, Heard, and Preached Becomes an Invitation to Conversion and Fitting Worship

Of all the theologians working to reimagine a sacramental theology founded on the notion of the church as the basic sacrament and on the sacraments themselves as expressions of the proclaimed Word enfleshed in our ecclesial identity, Jesuit Otto Semmelroth has provided the clearest theological outline. He roots this dynamic in the redemptive action of God and the rhythm of the liturgy itself. A brief look at his often unnoticed work in the middle of last century will provide a framework for exploring effective liturgical practice and spirituality as it pertains to the presence of Christ in the proclamation and preaching of the Word. In order to enter into the dynamic Semmelroth proposes, let us first situate ourselves by looking at a familiar passage from chapters 8 and 9 of the book of Nehemiah, which records an occasion when the sacred texts of the covenant were read in the assembly of the people of Israel. The account movingly describes the relationship between the ritual reading of sacred texts within the community's prayer and their subsequent self-offering as a people in service to the faithful God who speaks that Word.

In Nehemiah 8, after the people had gathered at the Water Gate and instructed Ezra "to bring the book of the law of Moses, which the Lord had given to Israel" (8:1), Ezra stands "in the presence of the men and the women and those who could understand; and the ears of all the people were attentive to the book of the law" (8:3). Standing on a wooden platform in their presence, surrounded by the elders of the people, Ezra proclaims the Word that the people asked to be brought to them (8:1b), as the author describes this powerful liturgical event:

> And Ezra opened the book in the sight of all the people, for he was standing above all the people; and when he opened it, all the people stood up. Then Ezra blessed the Lord, the great God, and all the people answered, "Amen, Amen," lifting up their hands. Then they bowed their heads and worshiped the Lord with their faces to the ground. Also, [certain leaders of the people] helped the people to understand the law, while the people remained in their places. So they read from the book, from the law of God, with interpretation. They gave the sense, so that the people understood the reading. (8:5-8)

Notice the rhythm of the proclamation here: the elder receives the book from the people, who desire that the law be read in their assembled presence. Ezra stands in a place that enables all to see and hear. The assembly likewise stands in an act of reverence and communal solidarity that this Word is not only *from God* but also *for them*, in this time and place. The leaders charged with preaching accept the responsibility in this setting to help the people to see that connection. They do not give a talk *about* the Word so much as they "give the sense," which suggests an artful breaking open of the depths of connection this Word has with

God's saving deeds and also with their own lives as bearers now of the covenant that God made with the people for all time. This ritual act of encounter with the sacred text describes a great transformation of the law that is written in stone, which then becomes a saving Word written on human hearts, who then feed upon its wisdom and live the truth it proclaims. Nehemiah goes on to describe the action that flows from this communal hearing in the context of the great feast:

> And Nehemiah, who was the governor, and Ezra the priest and scribe, and the Levites who taught the people said to all the people, "This day is holy to the LORD your God; do not mourn or weep." For all the people wept when they heard the words of the law. Then he said to them, "Go your way, eat the fat and drink sweet wine and send the portions of them to those for whom nothing is prepared, for this day is holy to our LORD; and do not be grieved, for the joy of the LORD is your strength." . . . And all the people went their way to eat and drink and to send portions and to make great rejoicing, because they had understood the words that were declared to them. (8:9-10, 12)

Contemporary worshipers need to pay attention to what is happening here, given our own experience of gathering as an assembly to hear the Word and share in the table feasting. The Word is "taken" by the people and "blessed" as holy by the reverence and prayerfulness in which they gather to hear it. They experience this Word as "broken open and shared" by the priest Ezra. They allow this proclamation to enter into their self-identity to such an extent that they weep in communion with its challenge and promise. Surely, the community expresses penitence for their shortcomings in keeping the law. But the passage suggests something more, a stirring of the heart and a transformation in the hearing, that enables them to spread the feast, to bless God for the abundance they received, to sing and dance in praise of such bounty, and then, in the spirit of their own consecration, to bring the food to those "for whom nothing is prepared." What an ancient, venerable, and vulnerable model for hearing the Word in the context of the festal memorial! There is, to use the language and imagery of Donoghue, the *breathing rhythm* of proclamation and response; their *bodiliness* is essential to the ritual action; this, in turn, creates an interior *vulnerability* as the promise and challenge of the proclamation takes hold of contemporary life and meaning.

Chapter 9 goes on to describe the prayer that flows from the assembly's gathering in a communal recognition of their sinfulness and desire to be reconciled to the God of the covenant. After fasting and expressions of common need, not only for themselves but also for the sins of their ancestors, the appointed readers "stood up in their place and read from the book of the law" (9:3). This leads to worship and praise of God who is recognized and proclaimed in this reading as "ready to forgive, gracious and merciful, slow to anger and abounding in steadfast love" (9:17). The content of the blessing prayer here has a wonderful and curious resonance with our contemporary eucharistic prayers that the presider prays in the assembly's name at the table:

> And Ezra said: "You are the LORD, you alone; you have made heaven, the heaven of heavens, with all their host, the earth and all that is on it, the seas and all that is in them. To all of them you give life, and the host of heaven worships you." (9:6)

We can almost hear ourselves adding the harmony of our own ancient hymn of praise, "Holy, holy, holy Lord, God of power and might. Heaven and earth are filled with your glory." We find it easy to be in rhythm with the assembly's one body and one voice in their response to the power that flows forth from the mouth of God, when their leaders bid them sing their praise:

> "Stand up and bless the LORD your God from everlasting to everlasting. Blessed be your glorious name, which is exalted above all blessing and praise." (9:5b)

Contemporary worshipers would also resonate with the eucharistic character of the memorial of God's saving deeds that the leader then proceeds to enumerate in this prayerful address to God, which is the ground of their own meaning and future hope. For Ezra goes on, in the presence of this standing and praying assembly, to tell of God's fidelity in choosing a people and giving them life, calling them into freedom, hearing their distress, and fulfilling the promises of old (9:7ff.). Time and again, he prays, the people have forgotten and turned back, "but you did not forsake them" (9:17). We know this pattern of praying in our bones, generations later. Just as our tapers cast their warm glow off the walls of our temples of prayer when we gather for the Easter Vigil and hear these same stories, we also understand the rhythm of this proclamation and response in word and deed. We are in tune with Ezra and the whole assembly, as he praises God for the wonders of his deeds against Pharaoh and in God's sending the Israelites off to walk dry shod through the sea, so that they can then be led "by day with a pillar of cloud, and by night with a pillar of fire, to give them light on the way which they should go" (9:9-12).

The reading of these sacred stories of redemption and liberation, passed on in faith "age after age," localizes the revelation in their midst and in ours, which leads necessarily to prayer and feasting for the people gathered. Even more, we know only too well the source of the well of weeping that flows out of the communal experience of hearing this good Word together (8:9). The tears express their engagement with this proclamation with new depth of faith, of true repentance, and of nourishing sustenance as they hear how Ezra blessed God for the power of this Word of promise, fulfilled in the people:

> For their hunger you gave them bread from heaven, and for their thirst you brought water for them out of the rock, and you told them to go and to possess the land that you swore to give them. (9:15)

In the context of the people's vulnerable recognition of sinfulness and their utter confusion that God has somehow forgotten them in this time and place, the Word takes flesh in a recounting of past deeds, spoken through the grace of God into a vulnerable present, which gives redemptive meaning and direction for the future. The dynamic demonstrates the power and presence of God in liturgical memorial and its expression in the ritual reading of sacred texts. What begins as a perceived absence culminates within the assembly's memorial prayer as a powerful, nourishing presence.

The familiar pattern strikes a resonant chord in us. God's word is living and active in that rhythm of public proclamation, of standing together to listen, of breaking the narrative open "so that the people understand," and of communal sorrow and conversion as the fitting response to a Word that has cut to the heart and laid bare the marrow and the bone of their imperfect hearts as well as their deepest longing. And the fertile movement of proclamation and response spirals toward fulfillment at the table and the abundance of the feast to be shared with "those for whom nothing is prepared" (8:10). We know this liturgical dynamism because the gracious action of the Holy Spirit inscripts its cadence into our ritual bones. How, then, can we appreciate and efficaciously embrace that integral dynamic of Word that leads to table in our contemporary celebrations? In postmodern culture, how specifically do the life, death, and resurrection of Jesus shape that proclamation and response? Most liturgical theology after Vatican II simply assumes the centrality of the paschal mystery in our worship, but the Word of God hovers on the sidelines. The vagueness of our theology and practice does not illumine how our communion in the Christ-event is rooted in the life of God, in the active presence of Christ who "reads" this into us, and is expressed in the liturgy we celebrate. These questions and ambiguities may be addressed now, for Otto Semmelroth outlines a way to see how Christ, the Word who comes among us, shares that redemptive event with us in the liturgy we celebrate in his name. Christian sacraments, we will see, embrace the fulfillment of that ancient dialogue of relationship and participation that our ancestors in the covenant shared with God, passing on that chosen identity to those who would come after them. Furthermore, he gives a liturgical framework to the burning focal points of Word and Sacrament that illumine the wholeness of the redemptive event. We will look at his contribution to this liturgical dynamic of Word and table more closely.

Incarnation and Self-Offering as God's Word and Answer in Christ

For Semmelroth, the saving presence of Christ in the sacraments is not one-dimensional, because the redemptive event of Christ's paschal mystery is itself multilayered throughout Jesus' life, worship, and mission. Everything about Jesus resonates with the One who loves him and shares the kenotic love of mutual surrender with him, for the life of the world. These saving acts certainly culminate in his sacrificing death and triumphant resurrection; yet the expressive moment of cross and tomb completes God's redemptive action initially proclaimed by the incarnation of Christ in the world. The embodying of God's love and mercy as a moment in history announces itself, in Jesus, as the kerygmatic new beginning promised of old, as well as the harmonious complement to God's original creation of the cosmos in love. Because the church stands in the power of the Spirit as the basic sacrament of God's redemptive act revealed in Christ, her "sacramental life functions" in the proclamation of the Word and sacramental worship work together to reflect the dense fullness of God's gift to the world in Christ.[23] Incarnation and saving death culminate in the person and eventful life of Jesus, who "has given us a new birth into a living hope

---

[23] Cf. Semmelroth, *Church and Sacrament*, 9–10, 41.

through the resurrection from the dead, and into an inheritance that is imperishable" (1 Pet 1:3b-4a).

The liturgy's unity as a "single work," therefore, finds its source and ongoing efficacy in the fact that the *incarnation* and the *sacrifice* of Christ together express a single event of grace, liberating and redeeming the world God so desires. This living, breathing dynamism gives resonance and shape to the word of God, which was sent forth into the world when Christ became flesh and which returns to its source by means of Christ's self-sacrificing response back to the Father, in which we are now invited to share through the Spirit's life within us. The Liturgy of the Word and the Liturgy of the Eucharist echo this rhythm of proclamation and response: *the Word announces the incarnation* of that saving presence fulfilled in Christ and heard now as a present offer of grace; the succeeding movement to *the table expresses the self-offering of obedient love that Christ offered back to the Father* in complete freedom, for the life of the world. The church, now gathered as Christ's Body, participates with him as consecrated gift to the Father. Word and table proclaim in one voice the totality and richness of God reuniting all creation to God's self, the source of all desire. To isolate the incarnation (Word) as merely a preliminary to the saving death and resurrection (table) misses the complementary wholeness of the Christ-event for the world, as well as our relationship and participation in its ongoing redeeming presence at work in our midst.

The integral relationship of Word and Sacrament, Semmelroth concludes, expresses a "redemptive dialogue in which God and [human-kind] are a living unity joined in a personal confrontation."[24] Christ is present in the fullness of redemption, as *"Wort und Antwort,"* the *word* of announcement and the *answer* of self-gift, in which we are invited to share.[25] In Word and Sacrament, Christ fulfills his mission as Alpha and Omega, God's self-communication *to, with,* and *for* us that is dialogical, relational, and participative in character. The liturgy bears the *totus Christus* and gives us a healed and wholesome image for worship that unifies Word and table as a single event of grace-filled

---

[24] Otto Semmelroth, *The Preaching Word: On the Theology of Proclamation*, trans. John Jay Hughes (New York: Herder and Herder, 1965), 232. His Roman Catholic perspective on the sacramental character preaching and its theological foundation was groundbreaking for its time. The liturgical implications of such a Catholic sacramentality of preaching remained to be explored.

[25] Ibid., 230–32.

communication. This *is* the "living unity" of which Semmelroth prophetically speaks, a theological truth about the community of God in which we stand together in thanks and praise.

In the years immediately prior to the Second Vatican Council, Semmelroth's analysis of the rhythm and harmony of the proclamation of the Word and the celebration of the Eucharist entered new territory for a church about to embrace a tremendous reform of her ritual life and self-identity. The liturgy's theological focus does not rest here on an isolated presence of Christ located in a host upon the altar but on the paschal fulfillment of an encounter with the God who desires to be in communion with us. Christ as the incarnate *and* saving Word gives multidimensionality to God's saving intention to share that presence in our sacramental life in a way that is best described as a beloved's embrace, a dialogue of love, and a participation in each other's desire. Such a "living union"[26] cannot be encapsulated completely in the physical presence of consecrated bread and wine that exists merely to be gazed upon and adored, as fruitful as those pious practices may be. Instead, the totality of the eucharistic action finds its well of desire streaming first from the community's faithful hearing of a Word that draws together the biblical story of mutual longing between God and creation. This dialogical and participative relationship has been acted out through history and its memorial narrative brings the proclamation to this liturgical moment where the community's self-gift and Christ's abiding presence meet in a "living union." In response to that same originating grace proclaimed, heard, and broken open, the gifts of food and drink then become a visible proclamation (*verbum visibile*)[27] of the abiding, sacramental presence of Christ. Eating and drinking the Body and Blood of Christ in grateful memory gives witness to the fidelity of God's promise through the ages and God's desire that this life abide now in us, and through us, for the whole world. The grace-filled unity

---

[26] Semmelroth speaks of this living union in the church's sacramental life as an arena of encounter between humankind and God, "just as a [person] carries something in physical closeness within the clasp of his arms." This shows how all the sacraments express the *three dimensions* of (1) God's relationship with the world (the "vertical"), (2) our relationship with each other (the "horizontal"), and (3) all this in relationship with the individual human heart and the human family who come to the church to seek this offer of life (the "depth"). See *Church and Sacrament*, 85, 19–28.

[27] Augustine, *Jo. ev. tr.*, 80.3.

of the Liturgy of the Word and the Liturgy of the Eucharist, therefore, draws all things together in Christ, through the power of the Spirit's unifying grace, who consecrates the church and these gifts in our gathering. Semmelroth concludes that the mutuality of preaching and table sharing must be seen as a "total effect" and not separate actions:

> For this grace proceeds from what has happened in Christ, that is, from his incarnation considered as a word, and from his sacrifice considered as an answer, the two partners in the dialogue being God and [humankind]. But both are portrayed in the single yet dual process of preaching the word and the cult celebration of the sacrament.[28]

We can see from these reflections why the Constitution on the Sacred Liturgy[29] seeks to broaden the notion of eucharistic efficacy, emphasizing that these are not separate presences but dynamic modes of encounter that together express one divine gift revealed to us in the sacramental presence of Christ's paschal mystery. In addition, the document emphasizes in its section on the revision of the Ordo that pastoral efficacy and "the devout, active participation of the faithful" demand that there be clarity "in a way that will bring out more clearly the intrinsic nature and purpose of its several parts, as also the connection between them" (50). All this is to restore the "vigor" of the tradition that has been passed down and the importance of contemporary catechesis to show that "the liturgy of the word and the liturgy of the eucharist . . . are so closely connected with each other that they form but one single act of worship" (56). John Paul II's 1998 apostolic letter *Dies Domini:* On Keeping the Lord's Day Holy quoted from this paragraph and strongly restated this fundamental relationship, emphasizing even more clearly the dynamism between Word and table:

> As in every eucharistic celebration, the Risen Lord is encountered in the Sunday assembly at the twofold table of the word and the bread

---

[28] Semmelroth, *Preaching Word*, 237.

[29] In this seminal paragraph on the four modes of presence (SC 7), the emphasis remains on the wholeness of these expressions as revelatory of the paschal mystery the church celebrates. Christ is present, as the Constitution says, "not only in this, but also in this, etc." This unfolding relationship of presence is the way the document introduces the recovery of the sacramental life as an expression of the *totus Christus*, the total Christ in all its fullness.

of life. The table of the word offers the same understanding of the history of salvation and especially of the paschal mystery which the risen Christ gave to his disciples: It is Christ who speaks, present as he is in his word "when the sacred scriptures are read in the church."[30]

What remains for us now is to see how the preaching and proclamation event itself, involving preacher and celebrating assembly, effectively signifies the reality of God's relational, dialogical, and participative engagement with us. A spirituality that gives shape and energy to that eventful proclamation can then be outlined as a contribution to this exploration of the presence of Christ in the proclamation of the Word. It is not enough to name the theology; it must be rooted in our *lex orandi*. Our practice must harmonize with its claims, and our spirituality must provide the passion that keeps theology and worship in this expressive whole.

LITURGICAL PROCLAMATION AS AN EMBODIMENT OF "GOD'S OWN SERMON" TO US

> In the liturgy the proclamation of the Gospel is preceded by "Alleluia,"
> . . . the joyful greeting of those who see the coming Lord, who know
> His presence, and who express their joy at this glorious "parousia."
> "Here He is!" might be an almost adequate translation of this untranslatable word.
>
> —Alexander Schmemann, twentieth century[31]

The Resonance of the Lectionary as a Ritual Vessel

The procession of the lectionary or book of the gospels into the assembly and its resting on the ambo or altar convey to us from the outset that the Scriptures we read and the homily of the preacher share a privileged place in a gracious, Spirit-filled act of communication of the Word in the world. The ritual book and the cycle of readings they set out reveal who we are and why we are gathered. If this were not so, such ritual gestures would be barren of meaning and we could simply carry the Bible around like a service aid whose purpose serves to give the speaker material about which to speak. The ritual solemnity of festal carrying, tasteful decoration, and reverent enthronement

---

[30] John Paul II, *Dies Domini*: On Keeping the Lord's Day Holy" (1998), 39.

[31] Schmemann, *For the Life of the World* (Crestwood, NY: St. Vladimir's Seminary Press, 1988), 33.

accompany the reading of the Scriptures to highlight the divine encounter taking place, a *kerygmatic* event that carries with it transformation and grace. Its efficacy as a sacramental act relies on these same sacred texts having been heard and reflected upon, affirmed and preached about, for generations before us. The contemporary struggle to hear the Word and to shape our lives around its challenge flows out of the Spirit's inscripting of our lives into its offer of grace. The social energy of our forebears' faith gathers us in and brings us to this sacramental moment.[32] We must remember that we are encountering a Word that breathes in and out, requires bodily engagement and sensible attentiveness, and stirs up vulnerability and desire precisely because, as the revelatory word of God, it uncovers the deepest truth about our baptismal identity as a communal Body redeemed by Christ. Semmelroth called the concrete proclamatory event and the liturgical context in which it takes place as the grace-filled moment of "God's own sermon, the incarnation of his Son as the word of God to [humankind]."[33]

We begin to see a sacramental communion taking place in the simple, rich action of reading from the book. Our fidelity to communal proclamation testifies to the presence of Christ as the enfleshed Word of God's redemption and mercy. Our gathering and standing together to hear its promise gives texture and shape to all that we will hear. The ritual context locates that revelation as living and active in this time and place. Affirmations such as "Alleluia" and "Thanks be to God" orient its hearers into a future guided by the Spirit, who vivifies that life-giving Word in the world in which it has been sown and "which will not return to God empty" (Isa 55:11). The lectionary book and the cycle that sets the rhythm bear this resonance. That is why we call such holy things "sacramentals."

Reverent Proclamation and Intentional Listening as Sacramental Actions

The Letter to the Hebrews provides a great example of this liturgical and sacramental understanding of God's word as *kerygmatic*, alive, and refreshed as it circulates among the lives and hopes and dreams of those who hear it age after age. As the author begins,

---

[32] On the "circulation of social energy" that moves through a community's hearing of social texts, see *Holy Preaching*, chap. 3.

[33] Semmelroth, *Preaching Word*, 222.

> Long ago God spoke to our ancestors in many and various ways by the prophets, but in these last days he has spoken to us by a Son, whom he appointed heir of all things, through whom he also created the worlds. He is the reflection of God's glory and the exact imprint of God's very being, and he sustains all things by his powerful word. (Heb 1:1-3a)

A cursory look at this passage would seem to suggest that the inspired revelation is now completed with the advent of Christ, and believers now are charged with safeguarding its unchangeable truth for the rest of time. For many periods of the church's history, we have approached our engagement with the Scripture testimony as merely the recounting of a past act and not an ongoing dialogue between Lover and Beloved. In fact, the lifeless enactment that often surrounds our proclamation of the Word and the preacher's insatiable urge to talk *about* the Word as if it were a lesson in biblical catechesis continue to lend credence to this static notion of sacred texts read in the gathered assembly of believing Christians. However, if we give serious assent to Semmelroth's understanding of a redemptive dialogue whose actual event of proclamation participates in a revelatory moment of communication between God and humankind, then we must pay greater ritual attention to the fact that something richer, deeper, and multivalent is going on when the Liturgy of the Word is celebrated in our worshiping assemblies. The liturgical context as the bearer of the presence of Christ among us transforms the act of reading and preaching into the announcement of God's activity in our midst, a revelatory moment of new grace for this time and place. The proclamatory event is the ritual vessel that holds the reality it signifies. This matrix of symbolic relationships includes the reverent way that ministers read from the lectionary, preachers preach from it, and the assembly listens to its riches, all a part of the essential components of that sacramental efficacy.

All of this suggests that a sacramental theology that is relational, dialogical, and participative urges the whole assembly to honor the vessels of proclamation God provides for us. The mutuality and integrity of Word and Sacrament as expressive of the totality of Christ's redemptive event challenges us to reimagine how Christ's sustaining presence as powerful Word might be more clearly expressed and faithfully celebrated in this central event of our Christian identity. This involves getting practical and honest about our liturgical practice and asks a challenging question: *Does our celebration of the Liturgy of the Word provide an instrument for the desire of God's heart to be in graceful dialogue with those who "long to see God's face" and hunger for a word to refresh them?* We will begin by looking at some general principles of liturgical practice that help to express this encounter with God's abiding, irrevocable offer of mercy in Christ, of which the proclamation and preaching of the Word is both sign and reality. Then we will look briefly at the actual event of hearing the Word and the role the assembly plays in "bodying forth" Christ in the proclamation and preaching of the Word.

Communal Reading and the Resonance of Sacred Texts

We have asserted that a Vatican II sacramentality holds that Christ comes in Word and Sacrament in order that God's offer of mercy might enter into the story of our salvation here and now as a communication event. From this perspective, the book we use in the ritual to proclaim these sacred texts is not simply paper and ink and fancy binding. Furthermore, the cycle of readings in the lectionary book, as a sacramental vessel, carries with it a grace-filled presence that conveys the life-giving summons that is encoded within them. Finally, the readers and those who listen likewise share a role as a liturgical vessel in this matrix. Everyone and everything matters here. How do these active agents cooperate in this process of naming grace in our midst?[34] A contemporary literary theorist, Stephen Greenblatt, explored the nature of focal texts as having the capacity to evoke "resonance and wonder." Sacramental theology concerning the revealed word of God can profit from the dynamic he explains concerning the enduring life of literary artifacts and their relationship to the community that reads and reveres them:

> By *resonance* I mean the power of the object displayed to reach out beyond its formal boundaries to a larger world, to evoke in the viewer the complex, dynamic cultural forces from which it has emerged and for which as metaphor or more simply as metonymy it may be taken to stand. By *wonder* I mean the power of the object displayed to stop the viewer in his tracks, to convey an arresting sense of uniqueness, to evoke an exalted attention.[35]

[34] For an excellent discussion of "naming grace," see Mary Catherine Hilkert, *Naming Grace: Preaching and the Sacramental Imagination* (New York: Continuum, 1997), esp. 44–57. I would include all the agents of this ritual proclamation as taking part in this "naming grace" in our midst, although the preacher plays a focal role in this when the community celebrates the liturgy.

[35] Stephen Greenblatt, *Learning to Curse: Essays in Early Modern Culture* (New York: Routledge, 1990), 170; emphases mine.

This example from secular literary theory provides important insights when we consider the Scriptures as inspired and identity-confirming. The material elements, even the words of the lectionary themselves, are not magical, but they *are* bearers of an original, embedded life, as Greenblatt describes this dynamism.[36]

The privileged ritual context and actors then move this "life" into dialogue with the hearers' own beliefs, hopes, and desires. The book of the Scriptures used within the sacramental rite, therefore, carries within it a specific, evocative meaning compared to a Bible sitting on a shelf in a library. Consequently, how this vessel is held and displayed, read from and revered, participates in the quality of the proclamation taking place. The lectionary, as resonant and bearing grace-filled "Good News," functions as a dynamic compilation of a historical faith experience in relationship to its readers and hearers. The ritual book gathers together in intentional sequence the scriptural passages for the assembly's year-long journey into the source and grace of their identity as believers. These passages together share integrity as a *kerygmatic* word, an expression of the church's ongoing communication event with God. What the community reads here from this book, in communion with the liturgical context and season, carries within it a powerful proclamation that God has entered into the world to redeem her in Christ. "Alleluia," we say. "Here he is," revealing divine presence through creation, through the lives of fidelity and betrayal recorded in these books, and through the psalms, prayers, and letters that characterize the community's faith life and worship. Furthermore, in and with Christ, the agents of this story invite us to share with them their complex, fierce relationship with a God who enters into relationship with them. The abiding presence of Christ in this proclamation calls forth our own response to all this, whether we accept the summons or not. Reading and listening to the Word, therefore, encompasses both "sign" and "reality" of God's self-communication with us, through the gracious gift of Christ's own willingness to be the Word we hear and affirm as a "lamp to [our] feet and a light to [our] path" (Ps 119:105). Most of all, because Christ's relationship with the church

---

[36] Stephen Greenblatt, *Shakespearean Negotiations* (Berkeley: University of California Press, 1988), 2; see also *Learning to Curse*, 164. A further discussion of this in relationship to the liturgy can be found in *Holy Preaching*, part II, esp. 71–77.

becomes immanent and dynamic through the outpouring of the risen life in the Spirit in every age, these age-old texts are always specific and personal, inviting a fresh response each time they are uttered in the midst of the worshiping assembly. Book and reader, people and preacher: all converge around this resonant sacred text, whose event-fullness evokes "an exalted attention," a wonder, and a challenge to transformation.

In light of this complex interplay of relationships, the rites surrounding the procession of the Word by the ministers through the assembly and the way the lectionary is adorned, placed, and taken up by its readers as a ritual vessel should reflect the profundity of this immanent encounter in the sacramental moment. How easy it is to simply forget the sacredness of the materiality involved here. Sadly, our little acts of ritual neglect and vagueness mute and hide much of the resonance of this proclamatory moment in our Sunday assemblies. All too often, the holy text competes for prominence with songbooks and announcements carried by the lector as the book enters the sacred space; auxiliary translations typed on paper are pulled out and the lectionary itself is relegated to being a flat surface upon which to place these secondary elements. The lectors often mitigate the dignity of their public role as liturgical vessels by inattention to physical details of presence. One might argue that the content of the scriptural passages and the quality of proclamation take precedence here to these mundane concerns. Over time, however, inattentiveness by ministers and the assembly becomes embedded in the ritual pattern, and lack of care for the details of the rite hinders the fullness of the expressive acts they serve. On the other hand, simple attentiveness evokes wonder: holding the book with respect, bowing gracefully before the ambo, or kissing the text with reverence and deliberate tenderness all help to communicate the solemnity and centrality of the divine encounter taking place when these Scriptures are proclaimed in the liturgical assembly. Mindful gestures communicate an entrance into something sacred, a presence "spoken in these last days now by the Son's own life, death, and resurrection," to echo the Letter to the Hebrews' account of the sustaining Word.

Reading and hearing liturgically conveys a shared life and witness, because the church now embodies that grace and gift of Jesus, "the Book of Life in Whom we read God." Generations before us testify to an experience of God, of Christ as Word of the Father's love, and of the Spirit as inscriptor of its truth, all of which shape these stories and hold them close in the identity of a people's heart "age after age." The relational covenant of faithful love is being proclaimed and heard in a church community gathered throughout the world in every time and season. Through faithful practice, the creative discipline of ritual behavior surrounding the Liturgy of the Word begins to create profound connections between text and hearers, between *kerygmatic* proclamation and the succeeding *verbum visibile*, that takes place at the altar and the font. Intentionality slowly transforms the quality of engagement of the entire Body of Christ, whose witness to this Word "constitutes the Church," to use Schmemann's image. Beautiful things used expressively, even if their materiality is worn from handling or from its patterned actions enacted week after week for decades, carry with them the respect accorded them. It is our ritual way. They truly become vessels for the church that bear the presence the sacramental event bodies forth in their hearing.

We must not lose heart at the hard work this entails, nor can we shirk our responsibility to cooperate with the grace being offered in the everyday care of the ministry of the Word. A trip to one's ancestral home or to the house of a religious community or pilgrim shrine that has served the gospel with integrity and fidelity radiates the resonance and wonder embedded in focal places and actions of communal identity. We honor the stewardship of the mysteries and treasure the life that this land and bricks and mortar express. Why, then, can we not consider the same possibility of sacramental resonance in the liturgical vessels and rites we use to proclaim God's unconditional offer of life and love for all time and all places? Consideration for all the details of worship does not argue for exaggerated, overly theatrical artifacts and gestures that are hollow and lifeless, intended only to dazzle and impress; God's love and our humble service of the gift we have in Christ must be transparent and unambiguous. Proclamation, because it is a dialogue between God and humankind, must be culturally specific and suitable for contemporary liturgical practice in the assembly in which it takes place. Yet, the current malaise in our assemblies and the longing for greater mystery and reverence can be traced, in part, to simple things that have eroded over time. "Keeping memory" always struggles for authenticity amid an environment of liturgical forgetfulness and inattention. A sacramental life that is relational, dialogical, and participative finds a recovery of liturgical resonance not only fitting but also necessary, if the celebrants are to be faithful to the sacramental economy that resides in their regular gatherings to offer the church's act of praise and thanks.

The voice of Christ "who speaks when the holy scriptures are read in the Church" (SC 7) sounds in the timbre and presence of ministers who stand for the community in the ambo and read the passages of the day. This sacramental principle demonstrates the seriousness of human participation in the divine-human communication event. Such recognition on the part of lectors and presiders should evoke humility and awe, as well as temper any notions of self-aggrandizement or power. "Good News" from the One for whom we wait and long certainly involves more than the mere recitation of words on a page. At the same time, the reader does not insert his/her own self as focus or chief arbiter of the message proclaimed. How often have we been dispirited or disengaged by Sunday readings that are proclaimed in a vacuum, as if they had no connection to the graciousness of this present gathering and the divine self-disclosure taking place? Sacramental proclamation requires art and prayerfulness, a willingness to hold the sacred and the material in creative tension and harmony. Lectors and preachers as liturgical vessels embrace a delicate balance between engaged bodiliness and surrender of self, so that the Word of God can be proclaimed with sacramental power in the midst of the gathered assembly.

Liturgical professionals may argue over the rhetorical qualities that characterize public reading at worship. However, most communities immediately intuit when the harmony and rhythm of the reading sings in tune with the entire liturgical event. The elements of effective sacramental proclamation are complex and interwoven, but when that balance takes place, something palpable happens in the gathering. A sense of communal centeredness and an easy, shared silence inhabits the worship space, resonating with the divine rhythm of the Spirit that hovers over the assembly. As partners themselves in this sacramental act, liturgical assemblies aid that sense of powerful communication by means of their own willing expectation of a Word of grace. Communities truly gathered around the Word are ready to hear something, an attitude that springs from a shared longing stirred up by artful and graceful reading, received over time and in every season. "Inclining their hearts to understanding," as Proverbs says (2:2), prepares the assembly in spirit, mind, and body to hear the message that will call them to deeper wholeness and greater surrender to the Desire that taps the desire within them. Breathing in and breathing out, as we have acknowledged, occurs between lectors, presiders, and the gathered People of God at worship. If we are sensitive to these sacramental dynamics at work within the liturgy and see them as Christ's voice speaking them anew in the power of the Spirit who gathers the Body in praise and thanks, that rhythm deepens and coalesces within all parts of the liturgy and forms that "one whole word of God" of which Rahner spoke.

The lectors and presider, therefore, speak the voice of Christ in a way that is rooted first in the assembly's identity as the Body of Christ and also in their ministerial vocation to serve that Body in his name. The sacramental presence of Christ becomes immanent in the Word that is heard through their voices in this mutual encounter of believers at prayer together with him (Matt 18:20). The liturgical assembly, through faith and hope and love nurtured through practice, becomes that fertile, receptive field where the spoken Word finds rich soil (Matt 13:23). The harmony that results from what is spoken and heard, what is preached and received, and how the community then approaches the table in a continuing revelation of praise and thanks truly encompasses what we can honestly call *holy communion*, the "well-spring" of our sacramental union with Christ, God's uttered Word of grace.[37]

The role of *preaching* in this incarnational act will be discussed more fully in the chapter on the presider that follows, but certainly we can assert at this point that transformative homilies flow out of the encounter between the revealed Word, liturgically proclaimed, and the concrete people and situations in which they are embedded. Preachers who ignore the relationality of the event obstruct the desire that emanates from the heart of God, who is the source of their utterance and the energy of grace that circulates through the gathering. Even more, the voice of Christ in the preacher can be muted if that sacramental vessel assumes a superior or exclusive relationship to the hearers, lacks interior wrestling with the meaning of this revelation for the community who hears it, or focuses on the preacher's eloquent dynamism rather than the Spirit's enfleshing of Christ as *"Wort und Antwort"* ("Word and Answer") to God's offer of love, mercy, and forgiveness to the world. "The pulpit is a hungry place," Thomas Long

---

[37] Kenan Osborne, OFM, in his book *Sacramental Theology* (Mahwah, NJ: Paulist Press, 1981), uses the specific term "well-spring" to describe Karl Rahner's notion of the intrinsic connection between Christ as sacrament of God and the church as the sacrament of that relationship to the world (91).

has said so succinctly,[38] and this hunger relates that pulpit to the whole assembly and not just the preacher as an isolated individual. Good homilists resonate with the vertical, horizontal, or depth dimensions of that hunger and thirst (Ps 42:1-2). Research into communities of faith has continually shown that meaningful and challenging preaching stands at the forefront of worshipers' highest hopes and expectations for their congregations.[39] The People of God have tasted the possibility of nourishment and so their hopes and desires are deep, because they are rooted in the relational life of the community of God from which they spring.

The *ambo*, the liturgical and sacramental *locus* of proclamation, bodies forth a vulnerable place as well, since love and transformation are the dynamics at work when one wrestles with the Word "fulfilled in our hearing." Dominican William Hill elaborates this so eloquently in his essay on "Preaching as a 'Moment' in Theology," where he insists on the role of conversion in the preaching act:

> In preaching, knowledge comes to language—but the knowledge in question is at bottom a knowledge born out of the love of God. It is not academic and abstract . . . but concrete, historical, and existential. It comes always as grace, which moves the heart first, occasioning a shift of religious horizons, and creating a world of personal decision and existential commitment. . . . Aquinas views what we are calling here "conversion" as involving a certain docility of intelligence to the illuminative power of the Paraclete, a docility rooted in a prior affective union with God by way of charity.[40]

There is a cost to such a heartfelt surrender in the Spirit of Christ, who emptied himself in gracious response to his Father's own *kenotic* love.

---

[38] Thomas Long, *The Witness of Preaching* (Louisville, KY: Westminster John Knox Press, 1989), 177.

[39] For example, cf. Dean R. Hoge, Jackson W. Carroll, and Francis K. Sheets, *Patterns of Parish Leadership: Cost and Effectiveness in Four Denominations* (Kansas City: Sheed and Ward, 1988). Significantly, preaching is the "highest hope and expectation" of all four denominations and, regrettably, also the source of the greatest disappointments in their worship experience. The second priority shared by these four denominations concerned the desire for a spirituality upon which they can anchor their lives. Both of these dynamics concur with the tenets of this book.

[40] Hill, *Search for the Absent God*, 182.

The preacher will find life and good company there in that vulnerable sign of encounter where life must be truthfully engaged; moreover, he or she must get to know that dwelling place of docility and communion as a personal call to conversion through faith and love. Hill refers to the Irish poet W. B. Yeats's words to describe the creative fragility of preaching the faith experience in our day:

> I must lie down where all the ladders start
> In the foul rag-and-bone shop of the heart.[41]

This invitation to grace-filled *kenosis* is not the preacher's vocation alone, because everything we say here about the preacher, in the end, echoes the whole assembly's call in the work of liturgy. We can truly say that the relationship of *lex orandi, lex credendi* expands into *lex orandi, lex credendi, lex predicandi, lex vivendi*. The vulnerability of entering into a redemptive dialogue with Christ, who is both "Word and Answer" for us as baptized Christians, brings the questions of life and love face-to-face with the Scriptures we proclaim and summons the whole community to a conversion. The stories of our ancestors and their own testimony of the fidelity of God's covenant love now fulfilled in Christ assure us that such vulnerability is worth the risk.

One final point here regarding lectors and preachers as vessels of Christ in this Word-event concerns the role of bodily presence in sacramental expression. "Our bodily presence in the world is as vulnerable as a heartbeat," as Donoghue noted at the outset of the chapter. Presence in the ambo in the role of one who proclaims God's word asks for an attentiveness and respect for the many layers of communication taking place through the body, voice, and sensibility of the one who speaks. Once again, the emphasis is not theatrical or self-focused. However, one stands and speaks and engages the assembly as if the text really embodies the Good News coming from the mouth of God as refreshment, challenge, and guidance for the people. The subtlety of this nuance clarifies itself over time, with practice in real liturgical events, but the characteristics can be described as the difference between reading an important communication from a revered and loved person whose message is life itself as opposed to a passage that simply imparts information.

[41] W. B. Yeats, "The Circus Animals' Desertion," in *The Collected Poems of W. B. Yeats* (New York: Macmillan, 1977), 336. See Hill, *Search for the Absent God*, 182.

Body language, eye contact with the hearers, and a gifted sense of allowing the life of the text to take precedence over the life concerns of the speaker create what Donoghue called a "vulnerability in common" in the gathered Body, arising from "dialogue, conversation, communication, and communion."[42] This assent to the communal act of breathing in and breathing out, which he describes as the most appropriate "understanding of presence" in the reading act, needs vessels of sacramental presence who understand the role they play in this divine dialogue of redemption and the enfleshed Word of grace, Jesus Christ, whose sacramental presence abides in this liturgical action of the church. Anything that gets in the way of that rhythmic flow and harmony must be abandoned whenever possible, and those responsible for preparing and evaluating the liturgy have to respond and evaluate what may seem at first glance to be "minor" issues, such as clothing, clarity and pace of expression, and personal habits while speaking. Bodily presence is the vehicle here, and lack of care can distract the assembly from the ritual space of hearing Good News together. It also can invite the hearers into the revelatory exchange and allow the *kerygma* to interact freely with the listeners' corporate and individual life experience. Obviously, the inevitable wandering of minds in free association during the proclamation can be a movement of the Spirit, allowing unexpected access to God's call to conversion and new life. However, dissonance occasioned by the minister's personal intrusion "peeks around the rite," breaks the dialogical flow, and lifts the assembly out of that grace-filled communication in which the lector's voice and bodily presence are pivotal. Real, human stories are essential to a preacher's work. However, if a personal story or observation leads the assembly out of engagement with the text into focusing on the preacher's quirks and foibles—physical or psychological—the engagement is hampered. As a footnote, the practical necessities of adequate amplification, lighting, and visibility cooperate with one's presence as a sacramental vessel. If the worshipers cannot see and hear, then their essential roles as hearers and responders in this communication event atrophy. We cannot emphasize this point strongly enough, yet it is the issue most easily forgotten: everything we use and everyone present matters in the sacramental celebration as an ordered, ritual action of the church. The resonance and wonder of the Word relies upon the shared life that circulates in this expressive moment and renders the

---

[42] Donoghue, *Ferocious Alphabets*, 98.

proclamatory event dynamic and redemptive. Christ, "the Book of Life in Whom we read God," unfolds that mystery through us, "when the holy scriptures are read in the Church."

CHRIST'S REAL PRESENCE IN THE WORD: SOURCE FOR A RENEWED SPIRITUALITY

> In a way that surpasses understanding, our duty in this time of famine is not to end the hunger and thirst for God's word, but to intensify it, until the whole world bangs its forks for God's food.
>
> —Barbara Brown Taylor, twenty-first century[43]

The living and breathing Word, the Christ who speaks as God's own sermon to us, the resonance and wonder of sacred texts revered and circulating social energy in the liturgical assembly: what does this particular matrix of symbolic relationships mean for a spirituality that holds together theology and practice? The tradition speaks often of a hunger for the Word as if the nourishment we receive from hearing the Scriptures together really does engage a matter of life and death for a people. But our concrete experience suggests that the Liturgy of the Word often does not provide such life-giving fare; often, in fact, it seems removed from the deepest passions of our lives. How do we bridge the gap between what God is offering us and our seeming inability to taste its fruits? This is the concluding focus of this chapter. The points outlined so far have been complex because the relational events taking place in the proclamatory event are themselves interactive on a variety of levels, not all of which are immediately conscious and accessible to every person at every moment of worship. The challenge here is to understand the richness of the theology at work, assess our liturgical practice according to the way it harmonizes with those claims, and suggest a way of imagining and celebrating the Word-event that brings forth the powerful mystery of Christ's presence in the liturgical proclamation of the Scriptures into our midst. Let us consider *hunger* and *eating* as appropriate images for the proclamation event, and we will see how the Word-table connection provides a crucial step toward bridging that gap between theology and practice.

---

[43] Barbara Brown Taylor, *When God Is Silent* (Boston: Cowley Publications, 1998), 120.

The Liturgical Word: Where Our Story Is Really a Nourishing Table and Our Communion a Sacred Text

The Scriptures, uttered out of faith in the presence of a community of faith, recall the manna experience in the desert that Jesus uses as a figure for "eating" him in the Bread of Life discourse in John 6:

> So [the crowd] said to him, "What sign are you going to give us then, so that we may see it and believe you? What work are you performing? Our ancestors ate the manna in the wilderness; as it is written, 'He gave them bread from heaven to eat.'" Then Jesus said to them, "Very truly, I tell you, it was not Moses who gave you the bread from heaven, but it is my Father who gives you the true bread from heaven. For the bread of God is that which comes down from heaven and gives life to the world." They said to him, "Sir, give us this bread always." (John 6:30-34)

The manna, of course, functions in the Hebrew Scriptures as "the figure of the word of God" that comes down and feeds the human heart in faith, because "one does not live by bread alone, but by every word that comes from the mouth of the LORD" (Deut 8:3). Jesus associates his own "identity and mission" with both manna and Word, as Louis-Marie Chauvet has noted.[44] But the scandal is compounded, Chauvet says, by the seeming blasphemy that God, whose very identity is at stake, could allow the chosen One to suffer and die as a redemptive act. The discourse does not focus simply on a *real presence* in the Eucharist species per se, but on how those who eat this bread become consecrated "in the Spirit" into the same *kenotic* life and mission that began in God's first utterance of love, which takes concrete flesh and blood in the person of Jesus. Chauvet gets right to the scandalous point of this Johannine passage for those who hear it today:

> We are told that faith is nothing less than the daily realization of what is lived in the symbolic experience of the eucharistic meal: we must eat, masticate to the point of accepting, in heart and body, the bitter scandal of a God crucified for the life of the world. For John, the eucharistic act of eating is the great symbolic experience in which we are given, to feel and live, this scandal of the faith until it enters our bodies, that is to say, our life.[45]

---

[44] Chauvet, *The Sacraments: The Word of God at the Mercy of the Body* (Collegeville, MN: Liturgical Press, 2001), 49–50.

[45] Ibid., 50.

The spirituality of bread in the wilderness (i.e., the Word of God) keeps showing up in the feeding of the hungry crowds in the gospels and always points to the unity between the Word of God promised in the covenant and Jesus' own life that he shares with us. Through their communion in this bread/Word, disciples learn that they are always able to feed others and to trust in the amazing abundance that emerges from the little they have (e.g., Mark 6:34-44; 8:1-21; John 6:1-14). John takes pains to emphasize how misguided the response of those who then wish to "take [Jesus] by force to make him king" (6:15), as logical as it seems to the apparently satiated crowd. "Do not work for food that perishes," he says, "but for the food which endures for eternal life, which the Son of Man will give you" (6:27). Jesus insists that the bread he gives is not about personal satiety, power, or control. Eating the bread as a sign of the reign of God opens up a ravenous appetite for God and a surrender to Jesus' life of obedient service in the Spirit of his Father's own loving. Jesus becomes bread *to be broken and shared*, the grain of wheat that falls to the ground as seed for our own prophetic fruitfulness (John 12:24). Jesus goes on to make the connection that the liturgy itself celebrates between this bread, the Word in our midst, and the table fellowship of Christians:

> Those who love their life lose it. And those who hate their life in this world will keep it for eternal life. Whoever serves me must follow me, and where I am, there will my servant be also. Whoever serves me, the Father will honor. (12:25-26)

And it is always enough. The Word leads to the table because self-offering in communion is Jesus' answer to the Father's Word of Love, as Semmelroth said. Communities that keep the "distinct-but-not-separate" connection between eating the Word and eating the Bread of Life deepen their participation in the passion that begins in the heart of God and flows through every aspect of life and worship. We chew upon the Word in a real sense, in that we wrestle with its tension and challenge for our forebears and for ourselves. We continue to digest its call to discipleship when the general intercessions give voice to the hungers of the world that still cry out for bread in the wilderness. Finally, we accept its offer of life at the table where our communion in Christ and one another provides the most fitting answer to the God who speaks. "Yes," we say. "Alleluia . . . we recognize him here." And finally, "Amen, so be it."

Presiders and *ministers* play a major role in enhancing this ritual harmony. They speak a word of grace primarily through their interior awareness that the Word they proclaim and around which they gather the faithful stands first and foremost as nourishing food that consecrates those who hear it into a sacramental life, embedded in their bones and enduring as the sacred texts out of which it is spoken. Without their own eating, their ministerial lives are hollow and ineffective signs of the reality they proclaim to the assembly that gathers. In turn, *the assembly*, like those at the festival in John 12 who "wish to see Jesus" (12:21), will only encounter him in the word/bread if they join Jesus in "the hour of glorification" (our common worship), when Word speaks truth about our lives as grains of wheat, consecrates our desires to be fruitful like his own, and shares that communion in him for the life of the world (12:23-25).

God's fidelity assures Christ's presence in the sacrament (*ex opere operato*), when the church acts intentionally in this regard (*ex opere operantis*). But the grace of the sacrament, redemptive and intimate unity in and with Christ (*res tantum*), reaches its expressive truth in *holy communion*, a relational event that necessarily moves from hearing the summons as a personal address, through the physical act of eating and drinking in grateful thanksgiving, to the soul-full conversion of life and mission. That is why the words of the institutional narrative in the eucharistic prayer—"Take and eat . . . Take and drink . . . "—announce within the context of table-sharing with bread and wine the presence of Jesus on all those levels around which the story is a nourishing table and our communion a sacred text. The entire liturgy must be intentional and multivalent enough in image, gesture, and space to allow that matrix of symbolic relationships to inhere among the gathered faithful, both assembly and ministers. As Chauvet reminds us, rituality involves "action language" whose symbolic force lies in its "establishing communication between the participants and God and as a consequence, among themselves."[46] Liturgical gestures and words throughout the celebration merge in this harmony of action and follow this primary *way of proceeding*: "do not say what you are doing; do what you are saying," he pleads. In this sense, attentiveness to the rhythm and harmony of the whole event moves the argument beyond liturgical taste and verbose explanation to the ritual enactment as the locus of primary theology. Hence, Chauvet goes on to argue that

[46] Ibid., 99.

the attention given to the proper use of symbols is not based on a mere concern for aesthetics, but on a theological motivation. That the liturgy is seen as the place not for discourse on God but for reception of God's action corresponds in depth to what the Bible understands by "word of God"; this is not an abstract word, such as the Greek *logos*, but a word which is *action and event*. It is by God's word that God creates the world (Gen 1). When the word comes to the prophets, it invades them to the point of working violence on them (Amos 7:15; Jer 20:7ff.; and so on); it is the messenger that God sends (Isa 9:8; Ps 107:20). The liturgy is the means by which this "performance" of the divine word is symbolically given to be seen and lived by.[47]

We would add that when this sort of integrity between eventful word and revelatory action begins to mold the assembly through its faithful practice, communities are transformed, preachers easily find "words to rouse" the church to deeper faith and committed living, and devotion to the sacred mysteries deepens. "The symbols effect the reality they signify"; the proclamation resounds on all levels as a communication event worthy of its claim of Christ's *real presence*. Chauvet's conclusion affirms the claims we have been making throughout this book:

In the liturgy, the word is made not only of words but of materials, gestures, postures, objects; the words seek not only to be there but to be "seen" and "touched"; the word aims at becoming a gesture, at being inscribed on everyone's body (baptism) or placed inside everyone's body (eucharistic communion). This intentionality is not accidental in the liturgy; actually, it is essential to it. As such, it is for the believer the expression of the dynamic nature of the word of God. In the last analysis, are the sacraments anything else than the unfolding, down to the today of each generation and each person, of this efficacious character of the word as word of God?[48]

The hunger in our assemblies for a good word and a spirituality around which to anchor our lives stands waiting for us to "do what we say" and live the reform the Vatican II documents set forth. It can be done. We start by imagining that every person and sacred thing matters to the integrity of this gracious proclamation. Then we allow

---

[47] Ibid., 100–101.
[48] Ibid., 101.

the Word into the depth dimensions of life and love, fear and joy, trust and doubt. The Spirit and Advocate who pleads our cause (Rom 8:27) then intervenes to make all this holy. As Yves Congar reminds us,

> The Word of God, whether written or preached, seems also to have a sacramental condition or structure. It is meaningful and effective beyond the material nature of the written or spoken words. In the case of the written Word, Scripture is actually there, rather like the Eucharist. There is, in other words, a "real presence" of the Word. Like the Eucharist too, it calls for a "spiritual eating" involving the intervention of charity and therefore of the Holy Spirit.[49]

God is faithful to this sacramental way of proceeding, and that, in the end, is all that matters.

Tending the Tables of Word and Sacrament

Liturgical reform that grounds a refreshed spirituality of worship requires hard work and consistent ritual exercise. Worshipers who have been lulled into inattentiveness and distance by paltry signs and symbols, lackluster and incoherent proclamation, and little exercise or challenge in the discipline of the Word fall out of rhythm with the paschal procession from ambo to table, in which Christ's presence testifies and "draws all people to himself" (John 12:32). As sacramental vessels, both ministers and assembly share a responsibility for the viability of this redemptive dialogue of the Word that comes down from heaven and will not return to the heart of God empty, as Isaiah sings so clearly (55:11). Its promise abides in the faithful context of hunger and eating in the face of the many levels of famine and abundance that impel us in our search "to see Jesus." A renewed spirituality of Christ's presence in the Word sees effective liturgical practice as the locale where the Word becomes food and people become what they receive, a living sacrifice of praise. Such profligate claims can only come from the mouth of God, whose heart overflows with a Word to revive the people in the wilderness journey into communion with the triune God and one another. The Liturgy of the Word and the Liturgy of the Eucharist cooperate together to proclaim the "one whole word of God" of which Isaiah speaks:

[49] Congar, *Word and the Spirit*, 25.

Ho, everyone who thirsts, come to the waters;
and you that have no money, come, buy and eat!
Come, buy wine and milk without money and without price.
Why do you spend your money for that which is not bread,
and your labor for that which does not satisfy?
Listen carefully to me, and eat what is good,
and delight yourselves in rich food.
Incline your ear, and come to me;
listen, so that you may live.
I will make with you an everlasting covenant,
my steadfast, sure love for David. (Isa 55:1-3)

What concluding remarks can we add to this renewed spirituality of the liturgical Word and the real and active presence of Christ in the proclamatory act? First, if we are to share more fully in God's passion for us and in the Spirit's inscripting of the Christ-life in us, *hunger* is necessary in order to recognize the food God offers. Furthermore, "*eating* the word" requires the rhythm of liturgical time and practice in order for it to nourish the Body in its eucharistic identity; the Word is not and *cannot* be fast food. We discover in the discipline of common practice that the two-edged sword of God's word lodges in both the "yes" and the "no" of our living, as well as the confusing spaces in-between, where only silence makes sense.[50] In the tension between what is being offered and who we are becoming, Christ is present as Word/bread and abides in the assembly's faithfulness to holy communion in all its dimensions. Finally, the liturgy provides a privileged arena for this sacramental communication event, in which there is a profound and integral movement from Word-to-table-to-world, which in turn becomes a new Word and an abundant table and a redeemed world, as the rhythm of the cycle continues. Word and Sacrament, then, embraces the mission of the church it sacramentally expresses: to echo the poet Hopkins again, "its end, its purpose, its purport, its meaning, is God and its life or work to name and praise him."[51]

[50] For a fruitful reflection on the tension between speaking "yes" in the midst of "no" and the need for silence as a vehicle of God's communication of the Christ-gift, see Timothy Radcliffe, OP, "The Sacramentality of the Word," in *Liturgy in a Postmodern World* (London and New York: Continuum, 2003), 133–47.
[51] Hopkins, "Further Notes on the Foundation," 129.

Chapter 4

The Gatherer of the Community into Communion: The Presence of Christ in the Sacramental Presider

God has enough of all good things except one:
Of communion with humans God can never have enough.

> —Mechtild of Magdeburg, thirteenth century,
> *The Flowing Light of the Godhead*[1]

Orchestras playing a symphony have conductors and the Christian liturgy employs presiders. The conductor's relationship with the score, the musicians, and the ensemble as a unity must be mutual and interactive in order for the music to release its beauty and harmony. The conductor must reverence all and find her or his proper identity and rhythm within that complex interchange. The same is true for the presider of the liturgy, with this added intensity: the matrix of symbolic relationships within the ritual enactment flows from the trinitarian life itself and establishes an identity for the presider, whose pattern of acting and manner of presence is one that is first *given* as a charismatic gift of grace. The attitude and manner is Christ's own way and truth and life, what we called in the first chapter as a presence *to*, a participation *with*, and a service *for* the life of praise and thanks that constitutes the church as the Body of Christ. Although such leadership is not the intentional or desired focus of the church's worship, the presider, nevertheless, communicates and cooperates with the sacramental economy in a powerful and often unconscious way. We will explore that unique mode of sacramental representation in this chapter.

[1] Sue Woodruff, *Meditations with Mechtild of Magdeburg* (Santa Fe, NM: Bear & Co., 1982), 56.

So we begin by asserting that the rhythm and harmony of the revelatory presence of Christ in the liturgy gather specific energy in the person of the minister of Word and Sacrament. The presider is a sacramental sign and symbol whose role is particularly communicated in his own unique personhood,[2] for he bodies forth both the *call and invitation of Christ the Good Shepherd*, now gathering the Beloved to himself, as well as the *unity of the ecclesial Body* assembled in this time and place, in which the *totus Christus*—the fullness of the gift of abiding presence—makes its home. The presider in the liturgy, and most poignantly at the Eucharist, bears through sacramental ordination the responsibility of *gathering the baptized community into communion*. Liturgical practice yields this theological fact, and attentive reflection bids us pay attention to how the ritual presence of the leader of prayer provides significant congruence with the way of proceeding of the triune life from which it flows. Simply stated, we must ascertain how the presider's acting *in persona Christi* is rooted in the church's unity in communion (*in persona ecclesiae*) of which the ordained leader is "sign and symbol of a sacred reality." We must ask if this sacramental dynamism, expressed focally at the community's worship, is *relational, dialogical, and participative*, both in the intentionality of the presider and in the perception of the gathered Body of Christ. Finally, we need to uncover the liturgical spirituality that flows from the generative heart of God that gives ecclesial ministers a fruitful share in God's passion to be in communion with us. Such are the issues we will pursue in this chapter.

But first, the current state of liturgical leadership and priestly identity rooted in a complex history needs to be addressed. In the name of the bishop and the universal church, this mode of sacramental presence embodies ordinary individuals, called and consecrated through the church's communal discernment, to "gather the family of God as sisters and brothers endowed with the spirit of unity and lead it in Christ through the Spirit of God the Father."[3] Out of that graced call, many levels of relationship *to* and *with* and *in* Christ manifest the *totus*

---

[2] For the sake of clarity, the masculine term for the presider will be used in this chapter. However, this does not hold true for those denominations who acknowledge women as presiders. Even more, much of what is asserted here applies to anyone who gathers the Christian community in prayer, precisely as a constitutive action of the church.

[3] Vatican II, Decree on the Ministry and Life of Priests (*Presbyterium Ordinis*, Dec. 7, 1965), 6.

Christus when the presider calls the assembly to prayer. In contrast to the praying and singing faithful and the Word that is proclaimed and preached, the presider highlights in a unique and sacramental way the specificity of fragile humanness, as well as social and cultural limitations of the church and the diverse societies in which she is embedded. This integrated way of proceeding we have embraced so far suggests that "gathering into communion" can perhaps give greater clarity to this complex liturgical, theological, and spiritual expression of Christ's activity within the church's worship and the ministry that flows from it.

CHANGING PARADIGMS OF SACRAMENTAL LEADERSHIP WITHIN THE BODY OF CHRIST AND THE CONFUSION REGARDING THE IDENTITY AND FUNCTION OF THE PRIEST

The contemporary church inherited a neoscholastic understanding of sacramental orders that focused almost entirely upon sacred powers conferred upon a man on behalf of a people whose access to the holy things was, at least from an official and institutional level, remote and mediated. The confection of the Eucharist and the power to forgive sins located the essence of priestly identity. However, such generalizations always must be nuanced, because sacramental priesthood clearly established an identity that went beyond function, that is, in the Catholic sense, the holiness of priests and their ministry to the people flowed to and from that sacramental identity and did not cease when the liturgical role ended or active ministry ceased. "You are a priest forever according to the order of Melchizedek" (Ps 110:4; Heb 6:20) proclaimed the prefigure David as the anointed one and echoed in the Letter to the Hebrews in the high priesthood of Christ, whose special relationship to the ordained defined both identity and function.[4] That

---

[4] Our focus is on the liturgical role and spirituality of the presider, but contemporary sacramental theology has provided a number of interesting perspectives to counteract the resort to the "ontological change" notion of identity and function. Theologians such as Louis-Marie Chauvet; David Power, OMI; and Ghislain Lafont, OSB, each respond with different approaches regarding the relational character of identity and function as a participation in an ongoing paschal narrative (the founding *récit*) handed down within the ritual enactment (Lafont), of a past event whose presence in absence (the "trace") is revealed in a "symbolic exchange" of gifts within the sacramental memorial

definition is always iconic of God's actions to redeem a people. Acting out of this promise, Hebrews says, "we who have taken refuge might be strongly encouraged to seize the hope set before us" (Heb 5:19). The enduring identity flows out of the enduring promise of God to us.

At the same time, this iconic relationship to an individual role and function within the Body contributes to the confusion regarding priestly identity in our present day, especially when liturgical presidency becomes the primary expression of that role, often divorced from close and regular immersion into the everyday lives of the community. Issues of gender and marital status (in the West) of priests who are imaged through these characteristics as "alteri Christi" assume focal emphases when the gatherer of the Body is understood in terms of "his" individual likeness to the human Jesus and the resurrected Lord.[5]

(Chauvet), and where the Spirit acts within the Body on the level of "poesis and praxis" and leaves us with awe and wonder at the mystery rather than clear, ontological categories (Power). They all seek to address both the neoscholastic categories they view as "static" and the postmodern rejection of all claims of metanarratives or philosophical categories that no longer speak to the contemporary human situation. "Sacramental memorial" and foundational stories of faith carried by the community over time are a shared concern of all three. For Chauvet, see *Symbol and Sacrament: A Sacramental Reinterpretation of Christian Existence*, trans. Madeleine Beaumont and Patrick Madigan (Collegeville, MN: Liturgical Press, 1995), chap. 4; for Lafont, see *God, Time, and Being* (Petersham: St. Bede's Press, 1993), part I, 3–117; for Power, see *Sacrament: The Language of God's Giving* (New York: Crossroad, 1999). Joy Harrell Blaylock's article "Ghislain Lafont and Contemporary Sacramental Theology," *Theological Studies* 66 (2005): 841–61, provides a thorough discussion of these contemporary sacramental approaches to neoscholasticism and postmodernism and I am indebted to her work in clarifying points that help understand the presider's role from a triune and relational perspective, instead of the "ontological difference" categories at the heart of much of the confusion about liturgical leadership today.

[5] Edward Kilmartin, SJ; David Power, OMI; Susan Wood, SCL; and others have treated the issue of sacramental identity in great detail. For an extended discussion of the iconic argument in contrast to a more ecclesial representational model, see Thomas P. Rausch, SJ, "Priestly Identity: Priority of Representation and the Iconic Argument," *Worship* 73 (1999): 169–79; Edward Kilmartin, SJ, "The Catholic Tradition of Eucharistic Theology: Toward the Third Millennium," *Theological Studies* 55 (1994): 439–440; Susan K. Wood, SCL, *Sacramental Orders*, ed. John D. Laurance, *Lex Orandi* Series (Collegeville, MN:

What, then, does the baptized community as the Body of Christ connote, especially when the community assumes a bridal role?[6] What is the relationship between the priesthood of all believers and the ordained priesthood and its sacramental expression as president of the liturgical assembly? These issues are part of the crisis of identity for priests in the church today and the tension they engender play themselves out during the liturgical gathering in many forms. Parsing out *distinctions* between the two priestly identities does not solve the ritual tension; however, beginning with the *inseparability* of the various modes of the presence of Christ within the liturgy (i.e., they are "distinct but not separate" in the classic sacramental sense) can bring the complex problems to a deeper level of engagement. Christ's presence in Word and Sacrament finds its expression (is "bodied forth") within that rich interplay between *the assembly praying and singing* and *the presider as gatherer of the community into communion*. The liturgy by its "nature" has a solid priority: all participants in the liturgy worship and act first as the baptized, the priestly People of God. As *Sacrosanctum Concilium* describes this, "in the liturgy the whole public worship is performed by the Mystical Body of Jesus Christ, that is, by the Head and his members" (7). We would add that the iconic roles within that Body give depth and texture to the wholeness of this sacramental event. The Vatican II document then proceeds immediately from this claim to emphasize the importance of the primacy of the *totus Christus* as the primary starting point for the liturgy:

> From this it follows that every liturgical celebration, because it is an action of Christ the Priest and of his Body which is the Church, is a

---

Liturgical Press, 2000); and Wood, ed., *Ordering the Baptismal Priesthood: Theologies of Lay and Ordained Ministry* (Collegeville, MN: Liturgical Press, 2003). Significant historical and theological work highlighting the current tensions, as well as the implications for ecumenical understanding, has been done by Kenan B. Osborne, OFM, *Priesthood: A History of the Ordained Ministry in the Roman Catholic Church* (New York: Paulist Press, 1988).

[6] For a spirited and contemporary discussion of both sides of the issue of imaging Christ and the question of women and orders, see the dialogue between Robert J. Egan, SJ, and Sara Butler, MSBT, in *Commonweal Magazine*, April 11, 2008, 17–27, and continuing in the July 18, 2008, issue. The theological starting points are very different and the debate itself demonstrates how gender, especially, muddles the liturgical issues we are considering.

sacred action surpassing all others; no other action of the Church can equal its effectiveness by the same title and to the same degree. (7)

This often repeated passage, in light of the integral relationship between presider and assembly, clarifies that the presider serves that gathering function *in persona Christi capitis* because he is acting *in persona ecclesiae*.[7]

Returning to the triune dynamic that is relational, dialogical, and participative, therefore, reasserts the role of the liturgical presider *within the context of Christ's presence in the church* as the fundamental sacrament of Christ the Priest. The Son's self-offering is proclaimed in Word and Sacrament, manifested in the communion of the Spirit-filled Body with her Lord in mutual self-surrender, offering praise and thanks to the Father as Giver of all good gifts. The liturgical leader gathers this dynamic mystery. As much current sacramental theology of orders has insisted, Christ's priesthood is threefold in its rich expression—in sacramental presence, in the priest who gathers, and in the community of the baptized. These multivalent relationships are inseparable, although they are distinct in the manifestation in which they are expressed. Within this complex of relationships, the presider invites the assembly "into the pattern of these good things" (Justin the Martyr)[8] through bodily presence and gesture, through the rite to which he gives voice and invites the assembly's active and responsive

---

[7] In terms of liturgical function and the relationship to the assembly, the term *in persona Christi capitis* more adequately describes the sacramental presence of Christ in the presider than the simpler form, *in persona Christi*. Following the thought of Thomas, Vatican II (PO 2), and the writings of John Paul II, David Power says: "It seems possible to pursue this issue of priestly representation by joining more closely together what is traditionally signified by the term *in persona Christi* with what is traditionally signified by *in persona Ecclesiae*. The twist given to the phrase *in persona Christi Capitis* would then have to do with gathering the baptized, through obedience to the gospel, into the one sacramental action, which is that of Christ and his body, the Church, or of Christ living through the Spirit in his Body. The diversification between the role of the baptized and the role of the ordained would still be clear, but in relation to the one ecclesial action rather than in relation to distinct acts within one action." Power, "Representing Christ in Community and Sacrament," in *Being a Priest Today*, ed. Donald J. Goergen, OP, 114 (Collegeville, MN: Liturgical Press, 1992). This is precisely the theological point underlying this chapter.

[8] *1 Apology*, 67.3b-4.

participation, and through the transparent heart that fosters the unity Christ so desired. As the *General Instruction of the Roman Missal* asserts regarding the duty of acting "within the Church . . . to offer sacrifice in the person of Christ" as presider, preacher, leader of prayer and fellow communicant:

> A Priest . . . presides by this fact over the faithful people gathered here and now. . . . Therefore, when he celebrates the Eucharist, he must serve God and the people with dignity and humility, and by his bearing and by the way he pronounces the divine words he must convey to the faithful the living presence of Christ.[9]

Role and identity, therefore, are necessarily intertwined here. The recovery of an ecclesial sacramentality at the time of Vatican II has called into question the manner in which the presbyter acts *in persona Christi capitis* and relates to the People of God who constitute the gathered *ecclesia*, the church. Returning to the dynamic of the liturgy as the wellspring of theology, practice, and spirituality suggests a movement away from an isolated individual and toward an active presence of Christ in the presider as gatherer of the community into communion. This precedes the power to consecrate the elements, baptize new members, absolve sins, and anoint and bless the assembly—which are all expressions of this primary sacramental presence of the Gatherer, the Shepherd, and the Tender of the garden of God's abundance.

The crisis of identity for the contemporary priest, the frustration of assemblies who lack the presence of adequate sacramental leadership, as well as the changing understanding of the role and identity of a pastoral leader instead of a dominant head have all muddied the

---

[9] GIRM 93 (2010). Once again, as in the previous chapter, it is interesting to note the difference between the English translations of the 1975 and 2010 editions. They reflect the growing tension in the theological and liturgical climate. The 1975 Instruction says (59–64), at the end of this paragraph, "by his bearing and by the way he recites the words of the liturgy he should communicate to the faithful a sense of the living presence of Christ" (60). In 2010 (92–94), the "authentic" context of the celebration is now spoken in terms of a "legitimate" one, and the "presbyter" is now referred directly throughout as the "Priest." "Divine words" are "conveyed" rather than their "sense communicated" through the relational enactment of the rite. The difference in these English translations is subtle but, I believe, indicative of a shift in understanding official liturgical documents.

waters regarding liturgical presidency.[10] Reaction and reassertion of sacral authority have resulted in some circles; outright dismissal of any specific ordained charism apart from the shared priesthood of all believers surfaces in others. Meanwhile, many faith-filled and earnest worshipers caught in the middle of this outright political and theological standoff suffer from the ambiguity and bad faith that result. Yet the desire for engagement with the mystery thrives beneath the professional and theological battles. The development of theology over the centuries suggests that styles of liturgical leadership and the sacramental nature of ordination cannot remain static and unyielding in the face of the actual reality of the church as a community of faithful people who embody the fundamental sacrament expressed in our ritual life. Recent crises about the nature of ecclesial authority and sacramental representation in light of the abuse crisis have heightened this tension. Yet, the power and grace of sacramental identity remains, or it would not be taken so seriously on all sides of this tragic dilemma. The promise and the mystery endure.

We can and must be true to the tradition of Christ acting in the person of the priest presider, and the sacramental dynamism of Vatican II enhances that tradition in a way that is faithful to its earliest expressions. If we remember that Christ abides in the liturgy in modes of presence that mutually enrich one another, then the presider's role garners depth and a breadth of expression in that interchange. The rhythm and harmony the ordained leader articulates finds expression only within the whole sacramental event—distinct but never separate, personal but never self-focused. God's way of proceeding speaks to us through the primary symbols and gestures of our worship. We now look to these for a deeper understanding of the Christ who gathers and the community gathered, sacramentally expressed in the ordained minister of Word and Sacrament.

Representing Christ in Gathering the Body of Christ

Vatican II was not of a consistent mind, nor did it resolve the tension, when addressing the role of the priest/presider within the church as the fundamental sacrament of Christ's presence in the world.[11] As

[10] Wood, *Sacramental Orders*, 119.

[11] *Lumen Gentium* considers the hierarchical nature of the church only after first asserting the "The Mystery of the Church" (chap. 1) and "The People of God" (chap. 2). *Presbyterium Ordinis* speaks of the "whole Mystical Body

David Coffey has expressed quite clearly in his study of the need for a deeper understanding of the pneumatological dimensions that bind together the priesthood of the faithful and of the ordained,

> Historically . . . the problem has been that the christological reference of the ordained priest, according to which he is recognized as acting in the person of Christ and even as being "another Christ" (*alter Christus*), has had the effect of lifting the ordained priesthood out of the ecclesiological framework altogether and situating it in a christological framework. This did not have to happen because of the christological reference, but it is what happened in fact. As a result, only the common priesthood was left in the christological framework.[12]

Coffey concludes that the "parallel rather than coordinated" understandings of the priesthood of the baptized and the ordained are rooted in a deeper confusion about the intrinsic relationship between the "missions of the Son and the Holy Spirit."[13] Although the Vatican II liturgical reform found its grounding in the notion of the gathered Body as the primary celebrants of the liturgy, the documents' various ways of describing the priest/presider retreat to a sacral model that mediates power to the faithful. This lack of solid congruity with the ecclesiological basis for ordained ministry stands in ambiguous tension with a notion of leadership being called powerfully from within the Body to represent its unity in the person of Christ. That call from "within" and not called "out of" the People of God is still clear in the Vatican II Decree on the Life and Ministry of Priests (*Presbyterium Ordinis*):

> Priests of the New Testament, by their vocation and ordination, are in a certain sense set apart in the bosom of the People of God. However, they are not to be separated from the People of God or from any person; but they are to be totally dedicated to the work for which the Lord has chosen them. (3)

[as] sharer in the anointing of the Spirit" and "in that Body all the faithful are made a holy and kingly priesthood" (2). However, the "nature of the priesthood" (chap. 1) still finds its origins in jurisdictional order instead of sacramental charism. *Optatem Totius*, from another perspective, strongly asserts the priority of pastoral identity in the training of priests (4).

[12] David Coffey, "The Common and the Ordained Priesthood," *Theological Studies* 58 (1997): 224–25.

[13] Ibid., 234–35. See also Rausch, "Priestly Identity," 177.

The warrant for both the christological and ecclesiological emphases still remains Christ—priest, prophet, and king. However, a sacramental foundation for ministerial leadership whose wellspring is the church illumines more clearly the Christ who offers himself in holy surrender as the firstfruits of the sacrifice, and who invites the community to find and claim its identity, through the Spirit's inscripting, by means of their intimate communion with the Son in praise of the Father that is the liturgy of the church. The sacramental priesthood of Christ that emerges from the ecclesiological foundation of sacramentality bodies forth a triune dynamic in which role and identity are intrinsically understood *in relationship*, are expressed in a *dialogical expression of a mutual giving and receiving of gifts*, and they *invite loving engagement*, rather than static or passive roles that express the essence of each Person's divine nature.

Given the premise of this trinitarian foundation we considered in chapter 1, we can understand with greater clarity Edward Kilmartin's insistence that "Christian worship, in all its forms, should be understood as the self-communication of the Triune God."[14] It follows that if Christ's presence in the liturgy flows from this communal context where personhood is expressed in loving relationship, it seems that the presider acting as the representative "sign and symbol of the sacred reality" of Christ the Gatherer must embody that sacrificial attitude of self-donation of which St. Paul speaks:

> Let the same mind be in you that was in Christ Jesus, who, though he was in the form of God, did not equate equality with God as something to be exploited, but emptied himself, taking the form of a slave, being born in human likeness. (Phil 2:5-7)

At the same time, kenotic self-offering finds its dynamism in the mutual giving and receiving of love, which enriches the identity of those who are willing to be so vulnerable with the Beloved. As Jesus'

---

[14] Edward J. Kilmartin SJ, *Christian Liturgy: Theology and Practice: I. Systematic Theology of Liturgy* (Kansas City: Sheed and Ward, 1988), 180. An excellent guide through Kilmartin's pneumatological theology of the liturgy can be found in Jerome M. Hall, *We Have the Mind of Christ: The Holy Spirit and Liturgical Memory in the Thought of Edward J. Kilmartin* (Collegeville, MN: Liturgical Press, 2001); and, particularly regarding priesthood and presiding, cf. Edward P. Hahnenberg, "The Ministerial Priesthood and Liturgical Anamnesis in the Thought of Edward J. Kilmartin, S.J.," *Theological Studies* 66 (2005): 253–78.

priestly prayer in the Gospel of John reminds the One who sent him, thereby prayerfully revealing the same relationship to and with us, "[Father,] I made your name known to them, and I will make it known, so that the love with which you have loved me may be in them, and I in them" (John 17:26). The revelatory exchange of mutual love, which we saw previously between Christ and the church who gathers in his name, continues its embodied expression in the leader of prayer. The presider's relationship with the assembly, therefore, gives flesh and breath to the foundational grace for which Jesus prayed. This strong and intimate christological identity in the presider is distinct but inseparable from the ecclesial. Further, it has significant consequences for the nature of presiding and the complementary roles that the acting assembly, the shared gifts, and the proclaimed Word all play in communicating the presence of Christ in the wholeness of the sacramental event. Edward Kilmartin, Thomas Rausch, Susan Wood, and others have brought to light the danger of a solely christological focus at the expense of the pneumatological and ecclesiological dimensions of the Christ-church relationship in which "the role of the priest is embedded."[15]

Edward Hahnenberg sums up the dilemma for Kilmartin and others, especially in regard to the liturgy and its celebrants:

> To view the priest as directly representing Christ, and so acting *in persona Christi* in an activity to which the passive community only subsequently relates itself (if at all), reduces the eucharistic celebration to a kind of sacral performance with the faithful as audience. This is not the case: the priest pronounces the words of institution as representative of the faith of the Church in a corporate act of worship, and because of this he represents Christ the head of the Church.[16]

Contrary to fears that such an ecclesially based notion of sacramental leadership diminishes the role of the presider by suggesting his inferior dependency on the worshiping congregation, the *relational*, *dialogical*, and *participative* qualities of sacramental leadership draw the priesthood of believers and the priesthood of Christ into closer intimacy precisely through the ordained minister's focal presence. Christ's self-offering in which we are invited to share takes on a

---

[15] Hahnenberg, "Ministerial Priesthood," 255; see also n. 14 above.
[16] Ibid., 256.

personal and incarnational expression in the actions and gestures of the one who gathers them. It is to these liturgical aspects to which we now turn. Specifically, we will see how relation, dialogue, and participation bodied forth in the leader of prayer express the presence of Christ in the sacramental event with efficacious clarity. The "manifest symbol" of the unity of the Body of Christ, universally represented in the ministry of bishops, as Vatican II reminds us, finds its greatest meaning in the dynamic at work when the presider gathers into communion the gifts received and shared through Word and table, in the midst of the faithful celebrants who constitute what *Lumen Gentium* (26) calls the "altar community" constituted as the church.

Relationality as a Sacramental Expression of the Presider Who Gathers
David Power's work *Sacrament: The Language of God's Giving* argues for a radical conversion in the ways that ritual life expresses or hides the mystery of Christ's gift of self to which our common life and faith give expression.[17] Paradigms that may have served sacramental life in the past must always adapt to the development of theological, social, and cultural understandings through history or else they cease to be incarnational. To be *in relationship* to this history and experience is the nature of the things that speak of God. In his consideration of the relationality of the presider to Christ the priest and to the assembly of the priestly People of God, Power speaks of *affective conversion*. He describes this call to integration in words that cut to the heart of the ordained minister's vocation as gatherer of the community into communion:

> Religious conversion involves deep affective commitment. The affective is that which enables a person to connect with others in mutuality, to develop a sense of belonging, to pledge oneself heart and soul to persons, to values, and to a sphere of action. Our emotions and our emotive tendencies are allied with the power to do and the power to act. They relate to those with whom we wish to live, or whom we wish to follow. They come into play in the religious commitment to God and God's kingdom. They are intimately bound with the personal values which we hold important and which we endeavor to realize in our personal actions and in consort with others.[18]

---

[17] Power, *Sacrament*, 264–73.
[18] Ibid., 269.

What else does this model than Jesus' own identity as Son, his real presence to us as the head of this Body, empowered by the Spirit to body forth the love of the Father? Such affective conversion, as well, characterizes the life and mission of the church out of which some are called to teach and preach, to sanctify in prayer and sacramental life, and to serve and lead the ordered Body as an embraced communion that reaches out to the world with the Good News of God's favor. Out of a matrix of symbolic relationships that expresses both the vertical, horizontal, and depth dimensions of the Christ-church relationship (Semmelroth), the presider stands as gatherer of the diverse gifts of God. Therefore, his own relationship to the treasure he gathers must invite the same affective conversion.

All of this suggests something about the *ritual gesture* and *bodily presence* essential to sacramental enactment. In the Spirit of Jesus, everyone comes from the community first as one who serves the needs of the whole rather than acting as "tyrants over them" (Matt 20:25). Gross mistreatment in one's role as ministerial leader, we would hope, is rarely seen and quickly addressed as contrary to the gospel. However, liturgical arrogance in gesture and presence comprises a much more subtle betrayal in one who acts *in persona Christi capitis*. Such dissonance of role may fester below the surface of the self-consciousness of the presider, who may earnestly interpret a strong, dominating presence as the embodiment of the prophetic, saving power of Christ, given to the presbyter as the representative closely configured to Christ through the sacral power conferred at ordination. But a strong, integrated liturgical spirituality confronts such dissonance. Liturgical presidency *in persona Christi capitis* demands more affective honesty than can be achieved when the priestly role generates its meaning first in the individual rather than in the ecclesial identity. The wellspring of the Trinity that waters the grace of leadership, as well as the fertile ground of the believing community as recipients of that baptized identity, cannot accept such excuses without addressing them in the context of the liturgical dynamic to which the ordained leader plays such a primary and representative role in communicating the presence of Christ as actively loving us and offering himself to us as gift. David Power affirms the trinitarian dynamic of this call to affective conversion and the solidarity that is intrinsic to the relationality of all believers:

> From this point of view, Christian symbol and sacrament serve to engage persons and communities wholeheartedly in the love of God,

made known in Jesus Christ, and the power of the Spirit who dwells within as a dynamic force of self-giving.[19]

By means of personal presence and human gesture, the presider must always *engage* the assembly as primary celebrants of the mystery. Bodily presence can be reverent but also humane; it can be expansively congruent with the public nature of the gathering rather than interiorly distant and isolated, as if the role primarily focused on one's own personal piety. As Louis-Marie Chauvet has said concerning the congruence of symbol and the wholeness of the relationship it signifies, "As long as the (symbolic) element remains isolated, that is, not fitted together with the whole to which it belongs, it does not function symbolically but *imaginarily*."[20] One can see the importance of this in terms of the person of the ordained leader and the gestures and bodily presence he uses as gatherer of the community and voice of the people's prayer in union with Christ. As Chauvet concludes,

> The symbolic element represents the whole of the world to which it belongs; better, it carries it in itself. That is why it *is* what it represents. Obviously, it is not "really" but "symbolically" what it represents, precisely because the function of the symbol is to *represent* the real, therefore to place it at a distance in order to present it, to make it present under a new mode.[21]

What the presider re-presents and sacramentally gathers together into communion signifies the *totus Christus*, both Christ the head and the Body of Christ, the members of his Spirit-filled resurrected presence in the world. No person can dare to possess the iconic perfection of the divine encounter with this world. However, the necessary *distance* is part of the efficacy, but only through the mediation of the concrete ministerial leader "who is what he is," bound to the Body and standing before her in order to present her "under a new mode."

In order to avoid what Chauvet would call "a semantic drift of symbol,"[22] such an affective connection—both interior and rooted in human, personal encounter—pertains to what we would call the

---

[19] Ibid., 270.

[20] Chauvet, *The Sacraments: The Word of God at the Mercy of the Body* (Collegeville, MN: Liturgical Press, 2001), 71.

[21] Ibid., 72.

[22] Ibid.

efficacy of the presider's sacramental function within the rite. The gatherer of the Body carries the Body in his own body, at a level of affection and solidarity that truly gives flesh to the virtue of compassion (*com-passio*, i.e., "to bear with, to suffer"). That relationship must not be "insignificant" or "only" symbolic, in the often misunderstood sense that it is disembodied from the divine/human connection the liturgy celebrates. A symbol, Chauvet maintains, "works with efficacy in the real world."[23]

"The sacrificial attitudes of Christ,"[24] the gift of the Spirit's indwelling embedded in the church by virtue of her members' common baptism, coalesce in a profound way in the one who leads by virtue of ecclesial call and charism. One could argue that halfhearted or distanced presiders may betray more about the inadequacy of their sacramental warrant to lead the community in its pastoral life than we first imagine. Sacramental symbols must not drift from the reality they signify without muting the proclamation of the *totus Christus* they are meant to communicate. Presiders, leaders of communities, and those who teach and pass on the sacramental tradition and prepare the rites that express it all have a share in this holistic nature of ministry as a congruent sign of the grace they bear. Liturgical preparation and enactment embraces, as Power says, "deep affective commitment."

So we can say unequivocally that *wholeheartedness* communicated through the body of the liturgical minister necessitates personal connection with those who gather, always conveying a sense of welcome and invitation, especially to those "who labor or are heavy burdened, offering Christ's rest" (Matt 11:28). Christ continually gathered the disciples and bid them come away and "rest a while," for "many were coming and going, and they had no leisure even to eat" (Mark 6:31-32). This reveals the compassionate heart of Christ, who teaches, sanctifies, and leads the Beloved. The presider/gatherer, in turn, communicates Christ's offer of intimacy in a focal way even at the door of the church, or in the ritual greeting of the assembly with outstretched arms that collect the Body's prayer as one, and in the terms of endearment directed toward sisters and brothers in the Lord, gathered

---

[23] Ibid.

[24] On the development of this notion in Edward Kilmartin, SJ, cf. Hahnenberg, "Ministerial Priesthood," 263. See also Robert J. Daly, SJ, *Sacrifice Unveiled: The True Meaning of Christian Sacrifice* (New York: T & T Clark International, 2009), esp. 21–22.

in the name of the Father and of the Son and of the Holy Spirit (e.g., "Beloved" or "Faithful Ones" are terms that awake an assembly to their true sacramental identity). "Peace be with you" is a benediction communicated through relational affect much more than disembodied words recited from a text. Christ's offer of graceful rest takes shape in ritual actions and presence that magnify the delight of God in the gathering, as well as solidarity with the intention of Christ to gather the busyness of contemporary lives into a prophetic space of stillness deep within.

Such attentive presidency cooperates with the sacramental encounter. Acknowledging this "holy ground" (Exod 3:5), expressed through the relationship between presider and assembly, announces the place where the church stands together in unity, so that all that gather can be attentive to God and to one another as Christ's Body, signed and signified here *in persona ecclesiae*. Affective connection between the preacher and the assembly proclaims the revelatory word of God spoken in Scripture as Christ himself, enfleshed in the concrete lives of the local and global situation out of which they gather, which thereby intensifies that union of minds and hearts. The Spirit, through all this, draws the gathered church into the sacrificial attitudes of Christ, as Kilmartin says, so that we are ready to listen and engage wholeheartedly in communion with Christ, particularly in the eucharistic prayer,[25] where the presider's voice must resonate with the communal self-offering. This rhythm of praise and thanks shapes the Body and hands her over for mission. The liturgical leader stands at the heart of this *exitus/reditus* rhythm of giving and receiving of self, what Kilmartin and others have called this "spirit-enabled dynamic of gift and return [in which] the priestly character of the people of God is most clear."[26] In affective surrender of body, mind, and spirit, the presider in this light represents Christ (*in persona Christi capitis*) because he is a "sacrament of the ecclesial community," as Wood so clearly describes this unique identity of the ordained leader of the liturgical assembly.[27] One could argue convincingly that *all* liturgical ministers, by virtue of the priest's ordi-

---

[25] Kilmartin, *The Eucharist in the West: History and Theology*, ed. Robert J. Daly (Collegeville, MN: Liturgical Press, 1998), 382.

[26] Hahnenberg, "Ministerial Priesthood," 267; see also Wood, *Sacramental Orders*, 137; Coffey, "The Common and the Ordained Priesthood," 219–21.

[27] Wood first articulates this notion in "Priestly Identity: Sacrament of the Ecclesial Community," *Worship* 69, no. 2 (1995); and continues it in *Sacramental*

nation in which gathering the community in prayer is focal, share in and body forth this active presence of Christ in worship, because their roles distinctly flow from the presider summoning the community into communion. Such a presence of Christ in the presider completes the redemptive dialogue the liturgy incarnates. God summons us in Word and we respond in union with "Christ, the sacrament of our encounter with God," as Edward Schillebeeckx so aptly described it.

From a relational understanding of the liturgy, therefore, the pneumatological and ecclesiological dimensions of presidency are not at odds with the christological identification with Christ. All of this takes place initially through the Spirit's inscripting into the body of believers, and it necessarily flows through the person of the one who carries the responsibility of gathering the local church in Word and Sacrament, united with the communion of the universal Body, "to accomplish our transformation into that which we receive" (LG 26).[28] Affective conversion to this way of presiding, far from being self-focused or dissonant with the solemnity of the rite, allies the leader of prayer, as Power describes the grace earlier, "with the power to do and the power to act" *in persona Christi capitis.*

A final example of the relational characteristics of sacramental presidency may clarify all that has been asserted here. Debates about presiding that occur in seminaries and schools of theology often include the simple question of the leader's eyes. Where does one look, particularly during the collect prayers and the eucharistic prayer? Rather than a minute issue of liturgical hairsplitting, the question embodies everything we have discussed about relationality. Some argue that the eyes at such a time should be lifted upward, since they are addressed to God and not the assembly. Others contend that true affective communion requires close and constant eye contact with the gathered celebrants. Employing the principle of liturgical theology, practice, and spirituality that maintains intimate connection between *all* the modes of sacramental encounter, one would answer that the presider stands in the midst of a complex matrix of symbolic relationships. Eyes raised to the heavens need not insist that God is only "up there" rather than embedded within the church and the world as a locus of revelation. Rather, such an upward gaze can be a way of drawing the

---

Orders, see 126; and "Presbyteral Identity within Parish Identity," in *Ordering the Baptismal Priesthood*, 175–94.

[28] *Lumen Gentium*, 26, is quoting St. Leo, Martyr, *Serm.* 63, 7; PL 54, 357C.

whole assembly's prayer into one, a "going out" from the common heart, and, in consort with outstretched hands of prayer, a willingness to receive the grace of the sacramental encounter the people at prayer represent. This "sacrificial attitude" conveys something very different than a lone mediator carrying on a personal dialogue with God while the passive congregation gazes upon this all in awe. The subtle difference here can be hard to explain in words, but congruence of body, mind, and heart in the presider communicates the reality that it signifies.

At the same time, the presider must also engage the assembly visually, within the rhythm of the communal prayer, because the relationality of "one heart and voice" also communicates the way Christ is present *in persona Christi capitis*, inviting the assembly to offer themselves "Through him, and with him, and in him . . . in the unity of the Holy Spirit." An expressive moment of this finds expression in many eucharistic prayers: "[W]e offer you, Lord, the Bread of life and the Chalice of salvation, giving thanks that you have held us worthy to be in your presence and minister to you" (II); "so that all of us, who through this participation at the altar receive the most holy Body and Blood of your Son, may be filled with every grace and heavenly blessing" (I); "Therefore, as we celebrate the memorial of your Son Jesus Christ, who is our Passover and our surest peace, we celebrate his Death and Resurrection from the dead, and look forward to his blessed Coming" (Reconciliation I); and many other instances. No hard and fast rubric inheres here. The mutual "looking" taking place comes from the heart of the assembly, which sees into the heart of the presider and joins in the loving gaze of God as Giver of the gift, the gift itself, and the bond of unity and charity that makes the gift what it is, the very presence of Christ. As Catherine of Siena said so profoundly, "I want to see us at the table of the Spotless Lamb, who is food, table, and waiter."[29]

There is so much to look at and to see that is holy. The locus of revelation is all around, if one takes incarnational and sacramental theology seriously. God's agenda transcends our battles of ecclesiologies and will not be controlled in terms of rubrical rigidity from any side, which either seeks to escape the world or to imprison us within our

---

[29] Saint Catherine of Siena, *Letters*, 49–50. Catherine returns to this multivalent activity of Christ often in her letters and prayers. See *The Prayers of ʿne of Siena*, ed. Suzanne Noffke (New York: Paulist Press, 1983).

own narrow confines. In the sacramental economy—in which we are both receivers and givers, hearers and preachers, called to repentance and redeemed, hungry and satisfied—God will not get caught by our efforts at apologetic manipulation. So, in the end, the Spirit is in the gaps and the presider knows where to look when the grace of the church praying in the power of the Spirit claims its proper relationship within the liturgy.

Dialogue as the Form of Liturgical Proclamation of God's Saving Acts in Jesus

The presider prays in the assembly's name, and his voice and person are engaged in gathering the community into communion. This demands attention and respect for the *dialogical* nature of the liturgy as God's way of communicating with us to proclaim the paschal mystery of Christ as both gift and invitation to "become what we receive." As we saw in chapter 3 concerning the presence of Christ in the Word proclaimed and preached, Word and Sacrament comprise the fullness of the redemptive event, in which God *speaks* first in the incarnate Word as a present offer of grace and in which Christ then *responds* as the Answer, by means of his obedient, loving, self-offering on the cross. Otto Semmelroth called this "a *redemptive dialogue* in which God and [humankind] are a living unity joined in a personal confrontation."[30] Such an incarnational encounter with the community of believers in the liturgy, Semmelroth goes on to say so eloquently, is literally "God's own sermon" to us.[31] We join the dialogue as an assembly of celebrating Christians. "Thanks be to God" and "Praise to you, Lord Jesus Christ" and psalmic responses acknowledging God's steadfast love give voice to our answer as the Body of Christ: "Amen. So be it." Our response continues in the profession of faith, broadens out to gather the needs of the world in general intercessions, and culminates in common praise and thanks in the liberating request for the Spirit "to hallow these gifts of bread and wine"[32] and to accept the holy and willing surrender of our lives in union with Christ, the Redeemer. "We

[30] Semmelroth, *The Preaching Word: On the Theology of Proclamation*, trans. John Jay Hughes (New York: Herder and Herder, 1965), 230–32. See also chap. 3, 107–10.

[31] Semmelroth, *Church and Sacrament*, trans. Emily Schossberger (Notre Dame: Fides Press, 1965), 57.

[32] Eucharistic Prayer for Various Needs and Occasions.

proclaim your death, Lord Jesus, until you come in glory." "Amen!" we say. "Forever and ever, Amen!" Such is the dialogical response of those engaged in "holy communion."

God initiates the redemptive dialogue, but the liturgy participates as the vehicle of this conversation in which each proclamation and response forges and nourishes the relationship between Lover and Beloved, in which Christ is at the center of this holy meeting.[33] The presider's role in the dialogue cannot be overemphasized here. Once more, mere recitation of words to this effect cannot capture the depths of proclamation and response that flow from the heart of God. Dialogue requires listening, respect for the grace that answers the summons, and always acknowledges the presence of Christ as embodied within the interchange of presider and assembly. The sacrificial attitudes of Christ in which the Spirit molds the liturgical assembly identify the character of presence a presider must embody in order for the dialogue to show forth the mighty deeds of God. Once again, the interior disposition of the presider must begin with these attitudes before they are translated into gesture and word within the liturgical enactment.

How does a leader of prayer listen from the heart, so that one may speak on behalf of Christ the Word and for this precious Body of Christ? The Scriptures are abundant regarding this teaching. "I sought the LORD, and he answered me, and delivered me from all my fears," the psalmist says (Ps 34:4), and ". . . if he calls you, you shall say, 'Speak, LORD, for your servant is listening'" (1 Sam 3:9). Moses voices the dynamic of listening so that one might speak when he tells the people: "The LORD will fight for you, and you have only to keep still" (Exod 14:14). One cannot imagine a leader of prayer who is not first the *silent one* in the depths of the heart, listening for the Word, "standing firm" and unafraid (Exod 14:13), engaged regularly in the dialogue that will take flesh in one's person when the assembly gathers in faith.

Rubrics and words can be learned, but the *attitudes* they proclaim are fashioned only in hearts that surrender in trust to the mystery taking place. Such bearers of Christ's mysteries place themselves into the

[33] For a more complete description of Semmelroth's understanding of Word and Sacrament as a "single work" bestowing grace, see Janowiak, *The Holy Preaching: The Sacramentality of the Word in the Liturgical Assembly* (Collegeville, MN: Liturgical Press, 2000), 20–27.

Heart of the only Word they will ever really require in order to be free for the self-surrender the liturgy enacts. The liturgical rhythm that emerges out of the heart of the gatherer carries over into the attitudes of public presiding, in which Christ is present as the bearer of all Good News and the food and drink that consecrates our identity in him. The leader of prayer must be led in prayer, be silenced first in order to call the assembly to stillness, and stand firm in the faith that God *will* speak and act through the fragile vessel that all honest presiders know themselves to be. God shapes a listening heart through the dynamics of proclamation and response that echo first within and then take flesh in the presider's own person, as Christ the Priest draws the assembly into the mystery they celebrate.

Dialogue requires response. Listening that occurs in the heart must then carry over into the way the presider listens and expects to hear a word of grace to be spoken in conversation with the Body of Christ. Listening to God and listening to Christ's Body, the presider is "all ears," so that the Holy One can *be* the mouth "and teach you what to speak" (Exod 4:12). A leader of prayer who does not expect that God will be communicating in many ways and means besides his own mouth alone (Exod 4:15), or who considers the faithful community as mute spectators in the redemptive dialogue, simply halts the rhythm and harmony of the song that resonates throughout the whole liturgical event. Even in times of silence during the liturgy, the Spirit's exchange of loving conversation continues. One encounters this only through an attitude that St. Ignatius of Loyola called in his *Spiritual Exercises* "felt knowledge" (*sentir*).[34] A presider who immerses self in the dialogue of the liturgy is always hearing that rhythm and cooperating with its flow. Such synergy, to use Jean Corbon's description, creates a harmony that transcends the rubrics and words on the page and "gives them breath and speech, so that all the living might find a voice to sing [God's] praise," as a study text of an American eucharistic prayer once described it. The Spirit forges this dialogue through the willingness of both presider and assembly to expect a visitation, listen for its cadence in word and enactment, and allow it to direct the flow of proclamation and response embodied in the liturgical rite itself.

[34] Saint Ignatius of Loyola, *Spiritual Exercises*, see, e.g., 118, 313, on *sentir* and its role in discernment.

Listen! I am standing at the door, knocking; if you hear my voice and
open the door, I will come in to you and eat with you, and you with
me. (Rev 3:20)

The interior dispositions of both presider and assembly cooperate with the ritual movement and deepen the resonance of the whole
event as a proclamation of God's saving acts in Jesus. The ordained
presider, as sacramental referent of the ecclesial community, accepts
the responsibility to orchestrate the ebb and flow of proclamation and
response by the manner in which he leads the Body in a ritual rhythm,
rather than simply following a linear progression from one part of the
liturgy to another, as if there were no fluctuations of emphasis that
integrate the whole. All elements of the rite cannot assume the same
importance and ritual intensity or else the dialogue languishes with
too much speaking and acting on the part of the presider and assembly and not enough receptive listening to the Spirit's hallowing. The
primary symbols and significant moments of sacramental expression
take precedence. The presider orchestrates this dialogical emphasis
when he acts sacramentally *in persona Christi capitis*. Proclamation and
response carried out through "taking, blessing, breaking, and sharing"
cannot be overshadowed by ritual digressions that may be meaningful
to some or anachronistic appeals to others, and they do not serve the
wholesome proclamation of the presence of Christ. A few examples
will help to illustrate such digressions that hinder the flow.

When the liturgical procession moves through the assembly, the
liturgy has already begun. A presider who intrudes with descriptions
about the liturgy, such as *"We begin our prayer* in the name . . . ," or
digresses into a peripheral commentary on the weather or personal
fatigue, or any other excursus from the focal actions of Word and
Sacrament, puts pedantic emphasis where the dialogical flow does
not belong. A needless and often extended synopsis of the homily
or the feast also seems misplaced at this point in the dialogue. The
temptation to be colloquial as a way of being human and personal is
understandable. However, such digressions are also not necessarily in
rhythm and harmony with the ritual dialogue that has begun.

The fact remains that God's gathering of the Body (the entrance
rites) is itself the primary proclamation taking place here. The assembly responds by naming and drawing herself into the triune mystery
through the presider's use of multiple images of the Scripture of the
day ("Lord Jesus, you healed the sick . . .") or by standing together

acknowledging the perennial desire of God to gather us in mercy, to heal our wounds and make us whole. Gathering together under the tent of mercy is what the dialogue expresses. Anything else mutes the ritual proclamation. Moses' dialogue with God in the desert, begging the Lord's sure presence, provides a rich analogy of this reconciling love that provides the context for hearing the Word and sharing communion in the Body and Blood of Christ at the table. Notice how God's assurance of presence, despite the fragility of the people and of their leader Moses, constitutes the heart of the following dialogue and the impetus for Moses to keep voicing the people's need as they travel the deliverance journey:

> [God] said, "My presence will go with you, and I will give you rest." And [Moses] said to him, "If your presence will not go, do not carry us up from here. For how shall it be known that I have found favor in your sight, I and your people, unless you go with us? . . . The LORD said to Moses, "I will do the very thing that you have asked; for you have found favor in my sight, and I know you by name. . . . and I will be gracious to whom I will be gracious, and will show mercy on whom I will show mercy." (Exod 33:14-16a, 17, 19b)

The gathering rites are disrupted all too often by the presider's inattentiveness to this dialogical focus that reveals the mercy that leads us into the mystery of worship. Other points in the liturgy can be noted as well. For example, the preparation of the altar and the gifts and the cleaning of vessels after communion often involve such an overemphasis that the assembly easily becomes disengaged with the fourfold movement we have named as central to the liturgical dialogue, culminating here in the deeds of the table. Communing should be the rhythm here, and not disconnection from the Body with fussing or cleansing! The inability of the presider to allow for adequate silence as a counterbalance to the verbal elements that accompany the gestures reduces proclamation and response to a stutter. Responsible liturgical leadership, therefore, always considers the importance of the dialogical nature of presidency and the intrinsic connection such a rhythm provides in allowing the interrelationship of the praying assembly, the proclaimed Word, the gifts blessed and shared, and the gatherer of the Body in fidelity to this invitation to render Christ's presence living and active in our midst. The "two-edged sword" of Christ's Word to us and our Answer in union with Christ requires skillful handling by the leader who orchestrates the sacramental dialogue that is the church's liturgy.

Participation as the Intrinsic Effect of Sacramental Leadership "in Persona Ecclesiae"

All that has been said regarding relationality and dialogue makes the participatory quality of presidency a natural conclusion. In short, the priest/presider does not celebrate "his" Mass, to use the common misconception. Since so much of the distinctive actions of presiding that cannot be separated from the whole enactment centers around the eucharistic meal, table presidency deserves closer scrutiny. The whole church "celebrates" the liturgy, we maintain, and the eucharistic prayer is the communal act of praise and thanks put into words through the presider's voice. To focus on an even more delicate and contentious issue, the institutional narrative in that prayer comes from this communal voice as well, rendered through the leader of prayer by means of the Spirit's agency. Edward Kilmartin emphasized this in many ways over the course of his years of study regarding the pneumatological and ecclesiological character of liturgical leadership as necessary dimensions that complement and deepen the christological character of acting *in persona Christi capitis*. As Kilmartin says,

> The words of Christ found in the liturgical account of institution are pronounced by the priest acting *in persona Christi*. But the priest is also the authorized minister of the Church. While conducting the Church's prayerful discourse with the Father, he pronounces the words which Christ pronounced in the unrepeatable situation of the Last Supper in view of the immediate future, and above all in view of the liturgical celebration of the Church. At the heart of the eucharistic worship, the authorized minister intervenes and in his oration pronounces the same words "in the person of the praying Church by the speech of Christ," that is, in the name of the Church which here prays with the words of Christ. The words of consecration are words of Christ not immediately in the mouth of Christ but in the mouth of the Church, authoritatively represented by its ordained minister.[35]

Eucharistic praying is a participative act, therefore, and the presider provides an integrating role in facilitating this characteristic of Christ acting when the church is at prayer. In a similar demonstration of the "distinct but not separate" relationship between *in persona Christi capitis*

[35] Kilmartin, *Eucharist in the West*, 348–49. The quoted term within is taken from Cesare Giraudo, *Eucaristia per la chiesa*, Aloisiana 22 (Rome: Gregorian University/Brescia: Morcelliana, 1989), 344.

and *in persona ecclesiae*, David Power appropriates Aquinas's understanding when he asserts that "to act in the sacrament in the person of Christ is to be Christ's instrument," not simply in individual likeness, but as one who embodies "the downward actions of Christ's humanity and mediation, those by which he brings the power of God to act in the community."[36] An engaged encounter is at play whenever Christ acts.

If, then, we could understand that this "heart of the eucharistic worship" (Kilmartin) is implicitly imbued with a participatory dynamic, we would go a long way toward rescuing ordained leadership from a sacral ontologization that remains such a lure for the contemporary church. To emphasize the role of the presider as the sacrament of the ecclesial community does not demean the priest's sacramental role. To insist upon elevated, "raised up" distinctions for the presider vis-a-vis the celebrants in the liturgy misses the necessary interrelationship of the modes of presence as revelatory of the *totus Christus* in our sacramental worship. In short, the presider's primary sacramental representation is to *gather the community into communion with Christ* rather than simply *to confect* the Eucharist. The preaching of the Word, as William Hill noted, "incarnates itself in human history, midway between the one who utters it and those who listen."[37] The sacramental gifts of bread and wine are consecrated as the Body and Blood of Christ, necessary food for the whole community to be in communion, "signs that effect the reality that they signify." From that perspective, participation necessarily comes to the forefront of the discussion. The *kenotic* act of the triune God remains the wellspring for this dimension, and the invitation of God to share this loving life in the Spirit remains its source and summit, to echo the Vatican reform (SC 10). Indeed, as we noted in chapter 2 concerning the inclusive dimension inherent in the Constitution on the Sacred Liturgy,

> The Church earnestly desires that all the faithful be led to that full, conscious, and active participation in liturgical celebrations called for *by the very nature of the liturgy*. (SC 14; emphasis mine)

[36] Power, "Representing Christ in Community and Sacrament," 100–101. He draws his ideas of Christ's actions of descent from I. Dalmais, "Theology of the Liturgical Celebration," in *The Church at Prayer*, vol. 1, ed. A. Martimort (Collegeville, MN: Liturgical Press, 1987), 227–80.

[37] Hill, *Search for the Absent God*, ed. Mary Catherine Hilkert (New York: Crossroad, 1992), 186.

Much liturgical reflection regarding this directive centers on the Christian people's engagement as a "right and duty by reason of their baptism," as the paragraph continues. However, one could make the same claim for the presider of the liturgical assembly, who represents both Christ the head and the Body of Christ in an intrinsic relationship bodying forth the fullness of the sacramental presence. In other words, a presider must himself be participating with the assembly in order to fulfill his sacramental mandate. Participation is the ordained leader's "right and duty by reason of ordination," which flows from a baptismal call to embrace the charism *in persona Christi capitis*, to facilitate and immerse oneself in the participation that characterizes the very nature of the ritual enactment he shepherds. As we maintained in chapter 3, charism and authority issue from the incarnational mode of the *kerygma*. The *kenotic* act of ordained service makes no sense unless one surrenders to the other, to Someone. The coordinates for this self-emptying can only be the common, holy People of God and the Lord God who called them out of darkness into such wonderful, grace-filled light. Participation in service means *participation with the other* to enact the mighty deeds of God in sacramental encounter. Again, this is the church's worship, not the priest's, "called for by the very nature of the liturgy." Recognition of the whole assembly's summons to enter into the sacred mysteries is clear; the presider's concomitant charge to *participate* in their participation is a sacramental "right and duty" and not something he may choose or not according to personal whim. This ordinance inheres in order for the faithful exercise of sacramental priesthood to occur. Participation with and by the presider expresses "orthodoxy," that is, "right praise."

So, we ask again in the same vein as before, what qualities represent such a participative ministry in the church's liturgy? *Interior disposition* and *bodily presence* again stand at the forefront of this public, ecclesial role. The Second Letter of Peter authenticates the interiority that directs liturgical presence of the presider. The promise of faith revealed in Christ allows us all to "become participants in the divine nature" (2 Pet 1:4). Christ participates in our participation through the "divine power" (v. 3) flowing from the heart of God through his own self-offering. The presider can do nothing less than model this action of Christ, whose mystery he appropriates by affective immersion into the Spirit-filled resurrected Body of Christ. The Shepherd knows and speaks what he himself has heard (John 8:26) through divine engagement with the One in whom he is begotten. The presider acting *in persona Christi capitis* acts in consort and rhythm with Christ's own mission. Even more, since the grace of ordination is conferred in the power of the Spirit through the church, presiding out of that Spirit draws him into engagement with the primary sacrament of that revelatory word of God, *in persona ecclesiae.*

"Participation in these things" of praise and thanks, as Gordon Lathrop expresses it, "is participation in him."[38] A heart that finds its deepest affinity with Christ stands vulnerable in this regard, in that nothing he does "in the Spirit" begins at root in the individual memory or will but in and through the "household of God, which is the church of the living God, the pillar and bulwark of truth" (1 Tim 3:15). *Interior disposition* in the presider finds its centering nourishment in Christ's ecclesial embrace and in the model of Jesus, who enters into relationship with us as his brothers and sisters and mothers in faith (Matt 12:50). Shaping an interior disposition toward participation asks that the liturgical leader lay aside the inevitable fears and preoccupations of the ego and "put on the whole armor of God" (Eph 6:11), which is a strength and shield that comes from surrendering to the vulnerability of God, who shares the divine life with us so fully in Christ. With that same vulnerable heart, the presider looks to the assembly as the primary sacrament of our communion with Christ he so desires to represent *in persona ecclesiae.* "Let this same mind be in you that was in Christ Jesus" (Phil 2:5).

Bodily presence communicates this interior disposition to the assembly, for it is the incarnate instrument the triune God calls forth to invite and gather the community into sacramental communion. Beyond words and specific actions reserved to the presider, the leader of ecclesial prayer conveys through his body a willingness to be embraced in this encounter and find true relationship with Christ. Once again, such nonverbal dynamics are difficult to describe with precision, but the assembly knows and feels it in its bones when distance or emotional resistance characterizes the manner of engagement with the dynamic of communion in Christ and one another. This often reveals itself in an attitude that the presider is *administering* the sacraments or *giving out* something that does not first embed itself within the worshiping

---

[38] Gordon Lathrop, *What Are the Essentials of Christian Worship?*, Open Questions in Worship Series, vol. 1 (Minneapolis: Augsburg/Fortress, 1994), 9. An updated edition can be found in *Central Things: Worship in Word and Sacrament* (Augsburg, 2005).

church herself. Once again, the rhythm and harmony between gathering, listening and hearing, proclaiming and responding, and eating and drinking in grateful communion with Christ and one another stutter when the sacramental embodiment of that unity dissociates bodily and personally from the grace-filled action. Despite a presider's weaknesses in this regard, God's offer remains sure, *ex opere operato*, but the fullness of the *totus Christus* can be muted and veiled. Christ's Body, in its totality, suffers when presiders do not take part in "full, conscious, and active participation in liturgical celebrations" that shape "the very nature of the liturgy" (SC 14).

Sharing in the Fruits of God's Passion to Be in Communion: The Presider's Portion and Cup

The eleventh-century mystical poet Symeon the New Theologian provides a vision of a liturgical theology for presiders that is rooted in the real and active presence of Christ in sacramental life:

> We awaken in Christ's body
> As Christ awakens our bodies,
> And my poor hand is Christ, He enters
> My foot, and is infinitely me.
>
> I move my hand, and wonderfully
> My hand becomes Christ, becomes all of Him
>
> . . . .
>
> I move my foot, and at once
> He appears like a flash of lightning.
> Do my words seem blasphemous?—Then
> open your heart to Him
>
> and let yourself receive the one
> who is opening to you so deeply.
> For if we genuinely love Him,
> We wake up inside Christ's body
>
> Where all our body, all over,
> Every most hidden part of it,
> Is realized in joy as Him
> And He makes us, utterly, real.[39]

[39] A copy of the whole prayer can be found in *The Enlightened Heart: An Anthology of Sacred Poetry*, ed. Stephen Mitchell (San Francisco: Harper and Row, 1989), 38–39.

This summons to union and communion in the Lord extends to all the Beloved, "in every last part of our body," as Symeon goes on to sing. The ordained leader in the church cannot claim special privilege in such intimacy, but the charismatic nature of his representation of Christ in the sacrament of orders consecrates his baptismal identity for service in the Body of Christ that points to and sacramentally re-presents such a grace-filled awakening. The gatherer of the community into communion bears the vigilant responsibility to recognize the Spirit's anointing of the Body, to witness to Christ's offer of redemption and new life, and to order the pastoral witness of the local church in such a way that a wider circle of God's beloved creation can find the source of all their longing. The presider stands as a beacon of that hope, "wakes up the assembly in Christ's body," as Symeon would attest, and gives voice to the community's praise for such a gift present among us.

As Paul proclaimed so eloquently in his remarkable dialogue with the Athenians, this often "unknown" God speaks through the human journey toward meaning and wholeness, "so that they would search for God and perhaps grope for him and find him—though indeed he is not far from each of us" (Acts 17:27). The church stands as the witness to this offer of grace, whose revelatory Word is Jesus. The ordained leader, who presides in the person of Christ and the church, is "woken up" to be the witness to the sacramental nature of Christ's life that transcends function to reach into the very shape of one's identity. As David Coffey describes this witness charism of ordination,

> The priest, then, is someone chosen by God out of the body of those who belong to Christ to be for the rest of his life an official witness to Christ for that body and for the world.[40]

A liturgical spirituality deepens when one's personal relationship with God finds in its corporate witness a profound grace of self-emptying love in the Spirit of Jesus' own pattern of life, death, and resurrection. The specific sacramental character of this relationship expressed in the gathered assembly at worship takes on a way of seeing, feeling, reaching out, and discerning the movements of the Spirit that course through the assembly as Christ bodies forth that presence through Word and Sacrament, leader and celebrants, all in a harmony

---

[40] Coffey, "The Common and the Ordained Priesthood," 227.

that proclaims the mighty acts of God for us now, in this time and place. Carrying the Body within the presider's body becomes a mode of being and acting that the church needs in order to be herself in her fullest sacramental truth. To assent to the Body and the Spirit's fashioning into the sacrificial attitudes of Christ impels the ordained leader and, at the same time, graces one's service in mission. The liturgy stands as a focal expression of that primary leadership in the community of Jesus Christ, which feeds upon the communion of the Trinity's mutual love that flows from the heart of God who is love. Such depths are awesome, and they do not require a reliance on ontological otherness to validate them. The place within the church out of which one sacramentally gathers this grace-filled reality joyfully "wakes the presider up" to be "utterly real" if he divests himself of everything else and surrenders to the mystery of it all. *Kenosis* embraces even our competence as liturgical presiders, or else it is "a noisy gong and a clanging cymbal" (1 Cor 13:1) of sacral arrogance. Some concluding remarks on such a spirituality of servant leadership will conclude the chapter.

A KENOTIC SPIRITUALITY OF LITURGICAL LEADERSHIP: A DESCENT INTO THE HEART OF CHRIST AND THE PEOPLE

Let the same mind be in you that was in Christ Jesus . . .
being found in human form, he humbled himself . . .

—Philippians 2:5, 7-8a

Anyone pulled from a source
longs to go back.

At any gathering I am there,
mingling in the laughing and grieving,

a friend to each, but few
will hear the secrets hidden

within the notes. No ears for that.
Body flowing out of spirit,

spirit up from body: no concealing
that mixing. But it's not given us

to see the soul. The reed flute
is fire, not wind. Be that empty.

> —Jelaluddin Rumi,
> thirteenth-century Persian mystic and poet[41]

If God desires this communion with us and chooses ministers of
Word and Sacrament to gather that Body into communion so that
they can receive the impelling Word of God and move to the table of
Eucharist to give praise and thanks by eating and drinking in grateful
memory, then a spirituality of liturgical leadership for our times must
embody the triune self-offering that unites this ministry with the assembly at prayer, the Word that is preached, and the sacramental food
and drink we share. Embedded within the liturgy as sign and symbol
of that sacramental unity, the leader of corporate prayer announces
by his presence as gatherer (*in persona Christi capitis*) that the church
constitutes herself in encountering Christ the head. The presider's attitude, therefore, is Christ's and the foundational expression of that is
kenosis, that is, self-emptying, servant leadership, radical vulnerability,
and a bodiliness that is not afraid to be human.

Identity, as we said at the outset, precedes function in this sacramental economy. Identity is both an interior disposition and bodily
in expression. Ordained presiders in this contemporary world can no
longer rely on images of being "raised up" to some spiritual plane
that is above the assembly gathered. True, there is great dignity and
blessedness in ordained ministry, but one is "raised up" only because
Christ "raises up the church" as the Spirit-filled Body in the world. "I
say to you, stand up, take your mat and go to your home," Jesus says
to the paralytic (Mark 2:11), and like all who have been touched and
healed in their encounter with Christ, the one who is raised up has
a summons: to live and preach the glorious power at work in Christ
Jesus through the Father's own self-emptying love revealed now to the
world in the power of the Holy Spirit.

From this model of gift and summons, a *kenotic* spirituality of liturgical presidency is best described as a *descent into Christ's own heart and
into the heart of the community* that bears his presence as the primary
sacrament of the church. One could assert even more strongly that

---

[41] Taken from "The Reed Flute's Song," in *The Essential Rumi*, trans. Coleman
Barks, et al. (Edison, NJ: Castle Books, 1997), 18.

such liturgical leadership is not a promotion but, in the sacramental reality, a *demotion* that bears depth and resonance precisely in its self-emptying. As Susan Wood says so clearly, the grace of Christ's presence in a sacramental understanding of orders must derive its authenticity from the network of relationships that constitute the church as the Body of Christ. A presider's sacramental efficacy flows from that relationship rather than stands above or outside of it. The summons resonates from within the *totus Christus*; this is God's mode of self-communication to us. From this perspective, an identity begins to emerge that has profound implications for liturgical spirituality.

> By virtue of ordination the priest sacramentally represents the ecclesial community, stands for the community, becomes a type of corporate personality in which the community recognizes itself; in short, he is a sacramental sign of the community. The truth has long been affirmed in saying that the priest stands *in persona Ecclesiae* as well as *in persona Christi*. This understanding underlines the importance of the reception, recognition, and even the call of the ordinand on the part of the community.[42]

The spirituality we are considering here is not of the priesthood per se, but the ordained leader's specific sacramental role "bodying forth" the presence of Christ as the gatherer of the community into communion. At the same time, leadership of the community at prayer cannot be divorced from the whole gospel life of ecclesial leadership, or else it migrates solely to function and not identity. This is what makes such a discussion fraught with ambiguity and complexity. These are not insurmountable hurdles, however, if we begin with the passion that flows from the heart of the Father, made manifest in the incarnational gift of Jesus, and the Spirit's outpouring of this identity of Christ in the church. *Out of* that rich relational, dialogical, and participative dynamic, the presider's identity is shaped and deepened and ultimately fruitful for the *totus Christus* out of which he is a representative sign and symbol. The discussion only becomes sidetracked and problematic when one begins with gender or marital status as the foundational requirements for ordained leadership. The tradition of the Roman church has maintained the latter as necessary, but a sacramental consideration begins with other primary considerations. Perhaps

---

[42] Wood, "Priestly Identity: Sacrament of the Ecclesial Community," 114.

this is why the discussion does not cease in communities of faithful believers. The sacramental body senses something more at stake here. At the same time, countless faith-filled priests still body forth the summons in a time of such complexity. Prayerful, embodied, and relational presiding gathers people and is an acknowledged "sign that effects the reality that it signifies." In these changing times, that in itself is a *kenotic* spirituality that deserves prayerful reflection.

Such a desire for this "mind of Christ" is alive and well in our own time. Benedict XVI, in his 2009 apostolic letter commemorating a "Year for Priests" (2009), noted that Pope Paul VI expressed so poignantly that "modern man listens more willingly to witnesses than to teachers, and if he does listen to teachers, it is because they are witnesses."[43] Interior disposition in "the mind of Christ," as we said, shapes good presiding and it really does "leave a mark on presiders' lives and shapes their thinking," as Benedict exhorted. The challenges of identity and efficacy of sacramental leadership remains central to the effective preaching of the gospel today. The liturgy is the primary instrument of such evangelization.

Everything we have said so far in this chapter coalesces in this *kenotic* spirituality, because it is in and through this fragile vessel, one "subject to weakness" (Heb 5:2; 7:28), that Christ acts and is seen to be acting in rhythm and harmony with all the modes of presence that constitute the "one whole word of God," Christ's real presence among us.

So what, then, *is* this identity that shapes the function of the presider in the liturgy and how does gathering the community in corporate prayer shape and deepen that sacramental sign of the presence of Christ that the leader represents as sign and symbol? Saint Paul offers some helpful images of the interior disposition of a disciple that give

---

[43] *Evangelii nutiandi*, 41. Pope Benedict XVI noted this point in Paul VI and commented further on this need for a self-emptying identity with Christ that requires, as we said above, an "affective conversion." Benedict goes on to say: "Lest we experience existential emptiness and the effectiveness of our ministry be compromised, we need to ask ourselves ever anew: 'Are we truly pervaded by the word of God? Is that word truly the nourishment we live by, even more than bread and the things of this world? Do we really know that word? Do we love it? Are we deeply engaged with this word to the point that it really leaves a mark on our lives and shapes our thinking?'" (Apostolic Letter of Benedict XVI, Proclaiming a Year for Priests on the 150th Anniversary of the "Dies Natales" of the Curé of Ars, June 16, 2009).

flesh to this descent that a kenotic spirituality of presiding calls forth. Paul's own struggles in 2 Corinthians 12 with the "thorn in the flesh" provide a key to interpreting this entrance into the heart of Christ and the People of God. An identity-shaping characteristic for the one who offers sacrifice in the name of the people is one that is in touch with the radical weakness in one's own self. Paul acknowledges the disparity between what he preaches and teaches and the sinful person he knows himself to be. Such radical honesty and reliance upon God allows him to be vulnerable in his humanness and to surrender his own lack of power or control into the hands of the One he serves. The power of Christ's own gift of self is sacramentally present as a "manifest symbol" (LG 26) *through* Paul, *with* him in his preaching and ministry, and *in* him, as bearer of the Good News that gathers the believing community into communion. The interior disposition of the liturgical presider can be nothing less. As Paul says about his radical vulnerability,

> Three times I appealed to the Lord about this, that it would leave me, but he said to me, "My grace is sufficient for you, for power is made perfect in weakness." So, I will boast all the more gladly of my weaknesses, so that the power of Christ may dwell in me. Therefore I am content . . . for the sake of Christ; for whenever I am weak, then I am strong. (2 Cor 12:8-10)

"For the sake of Christ," one gathers the assembly in such a kenotic frame of mind and communicates that in the reverence and attention one gives to the gestures and words that speak from such parabolic "strength." Assemblies intuit such power and grace and respond with a complementary self-offering, as the "priestly, prophetic, and kingly" People of God they truly are (LG 31).

To stand in the place of such an awesome proclamation, the leader must engage regular prayer and spiritual sustenance outside the liturgical context, or else the words and sacramental actions ring hollow and disengage from the relational, dialogical, and participative event taking place. The temptation in such a case is to find power in rubrics and disembodied proclamations rather than in the liturgy's own inherent power. The point is simple: presiders need to be praying before they lead the people in prayer; and *because* they pray, they are then ready to engage the mysteries the church celebrates. The experience takes on the Spirit's inscripting, for they see the face of Christ in the gathered Body; they encounter the Word as an event that is always new and not a static text to exegize; they set out the eucharistic meal as pure gift from the Giver of all good gifts. Because of this interior disposition, one is free to engage the rhythm and harmony taking place, knowing from the heart that "my grace is enough for you."

This interior disposition spills over into a bodily presence that is consonant and truthful and inviting to those gathered. Paul exhorts the community and uses the reality of the body to shape the Body of disciples:

> I appeal to you therefore, brothers and sisters, by the mercies of God, to present your bodies as a living sacrifice, holy and acceptable to God, which is your spiritual worship. Do not be conformed to this world, but be transformed by the renewing of your minds, so that you may discern what is the will of God—what is good and acceptable and perfect. (Rom 12:1-2)

Bodiliness remains the sacramental expression of Christ, acting in the presider *in persona Christi capitis*. Sacramental theologians, especially since the reform of Vatican II, have explored that essential element of communication within Christian ritual. In his focal work, *Symbol and Sacrament*, Louis-Marie Chauvet insists that the body itself is speech (a proclamatory act, we could also say), especially in the symbolic order. "Humans do not ex-sist except as *corporeality* whose concrete place is always their *own bodies*. Corporeality is the body's very speech." What is more, interiority finds its expression only by "taking up a position within the world of its meanings," as he quotes from the philosopher Merleau-Ponty. Interiority and bodiliness, according to Chauvet, are joined in a powerful way in the world of symbol and ritual and liturgical event. As he says further,

> Is it any surprise, finally, that culture or the symbolic order takes root in human beings as bodies? For their bodies in fact place humans in the world in a very particular way. The body is *the primordial place of every symbolic joining of the "inside" and the "outside."*[44]

Given the power of corporeality in the ritual action of presiding at the liturgy, one enters very vulnerable territory that requires great humility and openness to God's power acting through the "inside" *and* the

---

[44] Chauvet, *Symbol and Sacrament*, 146–47. For a rich discussion of Chauvet on this, see chap. 4, part IV, "The Symbol and the Body," 140–52.

"outside" of the person who is acting as a "sign and symbol" of a very graced whole. Oftentimes, those who are uncomfortable with such an expressive vehicle of the holy resort to a false solemnity instead of a profound awesomeness of the grace of God at work in these simple vessels of Christ's presence. A *kenotic* spirituality of liturgical presiding is not false humility—this also rings hollow. Rather, it is a reverent joy, an expansive hospitality, a willingness to engage, to see the "other" as a mirror of Christ.

Presiding from this perspective yields the "treasure hidden in the field" (Matt 13:44). The holiness of the gathering vibrates within the gathering and the presider is in tune with its resonance. The Word proclaimed and preached is "living and active . . . able to judge the thoughts and intentions of the heart" (Heb 4:12). The eucharistic food is not something to be distributed but a meal of joy and thanksgiving and mutual self-offering, set out and shared by all. The rubrics may provide the communal guidelines for such a "corporate personality" who is sign and symbol of the whole, but—much more important—this attitude of mind and body and spirit shapes its communal soul and the gatherer animates the integration between what we claim in our prayer and its consecrated reality in our midst. One can then affirm that the presider, as Wood says above, "stands for the community" in a way that "the community recognizes itself."[45] Such sacramental attitudes must be felt in the bones and nourished from a heart disposed to let the Spirit work. They are hard to legislate and even harder to teach. The only true prescription is to pray, to trust the church's call to such an awesome sacramental responsibility—embracing even the complexity of our times—and to be willing to gather the Body into communion as truly Beloved, gifts from the heart of God and sisters and brothers of Christ the companion. Paul reminds us,

> So also Christ did not glorify himself in becoming a high priest, but was appointed by the one who said to him, "You are my Son, today I have begotten you." (Heb 5:5)

This is "the mind of Christ" inside and outside, and it is out of that identity that function follows. Function is the fruitful expression of a sacramental identity that communicates the inner reality and truth of Christ's abiding presence.

[45] Cf. n. 43.

From this sacramental perspective, descent into the heart—not sacral arrogance—harmonizes with all the modes of presence that shape the real presence of Christ in the liturgy. Only then can one speak of being "lifted up" in the spirit of Mary's own *Magnificat*:

> for the Mighty One has done great things for me, and holy is his name. . . . He has shown strength with his arm; he has scattered the proud in the thoughts of their hearts. He has brought down the powerful from their thrones, and lifted up the lowly. (Luke 1:49, 51-52)

Two points conclude this chapter and prepare for our next consideration of Christ's presence in the feast of bread and wine, shared in grateful memory and thanks. The first issue is that the primary symbols of the liturgy do "work" *ex opere operato*, through God's promise and guarantee of grace-filled presence in Word and assembly, presider and gifts. But the *ritual clarity* of those primary symbols set out and in juxtaposition with one another, as liturgical theologian Gordon Lathrop would say,[46] as well as the spaciousness that circulates around them that attentive rhythm allows, remains primarily the presider's care and responsibility. If the leader of prayer acts in harmony with this relational, dialogical, and participative dynamic, the assembly acts with greater clarity and truth. "A Word that will rouse them" (Isa 50:4) preached with faith and conviction and love, bread that can be broken from the one loaf and wine poured out for all, and ritual leadership in prayer that empties itself out and allows itself to receive and be filled—the clarity of these in consort with one another allows the liturgy to release its beauty and harmony, as the conductor's hand orchestrates the music.

The final point involves the presider in these times of complex cultural and theological shift. A *kenotic* spirituality of liturgical leadership summons hearts with a willingness (rather than a willfulness) to live in ambiguity and even "cross-fire" status, because the social interactions in which the church is embedded often use the liturgy as a battleground to enact symbolic struggles much larger than any local assembly or particular rubric at issue. The worship of the People of God is always eschatological in its meaning and *more* than any role distinctions and symbolic boundaries of access to the sacred we may

---

[46] Gordon Lathrop, *Holy Things: A Liturgical Theology* (Minneapolis: Augsburg, 1993), see 10–11.

construct in order to insure fidelity to the tradition. As Mechthild of Magdeburg declared so strikingly, "God has enough of all good things except one: Of communion with humans God can never have enough."[47] Abundant communion flows from the heart of God and is generative and life-giving. Presiders who enter that pool of desire experience that fruitfulness. They are "Reeds of God," as Caryll Houselander reminded us so poignantly, that sing the song of the Spirit flowing through them. They are the spacious cups that hold the water of life and the cupped hands that nest the fledgling birds.[48] In turn, the priestly People of God respond in kind with joyful tending in return. If we trust the liturgy in its fullness, this *will* happen, *ex opere operato*. Christ is present, "the one whole Word of God." Presiders of the liturgy are "servants of Christ and stewards of God's mysteries" (1 Cor 4:1) in a way that gathers this multivalent treasure into holy communion. First Peter gives us food once again for consideration of the grace at hand:

> Like good stewards of the manifold grace of God, serve one another with whatever gift each of you has received. Whoever speaks must do so as one speaking the very words of God; whoever serves must do so with the strength that God supplies, so that God may be glorified in all things through Jesus Christ. To him belong the glory and the power forever and ever. Amen. (1 Pet 4:10-11)

---

[47] Woodruff, *Meditations*, 56.
[48] Caryll Houselander, *The Reed of God* (London: Sheed and Ward, 1976), 1.

Chapter 5

Eating and Drinking the Ineffable Mystery: Christ's Presence in the Holy Gifts

We taste thee, O thou living Bread, And long to feast upon thee still;
We drink thee, the fountain-head, And thirst our souls from thee to fill.

—Saint Bernard of Clairvaux, twelfth century[1]

The final part of our study moves to the sacramental presence of Christ in the consecrated gifts of bread and wine, broken and poured out at the table of the Eucharist for the community to eat and drink in grateful memory. This communion event intensifies all that has been unfolding throughout this book, for it is a ritual action that expresses the reality that it signifies: Christ actively present *to* us, *for* us, and *with* us as risen and glorified Lord, expressed in a sign and symbol (i.e., communing as one Body) of the unity in mission that participates in God's redemptive dialogue with all creation. Christ is essentially at the center of this "Mystery of Faith, that is, the ineffable gift of the Eucharist,"[2] as both the Father's Word of grace and the Son's obedient and loving Answer of complete surrender for the life of the world. The Spirit-filled dynamism of this paschal mystery of Christ present in the eucharistic bread and wine does not stand alone here, for the initiative began in the *kenotic* heart of the triune God, and it engages the relational, dialogical, and participative dimensions of the Trinity's way of being in communion with us. It is fitting, therefore, that the most

---

[1] The medieval hymn is from the Latin poem *Jesu, dulcedo cordium* ("Jesus, thou joy of loving hearts"), attributed, perhaps piously, to Bernard. This translation is that of Ray Palmer. See *Hymns Ancient and Modern, Revised* (Great Britain: Hymns Ancient and Modern, 1981), no. 387.

[2] Pope Paul VI, *Mysterium Fidei* (September 3, 1965), 1.

intense expression of this sacramental presence has been and continues to be the eucharistic gifts. The festal table at the liturgy gathers all these dynamic relationships into ritual clarity of expression.

Much scholarship and reflection have considered how and why and where such a presence abides. However, without the context of God's initiating desire, the assembly's coming together to "constitute the Church," the eventful Word spoken and heard that incarnates the mystery, and the presider gathering the community into communion, there is, quite simply, no Blessed Sacrament to commune. The importance of the process that unfolds in the sacramental economy must never be undervalued, for it bodies forth the wholeness of the eucharistic mystery. The tradition has maintained, and teaching documents such as *Sacrosanctum Concilium* (7) and the *Catechism of the Catholic Church* (1374) emphasize that Christ is focally and sacramentally present in the reality of body, blood, soul, and divinity in the species. Indeed, the Catechism goes on to say that in this integral sacramental reality *"the whole Christ is truly and substantially* contained."[3] This understanding of "the whole Christ" is particularly notable here, for it expresses, as well, the *totus Christus*, from which all four modes of sacramental presence derive their efficacy. Vatican II's Instruction on the Worship of the Eucharistic Mystery (*Eucharisticum Mysterium*) concurs that the eucharistic species expresses that presence in a "unique way, whole and entire, God and man, substantially and permanently."[4] The special nature of the "fullness" of this "substantial" presence is not at issue here. Nevertheless, the documents note that the other modes of presence are indeed *real*, and, as such, are distinct but inseparable from this *totus Christus*. A caveat in the Instruction tries to reconcile the unique and special presence with the reality expressed in the sacramental celebration, using the words of Paul VI in the encyclical *Mysterium Fidei*:

> The presence of Christ under the species "is called 'real' not in an exclusive sense, as if the other kinds of presence were not real, but *par excellence*."[5]

Yet, the documents and instructions do not say anything further in the matter, and the meaning of these different modes is left ambiguous. On one level, such ambiguity is understandable and even more

[3] See also Council of Trent (1551); DS 1651.
[4] EM (May 25, 1967), 9.
[5] Ibid., MF 39: AAS 57 (1965), 764.

faithful to the mystery. On another level, the "fullness of presence" is left with no sacramental context to hold its sacredness without the liturgy as the bearer of this meaning. Again, we ask the same question we explored in the first chapter: How can we hold the liturgical metaphors of real presence and abundant abiding in creative tension?

The liturgical relationships of these modes of presence provide a key to clarify the presence and to keep the tensive nature of pure gift in balance. Such *liturgical* understanding of these modes of presence precisely tries to avoid what de Lubac called "dialectical antitheses" and embrace the dynamism of the liturgy that holds them together as "symbolic inclusions." The wholeness of the "one whole Word of God"—Jesus Christ, risen and glorified and abiding in our midst (John 15:7)—keeps together the depth and meaning of the sacramental encounter. In fact, when theological discourse drifts toward precise definitions and philosophical distinctions of eucharistic presence, the essential presence of Christ in the Blessed Sacrament becomes, in our imaginations and practices, separated from the rich depths of relational, dialogical, and participative encounter that precisely bodies forth *communion* as the sign and reality of the Spirit-filled resurrected Body of Christ, who feeds the deepest hungers of the world. One could suggest here elements of an interesting *koan* of sorts: Do bread and wine need a body in order to be food? Is a body who thinks about food but does not taste the nourishing fare left satiated or hungry? Jesus insists, even at the risk of scandal, that this embraces the spiritual nourishment he offers for eternal life: "for my flesh is true food and my blood is true drink" (John 6:55). How does sacramentality as the mode of ecclesial identity necessitate relationship, dialogue, and participation in considering this eucharistic presence of Christ?

Papal encyclicals, council documents, and rigorous theological studies have wrestled with this wondrous gift and have nurtured centuries of devotional literature, rites, and practices to express what is, in the end, "an inexhaustible mystery which the Church can never fully explain in words," as the United States bishops remarked in their 2001 doctrinal and catechetical study titled The Real Presence of Jesus Christ in the Sacrament of the Eucharist: Basic Questions and Answers.[6] Christ's presence in the bread and wine at Eucharist is

---

[6] USCCB, June 15, 2001 (Washington, DC: United States Conference of Catholic Bishops). Of special and more recent note, see Pius XII, *Mediator Dei* (Nov. 20, 1947); Paul VI, *Mysterium Fidei* (Sept. 3, 1965); Vatican II's constitution

deep and unshakeable from a Catholic perspective and is a matter of growing consensus in ecumenical dialogue about the Eucharist.[7] We know this to be true in our bones, and yet there is still this hunger for the wondrous mystery that many feel was communicated more clearly in a Tridentine expression of the rite that yielded a profound cult of the real presence of Christ, understood primarily and especially in the sacred Host. Given the depth of a liturgical dynamic that sees these four modes of presence in rhythm and harmony at their very depths, an argument can be made that such a venerable eucharistic devotion still awaits our deeper appropriation of the "nature of the liturgy" that Vatican II envisioned and that will take long, faithful practice and prayerful reflection to appreciate.

Regress to a former period of eucharistic practice, especially one where the participative and dialogical relationship of the assembly with the presider in Word and Sacrament was not primary and clear, will not answer that ultimate longing over time. The Second Vatican Council, in word and deed, begged us to "listen to what the Spirit is saying to the churches" (Rev 2:7), particularly in our sacramental identity as an ecclesial Body in the world;[8] in how we hear and preach the Word as divinely revealed, especially its inseparability as part of "one table" of Word and Sacrament;[9] and in the manner in which we celebrate that fullness at the eucharistic feast as the source and summit

---

Sacrosanctum Concilium (Dec. 4, 1963); John Paul II, *Dominicae Cenae* (Feb. 24, 1980) and *Ecclesia de Eucharistia* (Apr. 17, 2003); Benedict XVI, *Sacramentum Caritatis* (Feb. 22, 2007). The theological and spiritual works will be noted throughout the chapter. The richness and variety express the centrality of this mystery in the identity and life of the Christian people.

[7] Taizé brother Max Thurian's ecumenical approach, *The Mystery of the Eucharist*, trans. Emily Chisholm (Grand Rapids: Eerdmans, 1983), is a classic in this regard to convergence in the churches regarding eucharistic presence, as well as the notion of a sacrifice of praise and thanksgiving. See also the World Council of Churches' document *Baptism, Eucharist, and Ministry* (Geneva, 1982) and the various Orthodox, Anglican, and Roman responses; George Hunsinger, *The Eucharist and Ecumenism: Let Us Keep the Feast* (New York: Cambridge University Press, 2008) is an important recent book from a Reformed perspective.

[8] Cf. *Lumen Gentium* (LG), esp. chaps. 1 and 2; *Gaudium et Spes* (GS), esp. the preface, introduction, and chap. 4.

[9] Cf. *Dei Verbum* (DV), esp. chaps. 2 and 3; on the one table, DV VI 21 and *Sacrosanctum Concilium*, 56.

of our Christian life.[10] Such a vision implies a reimagining of all those relationships and the centrality of the Eucharist within that sacramental economy. The current, and often bitter, tension in our practice is a tensive indicator of the importance of the Eucharist in our lives. Throughout all this, the Holy Spirit remains faithful, Christ abides abundantly, and the apostle Paul keeps confirming that "inexhaustible mystery" of God's ways with us when he utters out of that Spirit, "O the depth of the riches and the wisdom and the knowledge of God!" (Rom 11:33). Such trust and awe characterize the only attitude and gift the faithful can offer in this sacramental exchange of gifts (v. 35), a response to the abundance that comes from the heart of God. A contemporary spirituality and piety of liturgical practice, therefore, "gathers and does not scatter" (Matt 12:30).

Our present consideration of the eucharistic food and drink draws upon the dynamic of the first four chapters and is liturgical in nature, affirming the rhythm and harmony of all these sacramental modes that together resonate with God's mighty acts in Jesus now present in our midst and shaping us as the *totus Christus* in praise of God and in service of the world. Rather than diminish the focal reality of the real presence of Christ in the sacramental species, their liturgical role as food and drink that is life and pure gift for the people emerges with greater clarity and focus. Thomas Aquinas's text that stirred Christians for centuries on the feast of Corpus Christi still moves in our liturgical piety and spirituality, which remembers and celebrates and believes the future fullness in hope to which we commend ourselves in this meal of thanksgiving:

> *O sacrum convivium!*
> *in quo Christus sumitur:*
> *recolitur memoria passionis ejus:*
> *mens impletur gratia:*
> *et futurae gloriae nobis pignus datur.*
> *Alleluia.*
>
> O sacred banquet!
> in which Christ is received,
> the memory of his Passion is renewed,
> the mind is filled with grace,
> and a pledge of future glory to us is given.
> Alleluia.

[10] Cf. esp. SC 1–10.

Centuries of debate and anathemas have marred and muted that song of union and communion. They continue to the present day. A liturgical approach, the context in which the "inexhaustible mystery" unfolds, reminds us of its origin in God and of our humble and awesome responsibility to respond in praise and thanks, to unite ourselves with Christ, in what is pure gift, food for the journey, and a taste of the fullness to come. "O taste and see that the LORD is good; happy are those who take refuge in him" (Ps 34:8).

THE TRINITARIAN DYNAMISM OF CHRIST'S PRESENCE IN THE EUCHARISTIC MEAL

> In his longed-for shade I am seated and his fruit is sweet to my
>   taste.
> He has taken me to his banquet hall, and the banner he raises
>   over me is love.
>
> —Song of Songs 2:3b-4, Jerusalem Bible

In this chapter, the presence of Christ as food and drink will be explored through the communion of the trinitarian life itself. Father, Son, and Holy Spirit, in a self-emptying love, manifest that surrender and the life in which we are called to participate, through the relationship that binds them in a dialogue of mutual self-offering. Communion is the true nature of the Trinity. The generativity of that offering animates everything that is. That is why we will begin by acknowledging the Father's creative presence *to*, *for*, and *with* the Beloved of his heart, delighting and radiating the Love that can never be for itself alone but must be shared with the Beloved.

This naturally flows into a consideration of the Son's obedient response of love for the Father, which embodies the same *kenotic* expression, emptying himself and "being born in human likeness," humbling himself and being exalted in that self-offering in order to be life *to*, *for*, and *with* us (Phil 2:6-11). The character of this mutual sharing of gift and self characterizes the communion that we share as the bread of life and the cup of eternal salvation.

The Holy Spirit's role in the transformation of the gifts and the assembly will then be seen as this generative Love outpoured,[11] the agent and bond of that abundant and abiding presence in the bread

---

[11] Cf. chap. 1, n. 12.

and wine, which feeds and sanctifies and gives life to those who it. This is the occasion of the church's act of praise and thanks.

> Look, O Lord, upon the Sacrifice which you yourself have provided for your Church, and grant in your loving kindness to all who partake of this one Bread and one Chalice that, gathered into one body by the Holy Spirit, they may truly become a living sacrifice in Christ to the praise of your glory. (Eucharistic Prayer IV)

Finally, we will see how that communion draws us into holy communion on a level that is real and sacramental, because it consecrates the assembly to participate in the eucharistic event, not as bystanders, but as engaged actors in a redemptive mystery that gathers past into a present that orients the future wholeness, whose fullness we taste now as "the Mystery of Faith, the ineffable gift." The Catechism makes this clear by insisting,

> In the Eucharist the sacrifice of Christ becomes also the sacrifice of the members of his Body. The lives of the faithful, their praise, sufferings, prayer, and work, are united with those of Christ and with his total offering and so acquire new value. Christ's presence on the altar makes it possible for all generations of Christians to be united with his offering. (1368)

The trajectory of this final chapter draws that new reality of the *totus Christus* into the dynamism of the whole liturgy. The eucharistic elements are placed by Christ in relationship to himself and the community: we eat and drink in grateful memory, having heard a Word that will rouse us to approach the table in faith; we offer thanksgiving and intercession in the Spirit of that Word once again spoken anew; we open our hands to become what we receive because the invitation of the Beloved summons us. Edward Kilmartin describes this union of mutual self-offering:

> The comprehensive shape of meaning of the Eucharist reflects the fact that the Eucharist constitutes the central self-realization of the Church of Jesus Christ that occurs at the level of liturgical action. For this celebration has a katabatic-anabatic basic structure in and through which God and people are bound together. This binding happens through the actualization of the covenantal relationship in which the (katabatic) self-gift of the Father through Christ in the Holy Spirit to human beings finds the

faith response of the (anabatic) self-gift of human beings through Christ in the Holy Spirit to the Father.[12]

Separation has no reality here: "This is my Body. This is my Blood. Do this in memory of me." Nourished in a bond of identity rooted in God's own self-gift, the church is now consecrated and fashioned for mission. *Ite missa est. Deo gratias.*

GOD THE FATHER AS GIVER OF ALL GOOD GIFTS: EUCHARISTIC GIFTS THAT SPEAK COMMUNION

I know their sufferings, and I have come down to deliver them . . . and to bring them up out of that land to a good and broad land, a land flowing with milk and honey.

—Exodus 3:7b-8

How, then, does God, the Father, source of all life and love, draw us into communion with the Trinity's own life of mutual exchange of the gift of love, and how do the eucharistic gifts participate in that act of grace? As we noted in chapter 1, God is Love, and passion is the river of energy that unites us with the divine life. Such Love, infused with this passion for creation—which God saw and called "very good" (Gen 1:31)—is generative and self-emptying, and reaches out *to* and *for* and *with* the object of God's desire. Such loving is not a static state of being or reality but dynamic and life-giving precisely in its desire. Fresh from the activity of creation, God immediately proceeds to "plant a garden in Eden" and out of its ground growing things and the flowing river set the passionate mode of encounter in motion (Gen 2:8-15).

Such iconic images can never capture the immensity of pure desire at work here, but it should situate our eucharistic practice within its embrace. Food and drink, watering and feeding, and placing the Beloved in this fruitful place where they can wander in it and experience the gifts that Eden offers are apt images for what we do when we situate ourselves within the liturgical space of corporate worship, the

---

[12] Edward Kilmartin, *The Eucharist in the West: History and Theology*, ed. Robert J. Daly (Collegeville, MN: Liturgical Press, 1998), 341. Kilmartin says earlier that eucharistic praying "articulates a theology of covenant" that inaugurates the new dispensation Christ brings, i.e., "the mystery of the economy of the triune God in relation to the new people of God, the social body of which the crucified and risen Lord is head" (340).

sacramental expression of our gathering to "constitute the Church," as Alexander Schmemann has noted so poignantly.[13] For these holy things, "which earth has given and human hands have made," we bless the Giver as we prepare the table for the feast, and beg that they may become for us "the bread of life" and "our spiritual drink." Everything that is good, nurturing and nourishing, medicinal and life-giving, shares in that gifted passion that flows from the heart of the Creator and Lord of all the earth.

We spoke throughout the book of an interior disposition and attention that awakens the community to share in the flame of the burning heart of the Giver, which Jesus uncovers for the weary pilgrims on the road, after their deep disillusion leaves them wandering on the road to Emmaus in Luke 24:13-35. In Jesus' testimony of the Scriptures and in response to their desire to "Stay with us," his true reality as glorified Lord and abiding gift is "made known to them in the breaking of the bread." This liturgical context makes known a desire that is hidden from us when we rely upon our own reasoning and ways of proceeding. The Giver is revealed in the gift and the promise from which it flows. The disciples come to know him as present to them in a new mode through the dynamism of hearing the Word and sharing the table. "Then their eyes were opened, and they recognized him; and he vanished from their sight" (cf. Luke 24:28-35). Their interior disposition and outward attention to what he said and did is experienced and expanded with a new understanding. That same desire enacted in Word and Sacrament by the church today awaits the same reawakening. It is the fruit of faithful worship.

Easter is the defining moment and experience for all disciples, as Nathan Mitchell has explored so beautifully, employing postmodern theologians such as Louis-Marie Chauvet and Jean-Luc Marion. Out of what Mitchell calls a "new starting-point" for considering the sacramental economy and the "eucharist as 'presence' and 'gift,'" everything is utterly new, rewritten, and, following Marion's point, "we have to 'relearn everything.'" As he says about this Easter "innovation" spoken of by such contemporaries,

> Jesus' resurrection rewrites our world as the site, the space, the story, the new narrative that utterly surpasses any notions of presence and

---

[13] Schmemann, *For the Life of the World* (Crestwood, NY: St. Vladimir's Seminary Press, 1988), 27. See also chap. 2, n. 11.

causality based on empirical observation and measurement. This is, of course, supremely hard to conceptualize, because in our experience to be a body means one has to be *somewhere*, has to be *located*, has to *occupy space*, has to fill a site with the quantitative dimensions that make you a real, physical object in a real, physical world. Easter's innovation is counterintuitive because it compels us to talk "real presence" without relying on "empirical place."[14]

Christ's body, then, needs our communal body to embody the self-offering "in our time and for our flesh."[15] In terms of God's creative activity in the liturgical context of the relational modes of presence, we could add that Christ needs our liturgical body so that the mighty deeds of God revealed in the risen Lord Jesus can truly be, as 1 John says, "what was from the beginning, what we have heard, what we have seen with our eyes, what we have looked at and touched with our hands, concerning the word of life" (1:1b-2). The abiding promise of the Father takes flesh in the believing community communing the Body and Blood of Christ. The abundant food is not sufficient in and of itself to express this mystery. That is why the risen Jesus takes from the yield of the net full of fish and invites them: "Come and have breakfast" (John 21:12). The gifts must be engaged to reveal the sacramental dynamism for which they were consecrated. As we said at the beginning of the chapter, unless the passion flows from the heart of the Father and takes shape in the redemptive event of the Son, and unless the church hears the Word and is convicted by it so that they offer themselves in union with Christ's own self-offering and share the covenant meal in the hallowing of the Spirit, there is no consecrated species and no Blessed Sacrament.

---

[14] Nathan Mitchell, "Mystery and Manners: Eucharist in Post-Modern Theology," *Worship* (March 2005): 140. This piece, along with The Amen Corner series on "presence" Mitchell wrote for *Worship* in 2006, are deeply penetrating and poetic explorations of the notion of "real presence," for which I am most grateful. See esp. vol. 80, no. 6 (November 2006): 551–66. Mitchell's expanded version of *Real Presence: The Work of Eucharist* (Chicago: Liturgy Training Publications, 2001) did much to open up these contemporary studies of sacramental presence from a postmodern context.

[15] Mitchell, "Mystery and Manners," 141. He is quoting Jean-Yves Lacoste, "Presence and Parousia," in *Postmodern Theology*, ed. Graham Ward (Oxford: Blackwell Publishers, 2001), 395.

To return to Nathan Mitchell's insistence about the necessity of a body, he clarifies that sacramental reality in this way:

> Christ's *presence needs to have a body built for it*—and this is precisely the work of the Holy Spirit who acts in Eucharist, in church, and in the glorified humanity of the Lord who, by these very means, makes himself over to us as a gift, "gives himself as a *present*" by that same Spirit.[16]

Considering Marion's notion that our world then becomes new as a "Christic site," even more so "a manifestly trinitarian site," Mitchell speaks of the disciples' Emmaus experience as the journey of trust and companionship and engagement with the mystery—Word and meal—that allows them to break away from an idolatrous clinging to Jesus in the way they had hoped and desired, so that they can be transfigured and consecrated in a new reality that draws close and intimate precisely in his going away, his ascension, the gift that is now a "presence of absence." Following the similar thought of Chauvet in *Symbol and Sacrament*, he concludes:

> For this reason, Christ's presence to us in the eucharist may be (indeed, *must be*) inscribed on our bodies, although it can never be *circumscribed* in a place. Thus, too, the "here" of Eucharistic presence—while not an empirical "here"—always refers us back to the body, to its history and particularity, to its communion with others. Presence needs to have a body built for it, because God is "not 'nowhere in particular'; God is *somewhere*."[17]

Lest we find solace in a definitive location, "a closed object, an edible loaf," Mitchell adds this dynamic nature of the sacramental species:

> But of course that loaf is meant to be broken—so much so, says Chauvet, that "the great *sacramentum* of Christ's presence is not the bread as such in its unbroken state. Or rather, it is indeed the bread, but *in its very essence*, bread-as-food, bread-as-meal, bread-for-sharing. *It is in the breaking of the bread that its ultimate reality is manifested*," and

---

[16] Ibid., 141. He is following the insights of Marion in "The Gift of Presence," in *Prolegomena to Charity*, trans. Stephen Lewis (New York: Fordham University Press, 2002), 146.

[17] Ibid., 141–44. He is quoting Chauvet in *Symbol and Sacrament: A Sacramental Reinterpretation of Christian Existence*, trans. Madeleine Beaumont and Patrick Madigan (Collegeville, MN: Liturgical Press, 1995), 405.

hence "the breaking of the bread is the *symbol par excellence* of the *adesse* of Christ giving [us] his life."[18]

The necessity of the body requires, then, a dynamic nuance of a broken and shared loaf, a communal meal event, in order to be, as the ecclesial documents attest, a presence "par excellence."

The specifically trinitarian nature of this redefined place of Easter/ascension—the new garden of God's visitation—relies on the redefined order of relationships that Jesus' resurrection came to announce. This is where God's passion, the Father's *kenotic* sending of the Son, and Jesus' response in obedient Love are generative in the Spirit's overflowing of that passion and desire into all created reality. In this new reality, as the Pentecost gathering in Acts marveled at but could not control, the community is enabled to speak the wonders of God in diverse languages and experiences, and yet—what a mystery!—all can understand (Acts 2:6). The garden of God's creative passion now is in our midst, although it awaits its eschatological fullness. Yet, we glimpse it *here*, albeit "in a mirror, dimly, but then we will see face to face. Now [we] know only in part; then [we] will know fully, even as [we] have been fully known" (1 Cor 13:12).

As the scoffers in Jerusalem say in response to this mighty ingathering by the Spirit, "They are filled with new wine" (Acts 2:13). Perhaps this is truer than they thought. The garden and its fruits have come to us. We are no longer bound by the "old dispensation," as T. S. Eliot describes the magi's encounter with the incarnate Messiah.[19] We are "no longer at ease" in the isolated, separated, "theoretical antitheses" of Babel's confusion. In the liturgy, the garden returns. We make our way back home again. The never-ending road to Emmaus all makes sense; the ritual meal, as for the disciples, is the fullest expression par excellence of that encounter.

We can now with greater clarity return to the question posed at the beginning of this section: How, then, does God, the Father, source of all life and love, draw us into communion with the Trinity's own life

---

[18] Ibid., 144; Chauvet, *Symbol and Sacrament*, 406.
[19] T. S. Eliot, "Journey of the Magi." The poem ends with the lines:
> We returned to our places, these Kingdoms,
> But no longer at ease here, in the old dispensation,
> With an alien people clutching their gods.
> I should be glad of another death.

of mutual exchange of the gift of love, and how do the eucharistic gifts participate in that act of grace? The eucharistic meal, we can now affirm, begins at the moment of creation, when God's triune desire for communion with us is spoken: "Let us make humankind in our image, according to our likeness" (Gen 1:26). And this communal God immediately shapes the garden, and the garden bears the fruits of the earth and the river of life (2:8-10). This is the stuff of bread and wine. God the Creator, the one Jesus called Father, is encountered as the source and Giver of all good gifts.

This bringing together of the Beloved and the holy place, with the spoken Word of promise and the fruit of the field and the vine, inaugurates the procession into the heart of God that Alexander Schmemann says helps us understand how the eucharistic liturgy is "the journey of the Church into the dimension of the Kingdom."[20] Just as Mitchell, Chauvet, Marion, and others will highlight years later, this Orthodox perspective of the Easter experience of the church demands an *engaged faith* that is utterly new in language, vision, and way of living in the world. The liturgy, Schmemann says, is the privileged moment when this desire of God is so transparent that the worshiping church arrives "at a vantage point from which we can see more deeply into the reality of the world." Eucharistic praying, as we noted in chapter 2, is "our sacramental entrance into the risen life of Christ" and the "presence of Christ" experienced in a wholly new dimension. God's delight in creation, the radiating Love that is shared *to, with,* and *for* God's Beloved, now energizes and shapes creation's deepest harmony and rhythm. The liturgy is nothing less than a privileged moment of that vibrant song that God first uttered from the heart, that can never be for itself alone, and is spoken to us in that Word-made-flesh who dwells among us. As Schmemann has said, this "is not an escape from the world" but the arrival into reality at its deepest depths;[21] the liturgy enacts God's passion revealed, the garden promise to God's own beloved images (Gen 1:26). The food and drink of the garden celebrate the communion. Whenever the people forget this divinely creative activity, and the scriptural testimony Jesus recounts to the bewildered travelers is evidence of this, the summons is always announced anew, on any road and at any time. Slavery in Egypt, the people's hunger and enmity and meaninglessness, all find new form in every age, and so God's desire

---

[20] Schmemann, *For the Life of the World*, 26.
[21] Ibid., 27.

revealed to Moses promises that we too have a home in which to find our true identity and that houses a table where we will be fed:

> Indeed, I know their sufferings, and I have come down to deliver them . . . and to bring them up out of that land to a good and broad land, a land flowing with milk and honey. (Exod 3:7b-8)

We eat and drink our new relationship with God and one another within a new place, a new reality, and a new Word to speak its truth: "This is my Body . . . Take and eat. This is my Blood, poured out for you . . . Take and drink." The liturgy participates in God's desire and passion and tends the garden of visitation. As the seventeenth-century metaphysical poet George Herbert says of this insistent Love that abides despite our own resistance, "'You must sit down . . . and taste my meat.'/So I did sit and eat" ("Love"). Pure gift and real food in an "ineffable mystery" speak communion.

Liturgical Implications for Eucharistic Gifts that Speak Communion

What role does God's passion play in the practical enactment of the liturgy shaped by the Father's desire? The eucharistic liturgy should manifest the gift Giver's abundance clearly, given the dynamic of the creative act that makes everything that is good and shapes a garden to house creation, allowing the plants and living beings to grow and be food and drink for human persons, the image of God. Bread and wine, "fruit of the earth and work of human hands," ought to look and feel and be provided as food and drink. At the very least, it seems, a significant part of the bread should be one loaf or piece, "meant to be broken," as Chauvet has said. Indeed, the fraction rite must resume its important focal role in the enactment of the mystery, or else the dynamic nature of *our* participation and communion with Christ's loving Answer to the Father in mutual self-offering is muted and veiled by obfuscation. The wine mixed with water—Christ's *kenotic* sharing of our humanity so that we may be sharing in divinity—should be poured out in that fraction rite; the relationship between the lifeblood of Christ as "this fountain of sacramental life in the church" gives heightened clarity to the spiritual reality of the new garden's fruits in our midst and the new reality in which we live.[22]

---

[22] The arguments about the danger of spilling in the fraction rite are not strong enough to minimize the fraction rite. Trained eucharistic ministers

Furthermore, withholding the cup from the assembly or offering the eucharistic Body of Christ to them solely from the reserved sacrament in the tabernacle mutes the power of what Augustine calls this "sign of unity and bond of charity"[23] the sacramental elements express par excellence. As *Eucharisticum Mysterium* remarked so clearly,

> In order that, even through signs, the communion may be seen more clearly to be participation in the sacrifice which is being celebrated, care should be taken to enable the faithful to communicate with hosts consecrated during the Mass. (31)

> Holy Communion, considered as a sign, has a fuller form when it is received under both kinds. For under this form . . . the sign of the Eucharistic banquet appears more perfectly. Moreover, it is clearly shown how the new and eternal Covenant is ratified in the Blood of the Lord, as it also expresses the relation of the Eucharistic banquet to the eschatological banquet in the Kingdom of the Father (cf. Mt. 26:27-29). (32)

The examples demonstrate the insistence that the signs be employed in their fullness. The relationship of the eucharistic gifts to the covenantal promise that restores the garden to humankind in right relationship finds focal expression in *the wholeness and completeness of the primary symbols.*

Raniero Cantalamessa, in *The Eucharist: Our Sanctification*, notes how the early Christians reverenced and celebrated the wholeness of the signs, and so "we cannot but notice how far we have moved away from its original character." He goes on to speak of the slow movement toward withdrawing the cup from practice and devotion. In that light, he observes, "the Blood of Christ seems to be the 'poor relative,' an appendix of the Body of Christ, with the result that the Eucharist seems to signify more the mystery of the incarnation rather than the passion."[24] In terms of Semmelroth, the redemptive dialogue of incarnation (Word) and saving death (Answer) is cut off and muted in our celebrations and in our piety.

---

know their responsibilities. One might suggest such an injunction should be evaluated from the perspective of further "separating" the distinctive roles in an ordered assembly.

[23] See Augustine's "Commentary on the Gospel of St. John," John 6:51.

[24] Raniero Cantalamessa, *The Eucharist, Our Sanctification*, rev. ed., trans. Frances Lonergan Villa (Collegeville, MN: Liturgical Press, 1995), 40–41.

The procession of the liturgy moves into the new dimension of the kingdom, where the new way of being in the world has begun, and the "old dispensation" no longer holds. Any ritual enactment that devolves into what the presider has and does as opposed to what the worshiping assembly is allowed to have and do (and not do) does not honor the inseparable "distinctions" that are rightfully part of the order of celebration that proclaims "one whole Word of God." Rather, the distinctions are distorted, because they communicate "separations" that are enigmatic to the unity of the Body of Christ that the eucharistic proclaims. We will look at more of these issues in the next two sections, but suffice to say at this point that the actors and actions and material elements of the liturgy are sacramentally *significant*, and should be in harmony with the reality they effect.

The rhythm of participation, dialogue, and relationship with the Giver of all good gifts asks this attentiveness of us, given that we have been entrusted with the sacred mysteries so that the "new and everlasting covenant" always might be available in its integrity, for the life of the world. The Body needs a body built for it that is suitable and that sings the praises of God's saving acts in Jesus. Attention to the fullness of the signs of bread and wine respects this and sets itself within a garden that is unambiguously, as Marion has said, "a manifestly trinitarian site."[25]

CHRIST PRESENT IN BREAD AND WINE: REAL FOOD AND REAL DRINK IN A NEW REALITY

> . . . for my flesh is true food and my blood is true drink. Those who eat my flesh and drink my blood abide in me, and I in them. Just as the living Father sent me, and I live because of the Father, so whoever eats me will live because of me.
>
> —John 6:55-57

In many ways, the real presence of Christ in the bread and wine seems so ingrained in our liturgical bones that further discussion hardly seems necessary. How that happens and what it means, as we have mentioned, fills libraries of great thinkers and spiritual writers through the centuries. The importance in this exploration is not the reality or truth of the sacramental mystery in bread and wine but the

---

[25] Cf. n. 16.

spiritual richness of that presence *to, for*, and *with* us encountered in eucharistic praying. Jesus engages in the discussion of real food and real drink in the context of words that speak "spirit and life" (John 6:63), radically consecrating those who encounter his words. "Those who eat my flesh and drink my blood abide in me, and I in them" (John 6:56). The truth of the flesh and blood is essentially linked to *eating and drinking* in this passage, but this necessary and essentially corporal and vital act of life reaches to the level of deepest reality, of "substance," as the traditional teaching articulated it.[26] We are not simply gazing at a mystery but engaging it at the level of "spirit and life." Yet, this is not, as some Reformers claimed, a merely spiritual eating or a testimony of a once-and-for-all event, although these aspects are certainly present in eucharistic memorial. The utter materiality of this eventful action is the source of scandal and intense reflection by the disciples who hear it. As some say, "This teaching is difficult; who can accept it?" (6:60). Truly the divisions in the Body of Christ attest to that struggle to receive in faith a reality grounded in something as basic as eating and drinking, while at the same time speaking a new reality that is "inexhaustible" and "ineffable." Luther wanted to maintain the meal practice without resorting to what he saw as metaphysical wizardry. His desire was to maintain the pure giftedness of the event and to encourage communion.[27] Calvin and Zwingli, although with different emphases, focused on the sign value as a testimony to Christ's offer of redemption, the union with Christ that only the Spirit's interior transformation of the believer can accomplish, although they differed widely on the relationship between "symbolic memorialism/instrumentalism/parallelism" in the ritual act of the meal.[28] Indeed,

[26] A few recent examples of many include the 2001 catechetical instruction of the US bishops, The Real Presence of Jesus Christ in the Sacrament of the Eucharist, 3; John Paul II, *Eucharistia de Ecclesiae* (April 17, 2003); *Mysterium Fidei*, 3; CCC 1375–76. All refer to the Council of Trent (1551): DS 1651 as the primary articulation of the "whole Christ" present substantially in the sacrament.

[27] For examples of both Luther's belief in real presence (and his debates with others) as well as his critique of the Roman notion of transubstantiation, see *Luther's Works*, 36:29; 37:4–150.

[28] David Power maintains that for most Reformers, as well as for Romans, the disagreements over real presence involved a struggle to find words for a mystery in which they all fundamentally believed. See *The Eucharistic Mystery: Revitalizing the Tradition* (New York: Crossroad, 1992), 256. George Hunsinger, in *Eucharist and Ecumenism*, makes the same claim, while offering an Orthodox

the plethora of attempts to nuance this sacramental presence in eating and drinking accentuates the "substantial" nature of this act.

Roman Catholic tradition is not immune from this reluctance to engage the dynamic materiality of the meal, as evidenced by the growing infrequency of the reception of communion historically, as well as the prohibition of touching the Host and the excommunication of the faithful from drinking from the cup. All Christian denominations struggle both with our rational understanding *and* with the absolute intimacy of the act. Only faithful practice of eucharistic communion holds the two in tension and leads to that *sentir* ("felt knowledge") of which St. Ignatius always returns in the *Spiritual Exercises* as the fruit of deep companionship with Christ and the Father's desire he was sent to announce.[29]

The second-century African Tertullian cuts to the heart of the struggle here with a startling acclamation of the relationship we share to the gifts God offers, the very Body and Blood of Christ. Tertullian says, "The flesh is the hinge of salvation (*adeo caro salutis est cardo*) . . . the flesh feeds on the body and blood of Christ that the soul may also feast [lit. "be fattened"] on God."[30] The Latin here is illuminating, because *cardo* ("the hinge of a door") is also translated in classical Latin dictionaries as "the point round which anything turns, a pole of the heavens."[31] *Caro* ("flesh") becomes the way into "substance," the deepest reality where the "new dispensation," the marriage of heaven and earth, finds its anchor and direction. This is what the traditional doctrine means by Christ's sacramental and real presence "especially" or "par excellence" in the gifts of bread and wine. In St. Thomas's description, the eucharistic presence in bread and wine embodies "the

---

perspective to bridge the divide; see esp. part I on "Real Presence," 19–92. For an account of Calvin's insistence on regular eucharistic sharing and the drift of contemporary Reformed practice from this, see Laurence Sibley, "The Church as Eucharistic Community: Observations on John Calvin's Early Eucharistic Theology (1536–1545)," *Worship* 81, no. 3 (May 2007): 249–67. The World Council of Churches' *Baptism, Eucharist, and Ministry*, Faith and Order Paper No. 111 (Geneva, 1982), sets out the issues for much of the ecumenical discussion over the past few decades.

[29] Cf. chap. 4, n. 35.

[30] Tertullian, *De Resurrectione Carnis*, 8. This translation is from *Corpus Christianorum*, vol. 1, and is quoted in *The Real Presence Through the Ages*, compiled and edited by Michael Gaudoin-Parker (New York: Alba House, 1993), 27.

[31] Cassell's dictionary in many editions is a classic example.

perfection of the spiritual life and the end to which all the sacraments tend."[32] The material gifts, then, always and necessarily are related to the "end" (*res tantum*)—communion with God, sharing in the Father's communion with the Son, the Spirit's abundant pouring out of that Love upon all who come to taste her fruits. As we noted in the previous section, the "Body needs a body built for it." Bread broken and wine poured out are the hinge of the doorway where our flesh acquires a new reality and identity, *per ipsum, et cum ipso, et in ipso.*

It is only through the channel of this lowly "hinge," this doorway and polestar and centering point that anchors the dance of God's communion with us, that we can begin to contemplate how absolutely intimate and close to us the divine hovers. We do not escape our bodies to commune but enter into the very act that most signals our humanity and its relational bond with the gifts of the earth. Eating and drinking food that is itself so very basic, fruit of the fields and vine and work of human hands, shows how all the relational, participative, and dialogical components of the liturgy find focal expression in the gifts of bread and wine. On the night before he died, Jesus chose these things, in a gathering of Beloved in the Upper Room—the set-apart place where the festal meal is celebrated (Matt 26:17-19)—in the context of remembering another Passover meal (Luke 22:8), where the eating and drinking of food initiate the liberation journey out of slavery into freedom. We cannot underestimate the insistence with which Jesus uses food to embrace all the "symbolic inclusions" of the redemptive mystery, how it situates "the longing to share the Meal with the Beloved" (Luke 22:15), how everything he reveals about the Father and the unity they share (John 17:8) finds its apt expression in this act of eating and drinking in grateful memory. In union with his self-offering on the cross still to be accomplished, he hints at the "new time" when "it is fulfilled in the kingdom of God" (Luke 22:16). All these practical preparations and securing of meal provisions and the memorial context of celebration are bearers of a rich and holy proclamation. They set the stage for a manifestation par excellence.

A reflective reading of John's farewell discourse through the lens of this multivalent and relational perspective of real presence shows us that this really is an "inexhaustible mystery." In so many ways and images, Jesus' communion with the Father and with the Beloved is proclaimed in the context of this gathering. "Believe me that I am in the

---

[32] *Summa Theologiae* III, 73, 3c.

Father and the Father is in me" (14:11), Jesus says repeatedly, a rhythm of mutual self-emptying flowing from the heart of the Father and given flesh, the hinge, in the incarnation of Jesus (Word). That Word is then incarnated in obedient love by Jesus so that he, in the flesh, is revealed as the point around which everything—our flesh, the hinge into our deepest reality—then turns back to the Father in loving surrender and self-gift (Answer). This is not something Jesus does alone but a gathering he longs to enact where the communicants, essential actors in the drama, are gathered into its dynamism. The washing of the feet sequence unique to John 13:1-11 provides another multivalent expression of this mutual self-surrender.

> Jesus, knowing that the Father had given all things into his hands, and that he had come from God and was going to God, got up from the table, took off his outer robe, and tied a towel around himself. (13:3-4)

The mutuality deepens. "Do you know what I have done to you? . . . So if I, your Lord and Teacher, have washed your feet, you also ought to wash one another's feet" (13:13-14). Peter's reluctance to draw so close to the dynamism of this very corporeal and material act is not interpreted by Jesus as some humble deference but is rebuked as inimical to the relationship he came to inaugurate (13:8).

Through all this rich exchange, we see that the meal takes place in a dialogue of Word and Answer, proclamation and response, an invitation that is communal and participative. Semmelroth's redemptive dialogue of Word and Answer is revelatory on so many levels. Its harmony is complex and rich. We feed on it as branches draw life from the vine (15:1-7), so that its *synergy*, as Jean Corbon would speak of it, might be our very lifeblood, where "everything in the body of Christ is raised to life" through the bonding of the Spirit.[33] Even more, the feeding passages in the Synoptics keep returning to this food that

---

[33] Corbon, *Wellspring of Worship*, 147; see also p. 7, where he describes this synergy as a "joint activity" . . . "to express what is novel in the union of God and human being in Christ and, more specifically, what is novel in the energy of the Holy Spirit that permeates the energy of human beings and conforms them to Christ." This notion is inseparable from the term more familiar to the West, that of "epiclesis," as the hallowing of the gifts and the assembly by the Spirit. Such richness is part of the trinitarian dynamic that permeates all the modes of Christ's presence in the sacramental economy.

is discovered to be a divine encounter that always starts with hunger among those who come to Jesus, and with provisions that seem so meager and ordinary and inadequate. "Where are we to get bread in this desert to feed so great a crowd?" (Matt 15:33; also Mark 8:4), the disciples ask. And Jesus lifts his eyes, says the blessing over the fruits of the earth, bids them share it among the multitude, and it is enough—more than enough, miraculously abundant. "And all of them ate and were filled; and they took up the broken pieces left over, seven baskets full" (Matt 15:37).

This taking, blessing, breaking, and sharing of food and drink keeps the people alive in so many dimensions, if they simply realize that what they have "is enough." Food is the vessel for this Body of Christ to have a Body. From that "somewhere," the boundaries and depths of this "substance" reach the sacramental dimensions of union with the triune life and the Father's desire, our identity with Christ as Savior and Redeemer and Companion on the road, and the Spirit-filled, resurrected reality of the community of believers who bear that Body in the world. That communion is not limited to *this* time and *this* place, but it needs *this time and place* of our celebration to draw us into "the dimension of the Kingdom," as Schmemann says, where all the saints and faithful ones of all time gather:

> For this reason they are before the throne of God, and worship him day and night within his temple, and the one who is seated on the throne will shelter them. They will hunger no more, and thirst no more . . . for the Lamb at the center of the throne will be their shepherd, and he will guide them to springs of the water of life, and God will wipe away every tear from their eyes. (Rev 7:15-17)

What starts in the garden as fruit of the vine and field is now the hinge into the "inexhaustible mystery" that keeps unfolding in the church and in the world. The hunger for this "spirit and life" comes to us hidden and waiting to be disclosed on all levels through our communing this simple bread and wine, chosen by Jesus as "my Body" and "my Blood." This is "symbolic inclusion" that should draw us into silent awe and reverence.

Liturgical Implications for Eucharistic Gifts as Real Food and Real Drink in a New Reality

The celebration of the eucharistic liturgy truly participates in the sacramental incarnation of the flesh and blood of Christ, because they are set out within the liturgical economy that is the doorway through which the gifts are "taken, blessed, broken, and shared" in a communion that constitutes the church and consecrates the matter at hand into a new reality. If the sacramental presence of Christ is to be that hinge, "the point around which anything (and everything) turns" in this ritual realm, then what is in rhythmic harmony with that polestar "bodies forth" the proclamation of the "ineffable mystery." The meal elements of bread and wine cooperate with this embodiment. In the previous section, we spoke of the importance of the bread and wine, broken and poured out, to be what they are enacted to be. The fraction rite and the commonality of the gifts provided pertinent examples in liturgical practice that mirror the gracious garden of their fashioning in the Father's heart.

With those implications affirmed, we can consider additional aspects of liturgical practice that flow from the Christ's interpersonal and relational gift of self revealed in real food and drink, which gives a taste of the Kingdom (*res tantum*) and impels us toward its fullness. If we consider, for example, the Son's reality as the Father's pure gift and Word that comes down from heaven to feed all human longing, then some aspects of "manna" from the Scriptures may help to clarify such enactment. We remember the gracious act of God's feeding in the desert, and the people ask, "What is it?" (Exod 16:15)—and hence its name, "manna," that is, "What is it?" In the spirit of such wonder, we are reminded that the Eucharist of our liturgy is a gift that cannot be reasoned so precisely that its mystery is choked, becoming *our* property and not God's pure gift. It is interesting to note that if there is any recipe for this manna, it is taken from the ordinary elements of their nourishment and yet retains its mystery in the midst of that ordinariness. Exodus says, "The house of Israel called it manna; it was like coriander seed, white, and the taste of it was like wafers made with honey" (16:31). The giftedness was affirmed in the injunction that they were not to hoard it or it would putrefy (16:20). The practical implication is so simple. Unleavened bread as a sign and the matter of this sacramental reality need not be hidden by excessive concerns over minute elements that go into its fashioning. Current fears over dishonoring the integrity of the symbol with bonding agents to keep the bread from crumbling seems to put a focus on our fashioning and not God's. After all, the essential simplicity of the unleavened loaf as real food is what is at issue here as a primary sacramental symbol.

In a similar vein, allowance certainly must be made for sufficient quantities of hosts to distribute to large assemblies, but this has led to a suspicion that bread baked in our ovens with simple, unleavened ingredients are less appropriate or sacred. Coupled with the fear of crumbs or fragments, the distancing of the "real food" from the reality of the sign Jesus gave us inevitably begins to occur. While respecting a long-standing tradition of individual Hosts, could one not argue that at certain feasts and celebrations the hand-fashioned bread is not only appropriate but even desirable? From the perspective of "signs that effect the reality they signify," regular liturgical practice should include opportunities to remind us that *how* and *with what* the gift is fashioned need not be controlled so pointedly that its giftedness becomes a possession of liturgical canons and not from the ordinary stuff of the earth through which the signification takes place. The holiness is rooted in the pure abundance of the graciousness in which simple things, fashioned in the power of the Spirit, are consecrated and set out as a meal that nourishes the substance of our deepest reality, just as its sacramental substance transcends the boundaries of our own reason and even our longing. "Here you can find me," Jesus reminds us through our liturgical tradition.

> [The Lord] rained down on them manna to eat,
>   and gave them the grain of heaven.
> Mortals ate of the bread of angels;
>   he sent them food in abundance. (Ps 78:24-25)

The cup we share is also the chalice of salvation. The dignity and sacredness of liturgical vessels should be maintained. However, when the cup of the presider is separated so patently by design and setting from that of the assembly, who consume as focal expressions of that one Body, what does that communicate about the pure gift of this drink, which fulfills the water from the rock to quench the people's thirst (Exod 17:6), and now has been transfigured through Christ's own lifeblood? "For they drank from the spiritual rock that followed them," St. Paul says of our ancestors, "and the rock was Christ" (1 Cor 10:4). The communion we share in drinking from the cup of our salvation is, for us, the very presence of the life-giving blood of Christ that flows from his side and makes the covenant promise of nourishment an event of intimacy with the gift of Christ's self-offering in which we are invited to share. As St. Ambrose says in his mystagogical preaching,

For them, water came from the rock, for you there is the Blood;
the water quenched their thirst for a time, the Blood washes you
forever.[34]

Presiders communing in food and drink—proceeding to eat the
whole small, figurative loaf themselves and empty a private cup set
apart from the rest—who then clean up from the meal, and proceed to
distribute communion from other provisions, tends to suggest that the
children or the lesser guests are now to be served. We would never affirm that consciously; nevertheless, liturgical enactment that obsesses
over the presider and concelebrants' eucharistic communion as a necessary first act, and then demonstrably uses other elements and vessels for the assembly, mutes the wholeness of the sign.

Finally, the *totus Christus* rightly receives both the Body and Blood
of Christ because we receive the totality of all that Christ came to be
and to give and to bring to unity within the church who celebrates. We
have noted before in all the chapters the importance of the wholeness
of the relational, dialogical, and participative modes of Christ's presence in the liturgy. The "spirit and life" that Jesus' words of invitation
to eat and drink his Body and Blood offered to us suggest that the
movement to this table of God's abundance should be respected in the
wholeness that the sacramental symbols embody. The more faithful
the presider who gathers those who have heard the Word and been
convicted by its summons, the more the table of unity should be in
harmony with the grace of Christ the head, who desires and longs for
us to find the same unity in him that he shares with the Father and
that abides in abundance for us as "a new and everlasting covenant."
Everything matters in this important moment par excellence of our
communion.

---

[34] Saint Ambrose, *On the Mysteries*, 8.48. This passage is quoted in an excellent chapter on the spiritual significance of drinking the cup and the sharing of
the covenant in Cantalamessa, "'Unless You Drink the Blood of the Son of Man
. . .' : The Eucharist, Communion with the Blood of Christ," in *Eucharist, Our
Sanctification*, chap. 4, p. 49.

THE HOLY SPIRIT AS THE INSCRIPTOR OF THE HUNGER AND THIRST THAT BINDS US TOGETHER

> When the whole person is refreshed, this is abundant refreshment indeed.
>
> —Erasmus of Rotterdam, sixteenth century[35]

The Holy Spirit is the agent and bond of outpoured Love that effects the reality of Christ's presence to us in the holy gifts. This agency of Love, the firstfruits of the passion in the heart of God, is generative in the liturgy in a paschal sense. That is, what is offered up in obedient self-surrender by Christ is returned to the Father as a gift of eucharistic life, our own self-offering in union with him, through the outpouring of this Love that longs for communion. As Louis-Marie Chauvet has described this mystery embodied in the liturgy, "the Spirit clearly appears as the *agent of the Word's burial in the flesh*, more precisely, after Easter, as the agent of the *disappearance* of the Risen One into the flesh." In the liturgy, Chauvet says, quoting Karl Barth, the Spirit makes present "the moment of the appropriation of God by humans." Chauvet shows the transformative dynamism of this *kenotic* act of God by transforming *"what God has that is most divine by humankind in what it has that is most human"* through the Spirit's mission "of raising up for the Risen One a body of humanity and of the world. Through it, he who was raised now raises others."[36]

Any consideration, therefore, of the Holy Spirit in the transformation of bread and wine into the Body and Blood of Christ begins in generative Love, is impelled by a hunger and thirst such Love engenders, and "appropriates" everything into that economy of grace that renders communion and mutual sharing of real presence possible and life-giving. "We love because he first loved us" (1 John 4:19). Eucharistic thanksgiving gives voice to that Love bond: "[Y]ou have no need

---

[35] From *Ten Colloquies* (New York: Bobbs-Merrill, 1957), 150. Quoted in J. Robert Baker and Barbara Budde, eds., *A Eucharistic Sourcebook* (Chicago: Liturgy Training Publications, 1999), 85.

[36] Chauvet, *Symbol and Sacrament*, 526. He is quoting Barth, *Dogmatique*, I, 1, 2 (Genéve: Labor et Fides, 1969), 165. He adds a further aspect of this dynamism Barth notes: "Conversely, the Son represents 'the moment of appropriation of humankind by God.'" This is a fitting expression of the dialogic nature of liturgy we have been expressing.

of our praise, yet our thanksgiving is itself your gift."[37] Love begets gratitude; gratitude motivates the gift; Love becomes the bond of unity. As the preface for Pentecost affirms, "For, bringing your Paschal Mystery to completion you bestowed the Holy Spirit today on those you made your adopted children by uniting them to your Only Begotten Son." The risen Lord Jesus presents himself as gift of the mutual indwelling of the Trinity that the Spirit pours out upon the world as bread of life and cup of eternal salvation: "for my flesh is true food and my blood is true drink" (John 6:55). Such is the Spirit's inscripting in these sacred mysteries.

From the perspective of a liturgical spirituality of communion, *how* that transformation takes place yields to *why* such bounty is laid before us on the table. In the Western tradition, we ask God to "send the Spirit" and hallow the gifts so that "they may become for us the Body and Blood of our Lord Jesus Christ." The church's Great Thanksgiving Prayer also begs the Father for that same hallowing upon the assembly gathered in praise and thanks, so that we may be transformed ourselves in an act of self-offering and "become what we receive," as Augustine's dictum reminds us. The Eastern tradition has kept this deep and abiding role of the Holy Spirit in the consecration of both the eucharistic gifts and the receivers of these sacred mysteries by emphasizing the consecratory role of one *epiclesis* over both gifts and assembly in the eucharistic prayer. The focus for the East, therefore, is the Spirit's transformation of the gifts for the assembly to share, which includes the memorial words of Jesus but is not limited to them. Orthodox theologian Paul Evdokimov highlights this perspective in a way that is fruitful for ecumenical reflection:

> It is characteristic of the Eastern Church's Liturgy that it is not possible to isolate the precise moment when the miracle of the Eucharist takes place. From the beginning to the very end the Liturgy is just one single action in which the *epiclesis* appears as the final affirmation of the unique sacramental symphony.[38]

---

[37] Common Preface IV, "Praise, the gift of God."

[38] Paul Evdokimov, "The Eucharist—Mystery of the Church," in *In the World, of the Church; A Paul Evdokimov Reader* (Crestwood, NY: St. Vladimir's Seminary Press, 2001), 262. Although there are significant differences in eucharistic interpretations, particularly regarding the reserved Eucharist, ecumenical perspectives such as Evdokimov offers can only enhance ecumenical dialogue in this focal area of our common identity.

In terms of the four modes of presence as one proclamation, the Eastern Catholic and Orthodox tradition has much to offer us, especially for a spirituality and piety rooted in the rhythmic harmony of everything in the liturgy as a participation in the trinitarian way of communion.

What Jean Corbon calls the *synergy* of the liturgy—the union of the church with Christ who is in union with the Father—finds its deepest expression in the Spirit's action in this *epiclesis*. "To become what we receive," then, does not simply track the ordered transformation of an unredeemed reality to a new one. The consecratory action is revelatory of God's saving acts in Jesus available for us *here, in this time and place*, rather than relying upon a moment captured in time. The Western Christian tradition has tended to rely on that precise "moment," but the wholeness of the event gets isolated from the sacramental encounter when our piety and spirituality center on such precision. Rather, the *becoming* itself is an unfolding visitation that acts out of the rhythm of the triune life itself and permeates all reality, and, as we said, announces that mystery as available to us in our eucharistic praying in a way that feeds us now, as we are, and as God's desire is manifested in our midst. This is what other writers we have noted describe as the new reality of Easter/ascension, which Jean-Luc Marion says is a communion we share with Father and Son "accomplished in an inconceivable jubilation that the Spirit provokes (and attests)." It enables the believers to enter into Christ's own blessing of his Father "and so enter the space—the Trinitarian 'site'—where, in the ineffable communion of the Spirit, Father and Son bless and recognize one another."[39]

That visitation takes place as purifying and liberating fire in the heart of every worshiper and draws its energy from the Holy Spirit, who then gathers that love flowing from the Father and the Son into a Body in union with her Lord. Speaking of this journey into freedom in everyone who seeks the new life Christ offers, Corbon says,

> The Holy Spirit will have so fused the rebellious will with the will of the Father that prayer "to" Jesus will have become the prayer "of" Jesus himself. But this ceaseless prayer of Jesus is identical with the eternal liturgy which he celebrates before the face of the Father. The same Spirit who taught us how to breathe the name of Jesus will then

[39] Marion, *Prolegomena to Charity*, 134. Quoted in Mitchell, "Mystery and Manners," 145.

be able to open us, in the very prayer of Jesus himself, to wonder-filled adoration: "Abba, Father!" When the fontal liturgy wells up in the heart, it expands into "worship in spirit and in truth" (Jn. 4:14 and 24). And the epiclesis of the heart expands into an epiclesis over the world; this in turn is naught else than a participation in the great "work" (Jn. 5:17) of Christ in his ascension: that is, the pouring out of the Holy Spirit into the hearts of human beings in order to draw them to himself.[40]

The eucharistic gifts, therefore, through the Spirit-hallowing, announce this new dispensation where the liturgy becomes both the proclamatory event for Christ's abiding presence in the sacramental expression of food and drink (i.e., eating and drinking the *res et sacramentum* as "spirit and life"), as well as an intimate communion with Christ (*res tantum*) the meal effects and for which the world so desperately longs and needs to experience as real and active. We could say, then, that the Holy Spirit's inscripting bodies forth the abundant and abiding presence of Christ as Redeemer and Lord, whose sacramental presence draws near to feed us in that journey back to the garden, to right relationship, into the "dimension of the Kingdom" (Schmemann) of justice, love, and peace. Poetic metaphors can only hint at this awesome inscripting and ingathering:

> Each be other's comfort kind: . . .
> Divine charity, dear charity,
> Fast you ever, fast bind.[41]

The Jesuit Gerard Manley Hopkins speaks here of the marriage bond, but such powerful imagery is no stranger to Christ and the church as Bride and Bridegroom, and the liturgy itself as the marriage of heaven and earth. All of this happens in a communion of relation, dialogue, and participation, and the liturgy provides the vehicle of this visitation that unfolds over a lifetime and awaits its fullness in eschatological hope. Hopkins says it well in "God's Grandeur":

> And for all this, nature is never spent;
>   There lives the dearest freshness deep down things;
> And though the last lights off the black West went
>   Oh, morning, at the brown brink eastward, springs—

---

[40] Corbon, *Wellspring of Worship*, 148–49.
[41] Gerard Manley Hopkins, SJ, "At the Wedding March."

Because the Holy Ghost over the bent
   World broods with warm breast and with ah!
   bright wings.

The Spirit is the One who reveals the Father's flowing desire that "creates a thirst," as Corbon notes, and also "slakes that thirst with the Spirit, so that we become the Body of Christ."[42] The marriage of heaven and earth revealed in this sacramental Body and Blood of Christ hallowed by the Spirit proclaims the work of Christ laboring in the world in which we labor with him. The consecratory action of the *epiclesis* extends the boundaries of the triune visitation, embodied in these gifts of Christ's Body and Blood, because it is "somewhere" here *"for us,* and for all, so that sins may be forgiven. Do this in memory of me." We could not "Do this" unless the Spirit inscribes this longing of Christ in us to bless and offer himself with us back to the Father in praise and thanks.

The "distinct but not separate" action of the Holy Spirit, therefore, participates surely in the eucharistic mystery in the transformation of the gifts, but the action of the Spirit's relational generativity does not end there. In a synergistic response to this outpouring of Love, the church—the assembled community as representative sign and expression of that Body of Christ—also receives the Spirit's bonding when she "recognizes" her Lord in the breaking open of the Word and the breaking and pouring out of the bread and wine. The circle of the unfolding visitation of God's very life finds its expression in our receiving him, in our saying "yes" in that eucharistic action to the mystery we are, as Augustine remarked so well. This enables us to participate in Christ's giving of himself as "a present, according to the Spirit," as Jean-Luc Marion says. The meal set out is sacramental presence par excellence, for the wholeness of the Christ as Redeemer and Lord is available to us in a covenantal sharing of food and drink, a way that unites us with the communion of saints at all times and places. Our communion changes us (*metabolé*, in the Eastern terminology); we are "thrown or projected beyond"[43] into the new dispensation, which

[42] Corbon, *Wellspring of Worship*, 72. He is reflecting upon "The Holy Spirit and the Church in the Liturgy" in light of 1 Cor 12:13, i.e., "and we were all made to drink of the one Spirit."

[43] Paul Evdokimov and Alexander Schmemann both use this term for the action of the Spirit in the transformation of gifts and assembly in the *epiclesis*.

widens the boundaries of the tents of our meeting Christ and one another. Marion has similar words to express this "ineffable mystery," in which Christ "gives himself, as a present," which the Body of the Eucharist and of the church reveals and offers to all:

> If Christ had remained physically among us, according to the worldly economy of presence, he would have fixed himself in a place and a time; he therefore would have been inaccessible to [people] of all ages and all places. This empirical impossibility of encountering him would then have merely reflected a still more radical impossibility of recognizing him: had we approached him, we would not have been able—without the sending of the Spirit, because without trinitarian fulfillment—*to recognize him*; for we do not bless him, and in him the Father, except through the Spirit. We therefore owe our seeing him to the gift, through the Spirit and in the Trinitarian distance of the presence of Christ—in Spirit and in Truth, in all places and in all ages.[44]

In the worshiping community's recognition of Christ in the breaking of the bread and the pouring of the cup, the eschatological character of the sacrament finds expression, locates the grace, affirms the cosmic hunger and thirst for what only the Spirit can satisfy, and binds them together as one Body in holy communion. Past, present, and future coalesce in this sacramental body built for the redemptive mystery. The simplicity and immensity of it all—"buried in" these material gifts of bread and wine—reveals the action of the Spirit in revealing the God who "creates the thirst," as Corbon has said, and "slakes that thirst," which comes from the Love that keeps on urging us into "worship in spirit and truth" (John 4:23) that Jesus promised in this eucharistic meal. As Schmemann says, "The Eucharist is the sacrament of unity and the *moment of truth*: here we see the world in Christ, as it really is, and not from our particular and therefore limited and partial points of

---

See Evdokimov, "The Eucharist—Mystery of the Church," 251; and Schmemann, *For the Life of the World*, 43–44. Both Orthodox and Protestant insistence on communing the Body and Blood of Christ as the end and goal of our worship enriches the Catholic focus on the Eucharist as "source and summit of the Christian life" that Vatican II appropriated in the reform. It clarifies the Spirit's action in "hallowing" the gifts in an important way for contemporary Western liturgical spirituality and piety.

[44] Marion, *Prolegomena to Charity*, 146; emphasis mine.

view."[45] The Body and Blood of Christ feed the Spirit-filled resurrected Body of Christ, which is the church. Through this hallowing, we hand over our lives to be consecrated through the immensity of the gift we receive when we open our hands and say, "Amen. So be it."

The liturgical context keeps this pneumatological dimension of the mystery of faith before us and leads to a eucharistic devotion that unfolds over a lifetime of communing and that can only be fulfilled "in the age to come." The impelling Spirit, in our faithfulness to the Eucharist, urges us to a wholeness and purification in freedom that we could never imagine on our own. It happens in *this time and place* but transforms the liturgical encounter into grace-filled communion, the new dimension, which the Trinity's life is shaping in us. What more can be said? Faithful communicants know this in their bones. We simply surrender to the mystery of what God is doing in us in the freedom of the Spirit promised to us.

Liturgical Implications for Eucharistic Gifts That Bind Us Together

Three particular issues of ritual enactment will be noted here: (1) the wholeness of the rite as an appetite for communion in the Spirit, (2) the eucharistic prayer as communal praying in the Spirit, and (3) communing as a significant spiritual expression of the Spirit's hallowing. All three involve a mutuality between interior intentionality and bodily expression.

(1) Just as the Spirit's inscripting permeates the whole of liturgy and life and binds them together through the gifts that express this communion, the relationship between the Holy Spirit and Christ's presence in the eucharistic gifts of bread and wine is pervasive and worthy of intentional reverence. That relationship should be transparent throughout the celebration, because the liturgy "as celebrated and experienced"[46] makes available the wellspring that "creates a thirst in us and slakes that thirst with the Spirit," as we have noted. Attentiveness to this wellspring of hunger and thirst, of fulfillment and quenching, suggests that *everything about the meal gathering should participate and enhance such a profound moment of nourishment.* We affirmed such intentionality by the assembly and those who prepare and preside at the

---

[45] Schmemann, *For the Life of the World*, 44.

[46] Corbon, *Wellspring of Worship*, 72. The dynamism of the words is important here.

liturgy in every aspect of this study. The rites of the meal of Word and Sacrament commence, for better or worse, within the gathering. The quality of the gathering actions and how the symmetry of music and the fullness of the primary symbols echo the "sacramental symphony" unfolding in this time and space matters, as the taste for the meal unfolds throughout.

Of special note is the proclamation and preaching of the Word. Homiletic professors after the Vatican II reform made a great effort to teach preachers to reverence the "moves" from one dynamic proclamation to another.[47] In that light, many homiletics scholars maintained, the preaching should create an appetite for and lead to the table of Eucharist as a natural progression from the nourishment of the Word to its fullest liturgical expression par excellence in holy communion. Such rhetorical references cannot be shallow or forced, but the dynamism of every preaching cannot ignore what the Holy Spirit is revealing and how Christ is "fulfilling in our hearing" what we enact in the memorial prayer of Thanksgiving and the breaking and sharing together of the bread and wine. This requires a liturgical habit of interior attention to the hunger and thirst we bring to every worship, both assembly and presider.

Indeed, the very appetite for eucharistic action is stirred up by the Holy Spirit's fashioning in the Word, just as the prophet Ezekiel heard it prophetically addressed to him:

> O mortal, eat what is offered to you; eat this scroll, and go, speak to the house of Israel. So I opened my mouth, and he gave me the scroll to eat. He said to me, Mortal, eat this scroll that I give you and fill your stomach with it. Then I ate it; and in my mouth it was as sweet as honey. (Ezek 3:1-3)

Indeed, this is an invitation not only to preachers but also to the whole gathered church whose mission embraces Christ's own Word become flesh, sacramentally expressed in this gathering. In that sense, the hunger for God and the desire for communion in the Word of Life consecrate the assembly in the power of the Spirit to be that Word and work in the world. In Gerard Manley Hopkins's words we used in chapter

---

[47] David Buttrick uses this term of "moves" within the sermon structure itself. The argument in this book is that the whole liturgy is a proclamation. Hence, ritual "moves" bring the Body in procession to the table of both Word and Eucharist. See David Buttrick, *Homiletic: Moves and Structures* (Philadelphia: Fortress Press, 1987).

3, "its end, its purpose, its purport, its meaning, is God and its life or work to name and praise him."[48] The background, indeed the fundamental ground for approaching the table of Eucharist at all, finds expression in *creating an appetite*, in preparing the worshipers to eat and drink in grateful memory, and to open their hands to become what they receive. Intentionality of what the Spirit is doing in the gathering and in the preaching fosters deeper communion, signified in the sharing of the gifts. To cooperate with this binding Spirit is imperative for the whole end and fruit of true communion. Our lack of attention to this intrinsic relationship treats the gathering to preach and hear the Word as some separate event from the processive movement to eucharistic sharing of the Body and Blood of Christ. This disconnect inhibits and stifles that Spirit. The point here is simple and subtle: eucharistic anticipation becomes the assembly's attitude and ritual way of being when the Spirit's role in "creating and slaking the thirst" for communion permeates the hearts and minds of all who gather, with special responsibility for those charged with gathering the community into communion as a service of this Body. How can we taste the sweetness if there is no appetite? Uncovering the depth of Love at work intensifies the thirst for the meal, which is a nourishing event and not the consumption of a product of our production and distribution.

(2) The eucharistic prayer stirs into action the hunger and thirst that the memory of God's saving acts in Jesus engenders. The communal nature of the church's prayer draws Christ's offering into communion with our own. Its dynamism, the liturgical documents say, participates in a mystery of faith where all are invited into the mystery "with devotion and full involvement" (SC 48) so that "the unblemished sacrificial Victim to be consumed in Communion may be for the salvation of those who will partake of it" (GIRM 79c). This becoming or visitation, as we have called it, always links together the Spirit who transforms the eucharistic gifts and those who open themselves to receive it so that the *synergy* is coherent. Benedictine Ghislain Lafont, speaking from the Western tradition of the double *epiclesis* over the bread and wine and then of the assembly, notes this stirring of the appetite in the assembly by the Spirit's hallowing as setting the stage for the communion that follows. Commenting upon the words, "Grant that we, who are nourished by his body and blood, may be filled with his Holy Spirit, and become one body, one spirit in Christ," Lafont adds,

[48] See chap. 3, n.1.

> The prayer declares the meaning of the approaching sacramental communion, and it asks for its completion in us. We pray that we may be able to respond to the gift Christ has given us by the gift of our very selves.[49]

The manner of praying this prayer, therefore, is expansive in breadth and depth and the Holy Spirit's action not only consecrates gifts but also binds the receivers in its hallowing. A rote recitation hinders that dynamic. The gestures call for wide inclusion here, rather than a stiff projection of hands over the bread and wine as if the primary action begins and ends with the material gifts themselves. This is the church's prayer where her own "devotion and full involvement" are integral to the Spirit's action. The eucharistic prayer prayed with such an intentionality moves in power over both the gifts and those whose presence is consecrated into a self-offering inseparable from them. The Eastern Catholic and Orthodox practice of fluttering the corporal over the head of the presider at this time is not a mere affectation. As Schmemann has said, this *epicletic* action "transforms the Church into the body of Christ and—therefore—*manifests* the elements of our offering as *communion in the Holy Spirit*. This is consecration."[50] Such a binding between gifts and communicants requires engaged praying, clarifies its true nature in dialogic participation by presider and the assembly, and resists efforts to corral the Spirit's hallowing with narrow gestures and spiritless, formulaic recitation. Such praying is an art; it develops over time; it cannot happen without an interior spirituality and piety that respects "Divine charity, dear charity" that is acting in this communal prayer of the church to bind our yearning with the materiality of these material gifts of bread and wine into a sacramental presence of Christ that redeems and saves. Communal praying in the Spirit, at the table's "burning focal point" of God's passion made flesh and blood for us as pure gift, expresses its devotion more faithfully in lifted hands and hearts, soul-filled singing and gestures that gather and not isolate. Our current suspicion of such an attitude in favor of silence, hushed tones, and bowed heads may need some critical reflection, if we are to cooperate with full heart and mind and voice with the gift we celebrate in memory of Christ's own passion to eat this meal with us.

(3) The liturgical implications of the Spirit's inscription of this appetite for the gifts of God, our hungering and thirsting for communion

---

[49] Ghislain Lafont, *The Meal and the Word*, trans. Jeremy Driscoll, OSB (New York: Paulist Press, 2008; *Les Éditions du Cerf*, 2001), 102.

[50] Schmemann, *For the Life of the World*, 44.

that is the "hinge" and doorway into the new dimension, are significant. Do we process as one Body to receive the gifts of bread and wine, and are they offered to us and received by us as a pure gift that flows from this table of abundance? Such is the response to the Spirit's hallowing. We have spoken earlier of communion rites that express the reality for the assembly that they signify. They can only be reinforced here and outlined finally at the conclusion of this chapter. The generous attitude of ministers communicates much of the Spirit here. Offering the Body and Blood of Christ to one's sisters and brothers is not a right but a service that reflects the unity of the community who receives the Body and Blood as a common meal.

Even more, do these rites reflect the abundance the Spirit offers or the scarcity that often results from overefficiency and inattentiveness to the unity of the assembly who is communing? This is especially true of sharing in the Blood of Christ, the ritual act of receiving the covenant as a binding act of union—and choosing to share the lifeblood of its promise—in such a powerfully symbolic act of drinking from the ritual cup. Their placement and amount in large assemblies should reflect and reverence the thirst that we share. One wonders why this is so ritually self-evident in some communities and paltry, if at all, in others? Recent movements away from sharing the cup should signal concern for the integrity of the rite and the action of the Spirit the communion rites express. Something deeply meaningful is being communicated in what we do together in the power of the Spirit. Often it is not conscious or able to be put into words. This is especially true when the practice is withheld from whole communities or provided at some liturgies and not at others. As Cantalamessa insists,

> we may hope that the day will soon come when all those who so wish may receive Christ's Blood at communion. Indeed, how long can a practice last that discriminates between Mass and Mass and between one person and another within the same Mass, without the communion under both kinds itself becoming a sign of distinction and not of communion among the faithful?[51]

The reluctance to share the cup is explained often as a health concern, even in the face of much contrary evidence and the willing acceptance of communion from another's hand. At a deeper level, sharing the cup expresses a sacramental intimacy best reserved for the priest,

---

[51] Cantalamessa, *Eucharist, Our Sanctification*, 43.

a hearkening back to a more "mysterious" Tridentine rite. One may assert, in the face of such reluctance, that the pure gift of sharing in the blood of Christ *is* intimate, and it is precisely in view of our acknowledgment of the holiness of this sacramental sharing: "O Lord, I am not worthy to receive you. Only say the word, and my soul shall be healed." Communing in the Body and Blood of Christ is the sacramental *fiat* of the Word and Answer, and the healing act in which the redemptive mystery finds expression. The more we enter into that hunger and thirst that bind us together in the power of the Spirit, the more this act takes on sacramental significance.

In a similar vein, the relationship of the fragments to the one loaf should clearly be seen as part of the abundance required to satisfy this immense hunger. They are portioned out from the one table of communion; as far as is possible, significant portions are broken from the whole. These may seem like trivial matters for our attention. However, there is nothing more dispiriting than a lack of care for these simple expressions of our hunger and thirst and the binding to which we surrender in our shared meal. It *can* be done. Where there is respect and reverence for the presence of Christ in the bread and wine as food and drink of eternal life, there is abundance and it is enough. The signs which convey that sacramental reality should express that. Where the unity of the Body of Christ gathers around the Body and Blood of Christ, and ordinary fruit of the earth and vine are keenly recognized "in spirit and in truth" for the life of the world, the rites body forth this significance and the communion is experienced as a meal. The Holy Spirit draws spiritual meaning and liturgical expression together into one reality. The "spirit and truth of our worship" ask that of us.

HOLY COMMUNION: OUR ENGAGEMENT IN THE TRINITY'S SACRIFICIAL OFFERING

> She found herself eager for the next day's Mass—it would be Mary's day—because in communion the soul seems more sweetly bound to God and better knows his truth. For then the soul is in God and God in the soul, just as the fish is in the sea and the sea in the fish.
>
> —Saint Catherine of Siena,
> fourteenth century, Dialogue 27[52]

[52] Suzanne Noffke, OP, trans. and ed., *Catherine of Siena: The Dialogue* (New York: Paulist Press, 1980).

The real presence of Christ in the eucharistic bread and wine finds its deepest meaning and reality par excellence when the assembly receives holy communion. As we noted at the outset of the chapter, this fullness of presence of which the tradition insists holds the sacredness within this sacramental context and is the denouement of the "one whole Word of God," which the liturgy proclaims in the richness of its "symbolic inclusions" held in creative tension. For here, in the breaking of the bread and the sharing of the cup, the paschal mystery draws into intimate relationship *to us* and *for us* and *with us* and shapes us into the *totus Christus*, in which the true reality of the meaning of our life and mission is embodied. As the *Exsultet* exclaims so boldly of this redemptive intimacy of Christ, "What good would life have been to us, had Christ not come as our Redeemer?" What good would this tremendous outpouring be unless we taste its sweetness, unless we "do this" whole memorial complex in memory of Jesus? Lacking that ritual wholeness, holy communion would remain somehow a gift available as promised, but not received. Isaiah says to those who hunger and thirst for God's visitation, and God's prior passion to fulfill this feeding,

> For as the rain and the snow come down from heaven,
>   and do not return there until they have watered the earth,
> making it bring forth and sprout,
>   giving seed to the sower and bread to the eater, so shall my word be
>   that goes
> out from my mouth;
>   it shall not return to me empty,
> but it shall accomplish that which I purpose,
>   and succeed in the thing for which I sent it. (Isa 55:10-11)

Saint Augustine's famous homiletic plea makes the *synergy* of sacramental gifts and our eating and drinking in grateful memory the expression par excellence of that communion that flows from the heart of the Father as covenant, sign, and seal of our new identity in Christ. Augustine says, speaking of the sacramental meaning of these holy things we encounter,

> So, if you want to comprehend the body of Christ, listen to what the Apostle tells the faithful: "You are the body of Christ, his members" (1 Cor. 12:27). Since you make up the body of Christ and are his members, your mystery rests on the table of the Lord; you receive your own mystery. You answer "Amen" to the reality of what you are; your reply

gives consent to it. For on hearing the words, "The Body of Christ," you reply "Amen." Be in fact a member of Christ's body for your affirmation, "Amen," to ring true. . . . When baptized, you were moistened into dough. On receiving the fire of the Holy Spirit, you were baked. Be what you see; receive what you are.[53]

These startling images provide apt expression of the meaning of this culminating event as the "one whole Word of God," for now the elements themselves and the fashioning of the loaf become inseparable from the communion act of those who engage the mystery. In fact, the truth of our "Amen"—our reception in holy communion—is the ratifying truth of the mystery in its fullest sense, its sacramental "substance" united now with our own self-offering, the sign that effects the reality it signifies as real food and real drink "in spirit and in truth." Saint Athanasius, fourth-century Doctor of the Church, affirms this in a rich sense, where the Spirit's unfolding of all that is now comes to fruitful illumination in the hallowing work of the Holy Spirit that the Eucharist proclaims as real and active in our midst:

The Word took on Flesh so that we could receive the Holy Spirit . . .
God became bearer of flesh (*sarcophore*) so that we might become bearers of the Spirit (*pneumatophores*).[54]

That spiritual "bearing" we express in communion "recognizes him" and then, in this new dimension of which the sacrament is the doorway, fulfills the ascension promise of Jesus in Matthew that "I am with you always, to the close of the age" (Matt 28:20).

In the new dispensation where "Easter innovates," in Jean-Luc Marion's description, "this fleshly body disappears and leaves place for the Eucharistic body of bread that one eats, that one assimilates to oneself, and which, in this unique case, assimilates to itself those who assimilate it . . . Christ becomes present, not to the senses (which cannot see him or receive him), but to the heart, burning from now on, and the mind, from hereafter understanding." In this great giving away and going away of Christ in the physical flesh, Marion goes on, "it is accomplished as a gift of presence, which abandons itself in the

---

[53] Augustine, *Sermon* 272 (ca. 405–11); PL 38, 1247–48. Quoted also in Gaudoin-Parker, *The Real Presence Through the Ages*, 50–51.

[54] Athanasius of Alexandria, *De. Incarn.* 8: PG 26, 996 C.

heart and the body of the disciples."[55] Such divine *kenosis* is given expression for us in breaking and pouring out, and our communion and covenant is ratified in eating and drinking, to affirm in heart and body the "way and truth and life" Jesus shares with us. This is our touch point and entry into the dynamism of the trinitarian communion of mutual self-offering, of which Love is the fruit and in which passion and desire are the wellspring for Christ's presence as blessing, food, host of the banquet, washer of feet, and companion on the journey. We ask again in amazement and wonder of this holy communion procession, which draws us into this new reality and new meaning: "What good would life have been to us, had Christ not come as our Redeemer?" The answer is now here. It cannot be captured fully in words or ideas or creedal acclamations. Rather, we "do this" in all its fullness. We remember, we celebrate, we believe, and we feast, in the rich summons the liturgy embodies:

> The Spirit and the bride say, "Come."
> And let everyone who hears say, "Come."
> And let everyone who is thirsty come.
> Let anyone who wishes take the water of life as a gift. (Rev 22:17)

Liturgical Implications for a Spirituality of Communion and Sacrificial Offering: Engagement with the Mystery

Benedict XVI, in *Sacramentum Caritatis*, locates the church's eucharistic faith in the Trinity's communion of love. Indeed, our life of worship manifests the communion in love the triune God shares with us and to which our participation in communion affirms. Benedict says,

> The "mystery of faith" is thus a mystery of trinitarian love, a mystery in which we are called by grace to participate. We too should therefore exclaim with Saint Augustine: "If you see love, you see the Trinity" (*De Trinitate*, VIII, 8, 12).

At the outset, we can state unambiguously that a life of faithfulness to the Eucharist, in which the modes of Christ's presence are set forth and shared in relational, dialogical, and participative fullness, manifests its truth by the quality of love by which the Christian community is "recognized in their breaking of the bread." Liturgical divisions

---

[55] Marion, *Prolegomena to Charity*, 136–37. He is referring to Augustine in *The Confessions*, VII, 10.16.

and lack of charity that cling to eucharistic assemblies suggest that the sacramental presence of Christ to which we have been speaking throughout this book has been muted by this dissonance. Piety is only as rich as the fruit it bears. That fruitfulness is not tested in isolated perspective and doctrines but in the fruit of love that shares in Christ's own communion with his Father. "Liturgy wars" from any perspective summon a return to these foundational principles of the rhythm and harmony of the Body of Christ standing together in the community of God.

It follows that every action of the celebrating Body complements the communion of heart and mind we share in Christ. If our spiritual offering is united with Christ's self-offering and "the Body of Christ participates in the offering of her Head" (CCC 1368), then our material offering, our ritual eating and drinking in grateful memory, participates in this bodying forth as well. As the Catechism says, "With him, she herself is offered whole and entire." We already have established the essential act of communing to the efficacy of the eucharistic gifts themselves. However, the relational, dialogical, and participative nature of the liturgy goes much deeper than physical eating of real food. A concomitant spiritual communion inheres in the *totus Christus* by means of the radical sense of brokenness and being poured out in union with Christ's own self-surrender. Sharing regularly in the Eucharist consecrates the community and the individuals who are received into something that itself is a *becoming*, a progressive incorporation into the mind and heart of Christ (Phil 2:5-11) that is properly sacramental and very holy. The vessels are shaped by the mystery they bear and this *kenotic* refashioning leads to acts of worship in the name of Jesus. Bread and wine and all the symbolic inclusions they include regarding true solidarity, assimilation of Christ's ways into our own, being "given away" and spiritually in communion with our absent brothers and sisters—whether in diverse countries and communities or with those who have gone before us in faith—consecrate our manner and way of being in the world *here*, in *this time and place*, just as the eucharistic species announce that same real presence of Christ as *for us* and *with us* as an announcement of the promise whose fullness still awaits us.

This holistic perspective of "holy communion" illuminates what was noted at the outset of this chapter when the Catechism notes that "the lives of the faithful . . . acquire a new value" (1368). Such "immeasurable riches of his grace" (Eph 2:7) are the direct fruit of communion in the Body and Blood of Christ. Here, the liturgical reality and the interior union with Christ and all Christ saves and redeems "meet and fuse in an organic unity," as Yves Congar expressed so vividly.[56] Eucharistic praying changes the landscape of our faith reality. Congar provides a simple analogy for this "whole mystery of his Mystical Body":

> We have all of us seen a landscape, grey, gloomy and sullen, all at once lit up by the sun's rays. The whole scene changes in a moment: the fields are gay, the various features stand out clearly, there is a general impression of gladness and fecundity.
>
> In some such way, faith illuminates everything in a new way. To the eyes of faith, which illuminate everything they look at, the dull landscape of life appears in a fresh light coming from the "Father of lights." Life takes on a new meaning according to that which God gives it; all values are transformed. . . . We make our own Christ's way of looking at things; we apply ourselves to adopt his judgments of value, to let him direct and arrange our destiny.[57]

The church is the arena of this encounter, Congar goes on, "the fullness of his sacred humanity consecrated . . . that all may be, in him, consummated in glory to God."[58] This is the meaning of the doxology that culminates the eucharistic prayer. The gifts are raised high, and the significance is cosmic because there is now no barrier that can withstand this outpouring grace of Christ we receive in faith and trust and ultimate hope that "all will be well and every kind of thing will be well."[59] This mystical truth transcends creeds and canons and enters the realm of our deepest identity signified by the meal we are about to share. Eucharistic praying, therefore, reveals and participates in the meaning for which all people of all nations and creation long. God draws the Beloved now in ways we cannot imagine or bring together in terms of the old dispensation.

The world's diverse faiths and ethical perspectives already participate in this wholeness, and we but announce what God is doing, even

[56] Yves Congar, "The Mystical Body of Christ," in *The Mystery of the Church* (Baltimore: Helicon Press, 1960), 134.

[57] Ibid., 125.

[58] Ibid., 136.

[59] Julian of Norwich, *Julian of Norwich: Showings*, ed. Edmund Colledge, OSA, and James Walsh, SJ, 225 (New York: Paulist Press, 1978).

though we are not the fullness of its expression at any given moment and the church's own pilgrim road to holiness is not yet complete. Yet, as *Lumen Gentium* insists, "the renewal of the world is irrevocably under way; it is even now anticipated in a certain real way, for the Church on earth is endowed already with a sanctity which is real though imperfect" (48). Such global solidarity in love is the fruit of our changed reality that eucharistic practice engenders, or else the church is "a noisy gong or a clanging cymbal" (1 Cor 13:1). *Gaudium et Spes* rightly affirms this solidarity when the Constitution declares that the church—both in her structures and in her "spiritual community"—always "travels the same journey as all of humanity and shares the same earthly lot with the world: it is to be a leaven and, as it were, the soul of human society in its renewal by Christ and transformation into the family of God" (GS 40). The leaven of the community, nourished on the bread and wine we share, feeds human desire with God's own desire.

In celebration and affirmation of this, we raise the gifts before communion and then we eat and drink as the material expression of our "Amen" with which we conclude this great Thanksgiving. The church's worship, and the Eucharist par excellence, "is a sacred action surpassing all others," as *Sacrosanctum Concilium*, 7, maintains, and through this regular, faithful procession into the kingdom, in union with Christ and all the angels and saints and Beloved who share in this *sanctorum communio*,[60] the real presence of Christ and the Mystical Body of Christ are bound together in one sacred reality that is "distinct but not separate," as the sacramental tradition says, and "one whole Word of God," as Rahner describes it. Hence, as the Vatican document says,

[60] Henri de Lubac, SJ, "Sanctorum Communio," in *Theological Fragments* (*Théologies d'occasion*, 1984) (San Francisco: Ignatius Press, 1989), 16. De Lubac speaks of "the original meaning of *communio sanctorum* in the creed" and believes it designates "the source from which the Christian receives his personal saintliness—that is, from his communion with God, as well as his communion with his brothers." He insists further that in the sacramental economy, "this communication of the *sancta*, or this participation in the *sancta*, is not a completely individual event," but gathers into unity "a vast fraternal 'communion,' of which the series of 'harmonics' of the word as it is used in the New Testament has already informed us." This is an example of the harmony of multivalent meanings, the "symbolic inclusions," which we have noted throughout this study.

the renewal in the eucharist of the covenant between the Lord and his people draws the faithful into the compelling love of Christ and sets them on fire. From the liturgy, therefore, particularly the eucharist, grace is poured forth upon us as from a fountain; the liturgy is the source for achieving in the most effective way possible human sanctification and God's glorification, the end to which all the Church's other activities are directed. (SC 10)

We are back to the wellspring of God's desire, of Love incarnate as Word and Answer, and the fire of the Spirit that forges a union between what we do at worship and who we are as people fashioned by the union in communion we share. Christ is present in this matrix of symbolic relationships, which magnify the Lord in the world. This is the mind and heart of Christ who washes the feet of the Beloved at the Supper and is truly present, shaping our own way and truth and life. Such an attitude toward holy communion gathers and never scatters.

Our final reflections will look at two other implications of a spirituality of communion and the sacrificial offering we share with Christ: (1) the meaning of communion as a sign and reality of ecclesial unity; and (2) solidarity with the hungers of the world, especially the poor, the voiceless, and the marginalized. The summons to these realities should be obvious, but we present them as bold, yet modest, proposals to consider in light of this spirituality and piety of holy communion. The liturgical implications will suggest that *attentive faithfulness to the depths of relationships the eucharistic meal bodies forth both increases our hunger and solidarity* at the same time that we experience the nourishment the sacrament offers. This includes faithfulness in practice, the bonding of lives, the centrality of the meal, solidarity in hunger and hope, and the universal need for nourishment that a sacramental life offers. And this is as it should be.

Such participation in the redemptive mystery poses some simple questions for reflection. Would our desire, in union with Christ, "that all shall be one" suggest that at special times and celebrations it is fitting that we cross boundaries of eucharistic hospitality among other tables in the Body of Christ? The Week of Christian Unity or the celebration of the Solemnity of Saints Peter and Paul might include intercommunion among those who desire so deeply this union and communion to which Christ's presence impels us. Would this not be a foretaste of God's desire that transcends the limitations of our own histories and sinfulness? Without demeaning the sacramental economy that still divides us, or professing a unity we do not substantially share at this time, communal moments of reconciliation in the Body of Christ, embraced so readily in this day, might further accede to the Spirit's binding of heart and mind and express that proleptic desire for eucharistic communion to which our own desire is in harmony. At Vatican II, the Decree on Ecumenism (*Unitatis Redintegratio*) wrestled with "worship in common" (*communication in sacris*) and the two principles upon which it rests, namely, (1) "the unity of the Church which ought to be expressed," and (2) "the sharing of the means of grace" (UR 8).[61] The conclusion, such as it was decades ago, expressed the creative tension at work throughout the Decree:

> The expression of unity generally forbids common worship. Grace to be obtained sometimes commends it. The concrete course to be adopted, when all the circumstances of time, place and persons have been duly considered, is left to the prudent decision of the local Episcopal authority, unless the local bishops' conference according to its own statutes, or the Holy See, has determined otherwise. (UR 8)

Given the document's initial foundation regarding the unity of the church that the "highest examplar and source of this mystery is the unity, in the Trinity of Persons, of one God, the Father and the Son in the Holy Spirit" (2), would it be possible to start *there*, in the grace-filled passion of God's desire, before we disallow any testing of that movement by the Spirit in our time? We are not speaking about indiscriminate table sharing but mutually recognized moments of encounter that test the Spirit at work in all who seek to follow Christ in our triune unity of baptismal identity. If the "liturgical actions" of other communions, as the Decree also says, "most certainly can truly engender a life of grace, and, one must say, can aptly give access to the communion of salvation" (3), should there not be times of special recognition of our communion at the deepest levels of union that the *res tantum* of the sacrament fosters? This is simply a modest, but hopeful, proposal, in the spirit of the rhythm and harmony of Christ's presence

[61] For an illuminating discussion of the development of these issues during the council and immediately following the promulgation of the Decree on Humanism, see George H. Tavard, AA, "Praying Together: *Communicatio in Sacris* in the Decree on Ecumenism," in *Vatican II Revisited: By Those Who Were There*, ed. Alberic Stacpoole (Minneapolis: Winston Press, 1986), 202–19. Among the works of J.-M. R. Tillard, see *I Believe, Despite Everything: Reflections of an Ecumenist* (Collegeville, MN: Liturgical Press, 2003).

in these sacred mysteries, that certain times and celebrations might cast us beyond our denominational borders to proclaim God's mighty acts in Jesus to which we all cling and for which we give our lives in faith and trust. Those who regularly discuss and share faith at that ecumenical level would attest to this common hunger.[62] Unofficially, this occurs throughout the world. Official expression at appointed times of intercommunion removes the desire from the shadows and tests the relationship between the unity in Christ we so readily affirm and the sacred covenantal act of eating and drinking the Body and Blood of Christ, which announces that grace-filled visitation.

Secondly, solidarity with the hungers of the world, especially the poor, the voiceless, and the marginalized, provides an important implication that bodies forth a spirituality of communion and an identity with the sacrificial offering we share with Christ at the table. This also is a modest proposal. The liturgical trajectory of the procession into the mind and heart of Christ expressed by our gathering, hearing the Word, interceding for the world, and drawn to a common self-offering with Christ that consecrates us into the mystery we share cannot return to the Father as a true offering of praise and thanks unless our hearts go where Christ's heart can be found. The Scriptures are insistent on the place at the table Jesus always provides for those who are beyond the realms of the acceptable, the wealthy, and the righteous in the eyes of the world. Any Christian community for whom a vibrant liturgical life embodies the dynamics of the modes of Christ's presence *to us* and *for us* and *with us* also finds itself in harmony and real presence with the poor of her community and of the world. If this is not happening, something is dissonant. Divisions are muting the proclamation. A call to conversion regarding the integrity of worship must be examined.

How can such discernment take place? How does a worshiping community move beyond mere lip service to our solidarity with the poor of Christ and experience in that solidarity the relational, dialogical, and participative dynamic the liturgy embraces? A simple and honest assessment of the apostolic ministry of a community would reveal the depth of *synergy* between who we are becoming in union with

---

[62] Cf. Max Thurian, *The Mystery of the Eucharist: An Ecumenical Approach*, trans. Emily Chisholm (Grand Rapids: Eerdmans, 1983; Fr. 1981), especially "An Ecumenical Approach to the Mystery," 50–63. See also n. 7 for other recent ecumenical work on *communicatio in sacris*.

Christ and how that is expressed in ministry, resources, and engaged preaching that summons the community to a *kenotic* self-offering instead of maudlin examples that never move beyond the pithy story or emotional plea. Here is where a liturgical spirituality and piety might break through that impasse. David Power's work on eucharistic solidarity provides an important image here. He speaks of the sacramental memorial as an "event" in which all the chaos and alienation Christ came to dispel and make whole are present for us now in this time and place, in the sufferings and violence and alienation of our own world. As Power says, regarding the memorial in which the community finds her Lord as present and active,

> Through the narrative, Christ events again in the community, within the aspirations of its ritual expression, transforming them into a new being. . . . In its narrative and in its ethics and compassion, the Christian community finds the presence of Christ in suffering. . . . It does not however presume to offer a reason for suffering. It says in simplicity, in celebration, and in action that God is there, both revealed and concealed, and that those who suffer belong in the body of Christ, at the table of his body and blood.[63]

Such a perspective on the "real presence" of Christ and its relationship to the memorial meal suggests that the community finds her solace in a Lord that does not summon an escape from the world but a more intense immersion into its mystery, of which suffering is a constant companion. Just as the eucharistic gifts announce that *here* the promise is made available *to us* and *for us* and *with us,* that same descent into the suffering and marginalization of the world's forgotten and voiceless announce that same promise in a complementary rhythm and harmony with the Eucharist faithfully celebrated. In that sense, a liturgical spirituality and piety does not find an escape from suffering in

---

[63] Power, *Eucharistic Mystery,* 311. For a penetrating analysis of the relationship between the "Canon of Remembrance" and present-day solidarity and remembrance of suffering, see chap. 15, "Revitalizing Eucharistic Prayer and Practice," 328–49. Of special consideration is the role of diverse cultural expressions to articulate human need, God's presence, and God's gracious presence amid that cultural and symbolic matrix. The church's liturgical memorial and its rearticulation in the face of holocaust memorial, women's marginalization, and cultural repression and liberation all provide cogent examples of an "eventing" in this time and cultural reality.

the eucharistic mystery but—dare we say it—a *source* for the rending of our hearts and a call for lamentation, solidarity, and true acts of reconciliation and justice on behalf of those whom Christ loves and stands in faithful solidarity. The hospitality of the eucharistic community, the impetus of her preaching, and the summons to a life lived in service "for the life of the world" is the fruit of such an intimacy with Christ in the memorial meal, in the Blessed Sacrament that abides for adoration, and in the apostolic choices of time and treasure a community makes in order to fulfill her mission. "Zacchaeus," Jesus says, "hurry and come down; for I must stay at your house today" (Luke 19:2). A community never knows where Christ's banquet may lead them as they journey down the road.

Such a risky move from sacred table of Word and Sacrament to the table of the world and her hunger for God requires eucharistic faith, nourished in practice, and received as pure gift. As the *Exsultet* proclaims, "This is our Passover feast, when Christ the true Lamb is slain, whose blood consecrates the homes of all believers." Our home in the sacramental economy is the world but one in which the "new Jerusalem" embraces. Through Christ's presence, the tent of God's encounter with us broadens our horizons and expands our vision. This is not a gospel of success or wealth but of the beatitudes. Eucharistic praying can affirm the rhythm of God's way with us or it can be hijacked to bolster our own concerns and self-affirmation. Everything we have explored in this study suggests that the latter course leads to eucharistic ruin and a myopic piety. Transformation in the *totus Christus* feeds upon the wellspring of love we have opened ourselves to receive and to become. As St. Paul says,

> For the love of Christ urges us on, because we are convinced that one has died for all; therefore all have died. And he died for all, so that those who live might live no longer for themselves, but for him who died and was raised for them. . . . So if anyone is in Christ, there is a new creation: everything old has passed away; see, everything has become new! (2 Cor 5:14-15, 17)

Fear and hesitancy can hold a eucharistic community captive from such a new reality. A faithful liturgical piety and spirituality of communion in the Body and Blood of Christ, broken and poured out for the life of the world, clearly set out and made available in their ritual fullness, deepens our reverence and devotion for the mysteries we celebrate and the community we are called to be. The trinitarian dynamism we have explored in this chapter returns to the banquet hall of the Song of Songs (2:3b-4) with new vitality and a richer understanding of holy communion:

> In his longed-for shade I am seated and his fruit is sweet to my taste.
> He has taken me to his banquet hall, and the banner he raises over me
>   is love. (JB)

Benedict XVI concludes his eucharistic exhortation *Sacramentum Caritatis* with this same appeal to "the mystery of God himself, Trinitarian love" (7), when he urges the faithful:

> Our communities, when they celebrate the Eucharist, must become ever more conscious that the sacrifice of Christ is for all, and that the Eucharist thus compels all who believe in him to become "bread that is broken" for others, and to work for the building of a more just and fraternal world. Keeping in mind the multiplication of the loaves and fishes, we need to realize that Christ continues today to exhort his disciples to become personally engaged: "You yourselves, give them something to eat" (*Mt* 14:16). Each of us is truly called, together with Jesus, to be bread broken for the life of the world. (88)

We can only do this by surrendering ourselves to "the full human import of the radical newness brought by Christ in the Eucharist," Benedict says, which is nothing less than "the progressive transfiguration of all those called by grace to reflect the image of the Son of God (cf. *Rom* 8:29ff.)" (71). The liturgy holds out the promise that the "inexhaustible mystery" and the radical intimacy of the Christ-life can be held in a transformative tension to which, in the end, the creativity and graciousness of the love of God in communion with us engenders.

We return to the *sentir* of St. Ignatius of Loyola in the *Spiritual Exercises*, where the retreatant, after "pondering with great affection how much God our Lord has done and how much God has given of what He possesses, and desires to give Himself" in such a complete and intimate self-offering, is invited to make a mutual self-offering in return. The gathered Body of Christ as one communion shares this same invitation in the liturgy, and it is a fitting close to all that has been expressed in these pages:

> Take, Lord, and receive, all our liberty, our memories,
> our understanding, and our entire wills, all that we have and possess.

You have given all to us. To You, O Lord, we return it.
All is Yours, dispose of it wholly according to your will.
Give us only Your love and Your grace, for this is sufficient for us.
 (*Sp. Ex.* 234)

The vow of a Jesuit religious includes a *fiat* to this prayer, which finds its generative desire in the Father's own passion. Moving beyond the individual self-offering, let it be the eucharistic community's plea as well: "As you have freely given us the desire to make this offering, so also give us the abundant grace to fulfill it." We can expect good things from such a good God, who still acts in so many ways to feed the hungers of the people: "I am going to rain bread from heaven for you, and each day the people shall go out and gather enough for that day" (Exod 16:4). And it is always enough, more than enough, pure gift. May we be faithful to this, now and forever. Amen.

An Ecumenical Apologia:
For Visiting the Blessed Sacrament

O Salutaris Hostia,
Quae coeli pandis ostium;
Bella premunt hostilia,
Da robur, fer auxilium.

Uni Trinoque Domino
Sit sempiterna gloria:
Qui vitam sine termino
Nobis donet in patria. Amen

O Saving Victim, opening wide,
The gates of heaven to us below!
Our foes press on from every side:
Your aid supply, your strength bestow.

To your great name be endless praise,
Immortal God-head, One in Three;
O grant us endless length of days
When our true native land we see.[1]

Every morning, on my way to my office, I stop by our Jesuit university chapel to make a visit to the Blessed Sacrament, a devotional act close to the Roman Catholic sacramental heart. It is also a personal ritual unfolding over many years, with an intentional progression that I now see echoes the spirituality and piety of this book.

There are many layers of sacramentality at work in this simple practice. Remembering God's saving acts in Jesus, who we are and what we do in this house of prayer, I stop at the baptismal pool and dip my

---

[1] The text of this traditional eucharistic hymn is attributed to St. Thomas Aquinas (1227–74), trans. Edward Caswell (1814–78).

hand in the water and sign myself in the name of the triune God. I pause at the center aisle and bow before the ambo and the eucharistic table, in reverence and gratitude for the presence of Christ celebrated here as God's Word and Answer to us in Jesus Christ. It is in this place that the assembly hears the saving Word and is invited to enter into Christ's own self-offering at the table of praise and thanksgiving. As sacramental signs, font and ambo and altar are bearers of this sacred event we celebrate. The importance of what we do as a sacramental community remains within these walls and deepens the *anamnesis*. As Jean Corbon says of liturgical memory, "We do the remembering, but the reality is no longer in the past but is here: the Church's memory becomes a presence."[2]

The visit concludes at the Blessed Sacrament chapel, where the *fragmenti*, the sacred elements of the week's eucharistic celebrations, are reverently kept in order to be available to the sick and those who cannot join the Sunday assembly, and, in a particular nuance that has been retained most faithfully in the Roman tradition, for the community's ongoing prayer and adoration outside the formal liturgy. The sanctuary lamp announces that living presence and flickers with life, as a beacon and a sign that *here* we can rest in the mystery that announces Christ's promise *to us* of abiding communion, *with us* and *for us*. I kneel or stand in prayer for a few moments, calling to mind that God's passion is at the heart of this moment, that these fragments are a response to that desire, spoken as a Word of faith to this local church that has gathered, and that we have heard the summons and processed to the altar to offer ourselves in praise and thanks to God in union with Christ. This place for prayer resonates with that grace and the mystery of a God in communion with us and all creation.

"We taste thee, O thou living Bread, and long to feast upon thee still," as Bernard of Clairvaux sang.[3] It is this "taste" and the adverb "still" that sets the groundwork for another hopeful proposal for ecumenical dialogue regarding a common devotion of prayer before the Blessed Sacrament. In short, can Christians as one Body of Christ understand prayer before the reserved sacrament as a rich and dynamic sign, a revelatory moment of the rhythmic harmony of Christ's dynamic presence this book has embraced? Indeed, cannot a holistic

---

[2] Jean Corbon, *The Wellspring of Worship*, trans. Matthew J. O'Connell (New York: Paulist Press, 1988), 6.

[3] See the epigraph for chap. 5, from the hymn *Jesu, dulcedo cordium*.

approach to these modes of presence break down traditional divisions over this practice in our Christian past by seeing this contemplative stop along the journey as a profoundly *ecclesial* action that nourishes each person of faith? And finally, what difference does it make to "visit the Blessed Sacrament"?

The "taste" of the kingdom, the announcement of the new reality that Christ has begun and into which we are being formed and trans-figured, lingers sweetly when we sit before this awesome mystery, this presence par excellence of this "sacred action surpassing all others" (SC 7). Why is this so? The response that flows from this study is that such a presence reserved for prayer can only *be* because the Father first has allowed his pierced Heart to be emptied in love for us, that Christ has embraced this kenotic, saving mission with a mutual desire and in praise and thanks to his Father's outpouring, and that the Spirit's outpouring now empties itself out and invigorates us and draws us into a holy communion in what has been "taken, blessed, broken, and poured out." We have tasted this mystery and it lingers, when we pon-der the matrix of symbolic relationships of the Love that resonates in this place of reservation. All that God is, all that we are, and our fidel-ity to this mutual exchange of gifts, "seen and heard and tasted and touched," finds its testament here. As 1 John proclaims so boldly,

> this life was revealed, and we have seen it and testify to it, and declare to you the eternal life that was with the Father and was revealed to us—we declare to you what we have seen and heard so that you also may have fellowship with us; and truly our fellowship is with the Father and with his Son Jesus Christ. . . . so that our joy may be com-plete. (1 John 1:2-4)

What a grace and nourishment it is to be "still" before this mystery! In a world of endless work and striving and hunger and desire, to rest before the Blessed Sacrament is refreshment for mission and a signpost of our truest identity as a people baptized in the name of the triune God and claimed for Christ Jesus in the power of the Holy Spirit. Christians who share this belief may find a common heart by sharing in this devotion, rather than imagining some distracting focus on a practice that for far too long has been a sign of division, because it seemed not only "distinct" from the community's Eucharist but also understood to be "separate" from it. The one presence of Christ in four modes of relational, participative, and dialogical encounter, in which the sacramental gift of Christ is bodied forth, challenges that division

217

and offers a vehicle of a shared presence at a richer and deeper dimension than a sole focus on reserved, consecrated bread often have conveyed. Christ abides. The liturgy continues in the midst of our fragmented and hungry world. Praise be to God!

In light of this, personal prayer before the Blessed Sacrament is always an immersion into the life of the *totus Christus,* the whole Body of Christ, head and members. Whatever personal nourishment each person derives from such a "visit" always taps into that wellspring of grace, of which God's passion is the source and which Christ is the channel of mercy, who offers his very own body as a living sign of that mystery. The Holy Spirit gathers the church to celebrate that awesome act of Love and the Holy Spirit hovers as the agent and bond of that union proclaimed in ordinary gifts now consecrated and holy and real and true. In our past history, we Catholics have often forgotten the union of the community of believers that finds its meaning in this fragment of our holy communion. We have used the mystery to isolate ourselves over and against other people of faith and those who profess that same desire and longing.

From the perspective of those who are not from a "reservation" tradition, piety and practice has not dared to acknowledge that ecclesial and sacramental abiding of Christ, which the eucharistic action makes present and available *here* and *in this place* as pure gift, manna from heaven, and food for the journey. The reserved sacrament, we could insist here, does not alter or substitute for the wholeness of this graced action of hearing the preached Word and eating and drinking in grateful memory. Rather, the sacred elements announce our fidelity to the sacramental encounter and God's fidelity to us. However, there is always more to this dynamic gift. The pilgrimage we all share as Christians is still moving toward the fullness. Could we not stop together and rest in its promise? Even more, what might happen if we did this together, in silent praise and thanks, praying that Christ, who prayed so fully *"ut unum sint,"* might continue to "let the kingdom come and his Father's will be done," and to transform and reconcile us and lead us together in mission, broken and poured out for the life of the world? Such a possibility, nurtured in the arguments of this book, seems worth embracing.

Finally, on a very practical level, what difference does such a practice of visiting the Blessed Sacrament make in the large and expansive scheme of things? Is this not a matter best left to the traditionally pious and rigidly sectarian concerns of our shared and fractured history? A simple answer to this is a great leap of faith, but in an *apologia*, or "modest proposal," it is worth presenting. In such simplicity, what would be the harm? What might be the grace? It appears that in a world that desires to be so interconnected and relational and dialogical and participative, the profound silence of communion before the Blessed Sacrament is a profound way to center those desires first in God's preeminent desire for us. We do not ultimately "make communion" through what we do or say or feel on the outside or of our own wills. Tapping into the deeper wellspring by resting before this presence brings us back to the center of our individual and communal being, to the center of our hunger and joys and sorrows, and can only, in the end, invite us to let go and to let God have God's way with us. Letting go heals fractured souls and bodies on all levels. Silence before this sublime gift of the Giver transforms a culture that often seeks connection and communion with more words and images, texted and networked and recorded and projected. *Here*, in *this* place, the deeper mystery prevails. It comes with practice, faithful practice, over time. It is often without fanfare or dazzling insight, but is slow and sure and whole.

For three years I lived in a Jesuit community that was made up of good companions involved in a variety of ministries and works and ages and theological perspectives. Two members of that community began sitting in silent meditation before the Blessed Sacrament early in the morning two days a week. They invited others to join them. The number grew to nine over the course of the first year and the ritual was so terribly simple but affectively rich, especially for Jesuits who often live and evaluate situations from their practical heads. There was only the minor preparation of the space, some candles, the soft ring of a bell to begin and end, and the darkness of the chapel in the early morning to assist us. Over time, to a man, the community found that something important happened to us as a whole. We were in communion amid our differences in a way we could not describe precisely or analyze with surety. We loved being with each other more. The Eucharists we celebrated had a depth and a richness that were grace-filled, yet simple and profound. Our ordinary days of apostolic mission were grounded and centered in that silent adoration. Many said it was the most profound expression of communal prayer they had experienced. And every time we gathered, we still were sent out and scattered to do our work, teach our classes, and serve God's people. On that level, little could be observed that was different; on a level of interior communion, we were all profoundly changed, consecrated, and nourished.

This is my hope for all Christians. It does not solve all differences or exhaust the demands of reconciliation and reunion that our scandalous division has yet to heal. But it is a start, a hopeful proposal, an *apologia* for doing something different together. What would be the harm? Even more, what is the grace? Visiting the Blessed Sacrament is visiting heart to heart, individual and communal, a union with that sacramental mystery that has been "taken, blessed, broken, and shared." *Ut unum sint.*

Bibliography

Baker, J. Robert, and Barbara Budde. *A Eucharistic Sourcebook*. Chicago: Liturgy Training Publications, 1999.

Baldovin, John F. *Bread of Life, Cup of Salvation: Understanding the Mass*. Come and See Series. Lanham, MD: Rowan and Littlefield Publishers, 2003.

———. *Reforming the Liturgy: A Response to the Critics*. Collegeville, MN: Liturgical Press, 2008.

Benedict XVI. Proclaiming a Year for Priests on the 150th Anniversary of the "Dies Natales" of the Curé of Ars. Apostolic letter of Benedict XVI. June 16, 2009.

———. *Sacramentum Caritatis*. Apostolic exhortation. February 22, 2007.

Blaylock, Joy Harrell. "Ghislain Lafont and Contemporary Sacramental Theology." *Theological Studies* 66 (2005): 841–61.

Bugnini, Annibale. *The Reform of the Liturgy (1948–1975)*. Translated by Matthew J. O'Connell. Collegeville, MN: Liturgical Press, 1990.

Butler, Sara. "Women and the Priesthood." *Commonweal* 135, no. 13 (July 18, 2008): 8–10.

Buttrick, David. *Homiletic: Moves and Structures*. Philadelphia: Fortress Press, 1987.

Cantalamessa, Raniero. *The Eucharist, Our Sanctification*. Rev. ed. Translated by Frances Lonergan Villa. Collegeville, MN: Liturgical Press, 1995.

Catechism of the Catholic Church. Rome: Libreria Editrice Vaticana, 1994.

Chauvet, Louis-Marie. *The Sacraments: The Word of God at the Mercy of the Body*. Collegeville, MN: Liturgical Press, 2001.

———. *Symbol and Sacrament: A Sacramental Reinterpretation of Christian Existence*. Collegeville, MN: Liturgical Press, 1995.

Coffey, David. "The Common and the Ordained Priesthood." *Theological Studies* 58 (1997): 209–36.

Collins, Mary. *Contemplative Participation: Sacrosanctum Concilium Twenty-Five Years Later*. Collegeville: Liturgical Press, 1990.

Congar, Yves. *At the Heart of Christian Worship: Liturgical Essays of Yves Congar*. Translated and edited by Paul Philibert. Collegeville, MN: Liturgical Press, 2010.

———. "The Mystical Body of Christ." In *The Mystery of the Church*. Baltimore: Helicon Press, 1960.

———. *Tradition and Traditions*. London: Burns and Oates, 1966. Reprinted and retranslated. In *Theologians Today: Yves M.-J. Congar, OP*. New York: Sheed and Ward, 1963.

———. *The Word and the Spirit*. Translated by David Smith. London: Geoffrey Chapman, 1986.

Cooke, Bernard. *Sacraments and Sacramentality*. 2nd ed. Mystic, CT: Twenty-Third Publications, 1994.

Corbon, Jean. *The Wellspring of Worship*. Translated by Matthew J. O'Connell. Mahwah, NJ: Paulist Press, 1980 (San Francisco: Ignatius Press, 2005).

Cyril of Jerusalem. Mystagogical Catechesis IV, "On the Eucharistic Food." In *St. Cyril of Jerusalem's Lectures on the Christian Sacraments*, edited by F. L. Cross. London: SPCK, 1951.

Dalmais, I. "Theology of the Liturgical Celebration." In *The Church at Prayer*, vol. 1, edited by A. Martimort. Collegeville, MN: Liturgical Press, 1987.

Daly, Robert J. *Sacrifice Unveiled: The True Meaning of Christian Sacrifice*. New York: T & T Clark International, 2009.

Decree on the Ministry and Life of Priests. *Presbyterium Ordinis*. Dec. 7, 1965. *Acta Apostolicae Sedis* 58 (1966): 991–1024.

de Lubac, Henri. "Christian Community and Sacramental Communion." In *Theological Fragments* (*Théologies d'occasion, 1984*). San Francisco: Ignatius Press, 1989.

———. *Corpus Mysticum: The Eucharist and the Church in the Middle Ages*. Translated by Gemma Simonds, CJ, with Richard Price and Christopher Stephens. Notre Dame, IN: University of Notre Dame Press, 2006.

———. *The Splendour of the Church*. Translated by Michael Mason. New York: Sheed and Ward, 1956 (San Francisco: Ignatius Press, 1999).

Dix, Gregory. *The Shape of the Liturgy*. Westminster: Dacre Press, 1945.

Donoghue, Denis. *Ferocious Alphabets*. New York: Columbia University Press, 1984.

Egan, Robert J. "Why Not? Scripture, History and Women's Ordination." *Commonweal* 135, no. 7 (April 11, 2008): 17–27.

The Essential Rumi. Translated by Coleman Barks, et al. Edison, NJ: Castle Books, 1997.

Evdokimov, Paul. "The Eucharist—Mystery of the Church." In *In the World, of the Church: A Paul Evdokimov Reader*. Crestwood, NY: St. Vladimir's Seminary Press, 2001.

Ferrone, Rita. *Liturgy: Sacrosanctum Concilium*. Rediscovering Vatican II Series. Mahwah, NJ: Paulist Press, 2007.

Fink, Peter, ed. *The New Dictionary of Sacramental Worship*. Collegeville, MN: Liturgical Press, 1990.

———. *Worship: Praying the Sacraments*. Washington, DC: The Pastoral Press, 1991.

Flannery, Austin, ed. *Vatican Council II, Volume 1: The Conciliar and Post Conciliar Documents*. Northport, NY: Costello Publishing Co., 1996.

Foley, Edward. "The Eucharistic Prayer: An Unexplored Creed." In *Assembly* 28.4, Notre Dame Center for Pastoral Liturgy (July 2002): 28–32.

Foley, Edward, Nathan D. Mitchell, Joanne M. Pierce, eds. *A Commentary on the Revision of the Roman Missal*. Collegeville, MN: Liturgical Press, 2007.

Fox, Patricia A. *God as Communion: John Zizioulas, Elizabeth Johnson, and the Retrieval of the Symbol of the Triune God*. Collegeville, MN: Liturgical Press, 2001.

Gaudoin-Parker, Michael L., ed. *The Real Presence Through the Ages: Jesus Adored in the Sacrament of the Altar*. New York: Alba House, 1993.

Giraudo, Cesare. *Eucaristia per la Chiesa*. Aloisiana 22. Rome: Gregorian University/Brescia: Morcelliana, 1989.

Greenblatt, Stephen. *Learning to Curse: Essays in Early Modern Culture*. New York: Routledge, 1990.

Hahnenberg, Edward P. "The Ministerial Priesthood and Liturgical Anamnesis in the Thought of Edward J. Kilmartin, S.J." *Theological Studies* 66 (2005): 253–78.

Hall, Jerome. *We Have the Mind of Christ: The Holy Spirit and Liturgical Memory in the Thought of Edward J. Kilmartin*. Collegeville, MN: Liturgical Press, 2001.

Hildegarde of Bingen. Antiphon for the Holy Spirit. *Symphonia 141. Symphonia: A Critical Edition of the "Symphonia Armonie Celestium Revelationum" (Symphony of the Harmony of Celestial Revelations), Second Edition*. Translated and edited by Barbara Newman. Ithaca, NY: Cornell University Press, 1988, 1989.

Hilkert, Mary Catherine. *Naming Grace: Preaching and the Sacramental Imagination*. New York: Continuum, 1997.

Hill, William. "What is Preaching? One Heuristic Model from Theology." In *Search for the Absent God*, edited by Mary Catherine Hilkert. New York: Crossroad, 1992.

Hoge, Dean R., Jackson W. Carroll, and Francis K. Sheets. *Patterns of Parish Leadership: Cost and Effectiveness in Four Denominations*. Kansas City: Sheed and Ward, 1988.

Hopkins, Gerard Manley. "At the Wedding March." In *The Complete Poems, with Selected Prose*. London: Harper Collins, 1996.

———. "Further Notes on the Foundation." In *The Sermons and Devotional Writings of Gerard Manley Hopkins*, ed. Christopher Devlin. London: Oxford University Press, 1959.

Houselander, Caryll. *The Reed of God*. London: Sheed and Ward, 1976.

Hunsinger, George. *The Eucharist and Ecumenism: Let Us Keep the Feast*. New York: Cambridge University Press, 2008.

Hunt, Anne. *The Trinity and the Paschal Mystery: A Development in Recent Catholic Theology*. Collegeville, MN: Liturgical Press, 1997.

Janowiak, Paul. "*Lex Orandi, Lex Predicandi*: Preaching a Laboring Word." *Journal of Ignatian Spirituality* (Winter 2005).

————. *The Holy Preaching: The Sacramentality of the Word in the Liturgical Assembly*. Collegeville, MN: Liturgical Press, 2000.

John Paul II. On Keeping the Lord's Day Holy (*Dies Domini*). Apostolic exhortation. July 5, 1998.

————. The Supper of the Lord (*Dominicae Cenae*). Apostolic letter. February 24, 1980.

————. The Church of the Eucharist (*Ecclesia de Eucharistia*). Encyclical letter. April 17, 2003.

————. On Active Participation in the Liturgy. Address of the Holy Father Pope John Paul II to the Bishops of the Episcopal Conference of the United States of America (Washington, Oregon, Idaho, Montana, and Alaska) at their *Ad Limina* Visit. October 9, 1998.

Julian of Norwich. *Julian of Norwich: Showings*. Edited by Edmund Colledge and James Walsh, 225. New York: Paulist Press, 1978.

Jungmann, Josef. *Announcing the Word of God*. Translated by Ronald Walls. New York: Herder and Herder, 1967.

————. *The Mass of the Roman Rite: Its Origins and Development*. Translated by Rev. Francis A. Brunner. Dublin: Four Courts Press, 1951; 1986 ed.

Kerr, Fergus. "French Theology: Yves Congar and Henri de Lubac." In *The Modern Theologians*, edited by David Ford, 105–17. Malden, MA: Blackwell Publishing, 1997.

Kilmartin, Edward. "The Catholic Tradition of Eucharistic Theology: Toward the Third Millennium." *Theological Studies* 55 (1994): 405–57.

————. *Christian Liturgy: The Theology and Practice: I. Systematic Theology of Liturgy*. Kansas City: Sheed and Ward, 1988.

————. *The Eucharist in the West: History and Theology*. Edited by Robert J. Daly. Collegeville, MN: Liturgical Press, 1998.

Kubicki, Judith M. *The Presence of Christ in the Gathered Assembly*. New York: Continuum, 2006.

LaCugna, Catherine Mowry. *God For Us: The Trinity and Christian Life*. San Francisco: HarperSanFrancisco, 1991.

Lafont, Ghislain. *Eucharist: The Meal and the Word*. Translated by Jeremy Driscoll. New York: Paulist Press, 2008.

————. *God, Time, and Being*. Translated by Leonard Maluf. Petersham, MA: Saint Bede's, 1992.

————. *Imagining the Catholic Church: Structured Communion in the Spirit*. Translated by John J. Burkhard. Collegeville, MN: Liturgical Press, 2000.

Lamberigts, Mathijs. "The Liturgy Debate." In *The History of Vatican II*, Eng. ed., edited by Guiseppe Alberigo and Joseph A. Komonchak, 107–66. Maryknoll: Orbis, 1997.

Lathrop, Gordon. *Central Things: Worship in Word and Sacrament*. Minneapolis: Augsburg, 2005.

————. *Holy Things: A Liturgical Theology*. Minneapolis: Fortress Press, 1993.

————. *What are the Essentials of Christian Worship?* Open Questions in Worship Series, 1. Minneapolis: Augsburg/Fortress Publishers, 1996.

Long, Thomas. *The Witness of Preaching*. Louisville, KY: Westminster John Knox Press, 1989.

Marini, Archbishop Piero. *A Challenging Reform: Realizing the Vision of Liturgical Renewal, 1963–1975*. Edited by Mark R. Francis, John R. Page, Keith F. Pecklers. Collegeville, MN: Liturgical Press, 2007.

Marion, Jean-Luc. *Prolegomena to Charity*. Translated by Stephen Lewis. New York: Fordham University Press, 2002.

Martos, Joseph. *The Sacraments: An Interdisciplinary and Interactive Study*. Collegeville, MN: Liturgical Press, 2009.

Matthew, Iain. *The Impact of God: Soundings from John of the Cross*. London: Hodder & Stoughton, 1995.

McCabe, Herbert. *The New Creation*. New York: Continuum, 2010 (Sheed and Ward, 1964).

Merton, Thomas. *The Living Bread*. New York: Farrar, Straus and Giroux, 1956.

————. *Thoughts in Solitude*. New York: Farrar, Straus and Giroux, 1958; 1999 ed.

Mitchell, Nathan. "The Amen Corner: Real Presence." *Worship* 80, 6 (November 2006): 551–66.

————. "The Amen Corner: Revisiting Presence." *Worship* 80, 1 (January 2006): 55–68.

————. *Meeting Mystery: Liturgy, Worship, Sacraments*. Theology in Global Perspective Series. Maryknoll, NY: Orbis Books, 2006.

————. "Mystery and Manners: Eucharist in Post-Modern Theology." *Worship* 79, 2 (March 2005): 130–51.

————. *Real Presence: The Work of Eucharist*. Chicago: Liturgy Training Publications, 2001.

Mitchell, Nathan, and John Leonard. *The Postures of the Assembly during the Eucharistic Prayer*. Chicago: Liturgy Training Publications, 1994.

Mitchell, Stephen, ed. *The Enlightened Heart: An Anthology of Sacred Poetry*. San Francisco: Harper and Row, 1989.

Morrill, Bruce T. *Anamnesis as Dangerous Memory: Political and Liturgical Theology in Dialogue*. Collegeville, MN: Liturgical Press, 2000.

————. "Hidden Presence: The Mystery of the Assembly as Body of Christ." *Liturgical Ministry* 11 (Winter 2002): 31–40.

Norris, Kathleen. *The Quotidian Mysteries: Laundry, Liturgy, and "Women's Work."* 1998 Madaleva Lecture in Spirituality. Mahwah, NJ: Paulist Press, 1998.

Noffke, Suzanne, ed. *The Prayers of Catherine of Siena*. New York: Paulist Press, 1983.

Osborne, Kenan. *Priesthood: A History of the Ordained Ministry in the Roman Catholic Church*. New York: Paulist Press, 1988.

―――. *Sacramental Theology: A General Introduction*. Mahwah, NJ: Paulist Press, 1988.

Palmer, Ray. *Hymns Ancient and Modern, Revised*. Great Britain: Hymns Ancient and Modern, Ltd., 1981.

Pastro, Vincent J. *Enflamed by the Sacramental Word: Preaching and the Imagination of the Poor*. Eugene, OR: Pickwick Publications, 2010.

Paul VI. The Mystery of Faith (*Mysterium Fidei*). Encyclical letter. September 3, 1965.

Pecklers, Keith F. *The Genius of the Roman Rite: On the Reception and Implementation of the New Missal*. Collegeville, MN: Liturgical Press, 2009.

Pius XII. Mediator between God and Men (*Mediator Dei*). Encyclical letter. November 20, 1947.

Power, David N. *The Eucharistic Mystery: Revitalizing the Tradition*. New York: Crossroad, 1992.

―――. "Representing Christ in Community and Sacrament." In *Being a Priest Today*, edited by Donald J. Goergen. Collegeville, MN: Liturgical Press, 1992.

―――. *Sacrament: The Language of God's Giving*. New York: Crossroad, 1999.

Radcliffe, Timothy. "The Sacramentality of the Word." In *Liturgy in a Postmodern World*. London and New York: Continuum, 2003.

Rahner, Karl. *The Church and the Sacraments*. 3rd ed. New York: Herder and Herder, 1964.

―――. "The Word and the Eucharist." Translated by Kevin Smyth. In *Theological Investigations*, Vol. IV. New York: Crossroad, 1982.

Rausch, Timothy P. "Priestly Identity: Priority of Representation and the Iconic Argument." *Worship* 73, 2 (March 1999): 169–79.

Rubin, Miri. *Corpus Christi: The Eucharist in Medieval Culture*. New York: Cambridge University Press, 1991.

Russell, Norman. *Fellow Workers with God: Orthodox Thinking on Theosis*. The Foundations Series. Crestwood, NY: St. Vladimir's Seminary Press, 2009.

Schillebeeckx, Edward. *Christ, the Sacrament of the Encounter with God*. 3rd rev. ed. Translated by Cornelius Ernst. New York: Sheed, Andrews, and McMeel, 1963.

―――. "The Sacraments: An Encounter with God." In *Christianity Divided: Protestant and Roman Catholic Issues*, edited by Daniel J. Callahan, Heiko A. Obermann, and Daniel J. O'Hanlon. New York: Sheed and Ward, 1961.

Schmemann, Alexander. *For the Life of the World*. Crestwood, NY: St. Vladimir's Seminary Press, 1988.

―――. *The Eucharist: Sacrament of the Kingdom*. Crestwood, NY: St. Vladimir's Seminary Press, 1988.

Semmelroth, Otto. *Church and Sacrament*. Translated by Emily Schossberger. Notre Dame: Fides Press, 1964.

―――. *The Preaching Word: On the Theology of Proclamation*. Translated by John Jay Hughes. New York: Herder and Herder, 1965.

Sibley, Laurence. "The Church as Eucharistic Community: Observations on John Calvin's Early Eucharistic Theology (1536–1545)." *Worship* 81, 3 (May 2007): 249–67.

Smolarski, Dennis C. *Sacred Mysteries: Sacramental Principles and Liturgical Practice*. Mahwah, NJ: Paulist Press, 1995.

Tavard, George H. "Praying Together: *Communicatio in Sacris* in the Degree of Ecumenism." In *Vatican II Revisited: By Those Who Were There*, edited by Alberic Stacpoole. Minneapolis: Winston Press, 1986.

Taylor, Barbara Brown. *When God is Silent*. Boston: Cowley Publications, 1998.

Teilhard de Chardin, Pierre. *Hymn of the Universe*. New York: Harper & Row, 1965.

Tertullian. *De Resurrectione Carnis*, 8. In *Patrologia Latina* (MPL) 2, edited by Jacques-Paul Migne.

Thurian, Max. *The Mystery of the Eucharist*. Translated by Emily Chisholm. Grand Rapids: Eerdmans, 1983.

Tillard, J. M. R. *I Believe, Despite Everything: Reflections of an Ecumenist*. Collegeville, MN: Liturgical Press, 2003.

United States Conference of Catholic Bishops. The Real Presence of Jesus Christ in the Sacrament of the Eucharist: Basic Questions and Answers. Washington, DC: June 15, 2001.

Vasileios, Archimandrite. *Hymn of Entry: Liturgy and Life in the Orthodox Church*. Translated by Elizabeth Briere. Crestwood, NY: St. Vladimir's Seminary Press, 1984.

Wood, Susan. "The Eucharist/Church Correlation and Spiritual Exegesis." Chap. 3 (pp. 53–70) in *Spiritual Exegesis and the Church in the Theology of Henri de Lubac*. Grand Rapids: Eerdmans, 1998.

———. "Presbyteral Identity within Parish Identity." In *Ordering the Baptismal Priesthood*. Collegeville, MN: Liturgical Press, 2003.

———. "Priestly Identity: Sacrament of the Ecclesial Community." *Worship* 69, 2 (March 1995): 109–27.

———. *Sacramental Orders*. Edited by John D. Laurance. Lex Orandi Series. Collegeville, MN: Liturgical Press, 2000.

World Council of Churches. *Baptism, Eucharist, and Ministry*. Geneva: 1982.

Zizioulas, John. *Being as Communion*. Crestwood, NY: St. Vladimir's Seminary Press, 1985.

Index